Also by Fritz Stern

The Varieties of History
  From Voltaire to the Present   1956 *(ed.)*

The Politics of Cultural Despair
  *A Study in the Rise of the
  Germanic Ideology*   1961

The Responsibility of Power
  *Essays in Honor of Hajo Holborn
  1968 (ed. with Leonard Krieger)*

THE FAILURE OF
ILLIBERALISM

THE FAILURE OF
ILLIBERALISM

Essays on the Political Culture
of Modern Germany

FRITZ STERN

Alfred A. Knopf   *New York*   1972

ISBN: 0-394-46087-1

Library of Congress Catalog Card Number: 71-136317

Acknowledgment is gratefully made to the following publications which first printed these essays, some in slightly different form:
History, August 1960—"The Political Consequences of the Unpolitical German."
Central European History, Volume III, Numbers 1/2, March/ June 1970—"Money, Morals, and the Pillars of Bismarck's Society."
American Historical Review, October 1969—"Gold and Iron: The Collaboration and Friendship of Gerson Bleichröder and Otto von Bismarck."
Doubleday & Company, Inc.—"Bethmann Hollweg and the War: The Limits of Responsibility"—from the book *The Responsibility of Power,* edited by Fritz Stern and Leonard Krieger; "A Liberal Historian and the War," from the book *The Era of Tyrannies* (1965), by Élie Halévy, with a note by Fritz Stern.
Journal of International Affairs, Volume 22, Number 1, 1968, pages 126–34—"German Historians and the War," which appeared under the title "On Continuity in German History," copyright © by the Board of Editors.
Political Science Quarterly, 73, March 1958—"Adenauer in Weimar," which appeared under the title "Adenauer and a Crisis in Weimar Democracy."
Doubleday & Company, Inc.—"The Collapse of Weimar," from the book *The Path of Dictatorship,* translated by John Conway, introduction by Fritz Stern, copyright © 1966 by Doubleday & Company, Inc.
Commentary, February 1955—"Germany Revisited," which appeared under the title "The Fragmented People That Is Germany."

To the memory
of Richard Hofstadter
in abiding affection

Contents

Contents · *viii*

Acknowledgments

The publication of these essays gives me a chance to thank the many friends who over the years have given me their counsel and advice. Surely the best part of writing is learning, and in that process the criticism of others has helped me greatly.

Time and again, the following friends have been willing to read early drafts of my essays: Leonard Krieger, David S. Landes, Henry L. Roberts, and Robert K. Webb. To them, my warmest thanks for responding to my importunities with invaluable comments and suggestions.

In preparing one or the other of these essays I have also had the benefit of help from these friends and colleagues: Ralf Dahrendorf, Felix Gilbert, Beatrice K. Hofstadter, James Joll, Christoph and Flora Kimmich, Walter Sokel, Rudolf Vierhaus, and Philip M. Williams. At the beginning of my essay-writing and at the final stage of this enterprise, my teacher and friend, Jacques Barzun, gave generously of his still awesome expertise.

In the mechanics of assembling these essays I could rely on the meticulous assistance of Joan Karle. Ashbel Green of Alfred A. Knopf, forbearing and uncompromising at just the right moments, was a great and cordial help.

My family has helped me in ever increasing measure: my wife by all the intangibles that are of unsurpassed importance and by contributing her patient corrections to my often hasty formulations, my daughter Katherine by her ever cheerful, if sometimes impatient solicitude—as during a fall in Oxford when she asked regularly "How is Bethmann?"—and my son Frederick, by becoming a thoughtful critic of style and substance.

The book is dedicated to Richard Hofstadter. To him I owe more than I can say.

F.S.

Sils-Maria, May 31, 1971

Introduction

For my generation and for those older than we, the Third Reich was the central, collective experience of our lives. The shadow of Hitler fell on our youth, and we remember still the mounting terror of his rule. We remember the frenzied enthusiasm he aroused and the tepid opposition he encountered; we remember his Reich as the meanest and most popular tyranny the world has ever seen. Hitler was a challenge to our lives that we survived; he was also a challenge to our moral and political traditions, to our assumptions about man's nature, and that challenge we are still in the midst of meeting.

The experience of National Socialism has left most of us with a sense of the fragility of freedom, convinced that the legal and moral safeguards of freedom need unswerving defense. For many of the younger generation, however, Hitler is a memory that justifies drastic—and often utopian—action against the prevailing system and its deficiencies, regardless of the impact on prevailing and perhaps imperfect freedoms. The older generation fears the recurrence of tyranny; the younger generation seeks a New Jerusalem—and is willing to break with a civilization that could produce a Hitler. A quarter of a century after his death, Hitler continues to haunt and divide us.

The need, then, to understand the causes of National Socialism and to grasp its place in the history of our civilization has grown, not diminished, with time. In the last few years, paradoxically, the specific question of "Why Hitler in Germany?" has ceased to agitate Germans and the question of "Why Hitler in the Western world?" has come to be posed everywhere—by many out of a sense of shocked guilt, by some with the answer built in. To them, Hitler is proof of the rottenness of our civilization—and they invoke him to continue, for different motives, the attack on liberal civilization that Hitler himself had waged.

The memory of National Socialism lurks everywhere, though with ever diminishing precision and specificity. Memories always become selective, and the present tendency to distortion may be abetted by the avowedly anti-historical mood of so many of the young. A partial and partisan memory taunts and is made to taunt the Western world.

In this type of situation, historians have a special responsibility. They need to reconstruct the National Socialist era in all its complexity and horror, in its German as well as in its universal aspects. They must try to confront the selective and often polemically selective memory of a past trauma with as full and objective an account as possible. National Socialism as a vague and poisonous memory will increasingly weaken the present; an informed memory of the trauma, based on an intelligent and honest study of the past, may yet help to guide us in our present predicaments. Historians have grappled with this problem for a long time, but the need to do so is now more universal and more insistent than before. The present volume is intended as a contribution to the continuing effort of historical analysis.

Every disaster prompts inquiry into its causes, and for decades now historians have wrestled with the phenomenon of National Socialism. Most early answers tended to be trivial. "Pills to cure an earthquake," Élie Halévy called similar efforts to explain the origins of the Great War. It took some time before prejudices yielded to perspective, before the groundwork of research had been done and efforts could be made to integrate the monstrosity of National Socialism with the course of German and European history.

Early popular attempts at explanation clustered around two contradictory misapprehensions: first, that the Germans had always been cursed with unique deformations of mind and aberrations of history which made the triumph of National Socialism a logical development; or second, that Hitler's triumph was but an accident, an abnormality, and as such required no general reappraisal of the German past. The former view was a comforting illusion for liberals and non-Germans; the latter view offered a kind of retroactive immunity to Germans. It shielded the national past. Neither view is tenable. There is no easy or comfortable answer to the German question.

Historians have long realized that the German past is central to an understanding of our own era. For seventy-five years Germany dominated the politics of Europe; in the cataclysms of the twentieth century, she played a decisive role. Without the erratic thrusts of German power, neither World War would have occurred; without the two wars, no Bolshevism, no National Socialism, no Cold War, and no divided Germany. This is not to say that Germany was responsible for these events, but that if in the decades of its ascendancy, Germany had pursued a different policy, the configuration of the world would now be profoundly different.

Historians are also beginning to understand that the complexity of the German past is a particular challenge to their discipline. How does one account for the contradictory nature of so much of the German record? The historian remembers that German was the language of Heine and Rilke, of Helmholtz and Einstein, of Marx and Weber, of Gropius and the Bauhaus—as well as the language of Ludendorff and Hitler, of

Auschwitz and the concentration camps, of millions of "idealists" who thought their Führer could shape the world according to their monstrous fantasies. The German past is full of contradictions, some fused into a characteristic style, some unreconciled, pushing Germans toward one extreme or another. No wonder that so intractable and so complex a history has thwarted historians—and spawned a long line of simplifiers and system builders.

The very question now being debated by historians—that of continuity in German history—indicates a new perspective.[1] Historians now focus on the years before 1914, and there is a growing consensus that the nature of German society and the character of German imperialism before 1914 need to be examined if the collapse of Weimar and the emergence of Hitler's tyranny are to be understood. The major works of the last twenty-five years have already suggested certain links: Germany's militaristic traditions had been stronger than those of her Western neighbors; her conservative classes had clung more tenaciously to power there than they did elsewhere; her nationalism, her collective ethos had been peculiarly aggressive, xenophobic, anti-Semitic, anti-Western. The fact that these strains existed has been incontrovertible; their origins and their consequences remain in dispute. It is now a commonplace to say that Germany did not enter the liberal-Western path, that a belated attempt to do so in 1918 proved unsuccessful. One of the boldest analysts of the German past, Ralf Dahrendorf, posed the German question in this manner: "What is it in German society that may account for Germany's persistent failure to give a home to democracy in the liberal

---

1. See Andreas Hillgruber, *Kontinuität und Diskontinuität in der deutschen Aussenpolitik von Bismarck bis Hitler* (Düsseldorf, 1969). On this general problem, see also Hajo Holborn's fundamental essay, "German Idealism in the Light of Social History," originally published in 1952 and now available in Hajo Holborn, *Germany and Europe: Historical Essays* (Garden City, N.Y., 1970), pp. 1–32.

sense? . . . There is a conception of liberty that holds that man can be free only when an experimental attitude to knowledge, the competition of social forces, and liberal institutions are combined. This conception has never really gained a hold in Germany. Why not?"[2]

Dahrendorf's question, though central, may slight a related aspect of German history. What, we must ask, was the character of Germany's alternative to liberal democracy and what impact did it have on the terrible squandering of German power, as exemplified by the two World Wars? This is the question that prompted my essays on the unpolitical German and on money and morals in Imperial Germany, as well as the specific essays on the politics of Bethmann Hollweg and Adenauer.

Let us first of all remember that there was nothing preordained about the fact that an alternative to the Western pattern would fail or degenerate into self-destructive criminality. In the nineteenth century there was a presumption that liberal institutions would spread from England eastwards, but even then there were those who recognized that not every nation could duplicate the spirit and machinery of liberal politics. What Walter Bagehot wrote in 1874 about France fits Bismarckian Germany as well: "Parliamentary Government is not a thing which always succeeds in the world; on the contrary, the lesson of experience is that it often fails, and seldom answers, and this is because the necessary combination of elements is rare and complex. First, Parliamentary Government requires that a nation should have *nerve* to endure incessant discussion and frequent change of rulers."[3]

Bismarck loathed liberalism, and he believed (perhaps cor-

2. Ralf Dahrendorf, *Society and Democracy in Germany* (Garden City, N.Y., 1967), pp. 4, 17.
3. *Bagehot's Historical Essays*, ed. with an introduction by Norman St. John-Stevas (New York, 1965), pp. 449–50.

rectly) that Germans did not have the nerve for it. He believed the liberal system to be synonymous with instability, divisiveness, and eroded authority. He was determined that Germany should not follow that model. Indeed, if an alternative to liberalism could have worked anywhere, it should have worked in Germany. Where else was the authoritarian tradition still so strong, the bureaucracy so efficient and so incorruptible, the military so respected and so loyal, the populace so law-abiding and so unconsciously docile—and so far removed from being a politically mature citizenry? Bismarck assumed that these characteristics would remain unchanged for a long time to come.

Hence, in 1867 and 1871, Bismarck improvised a constitutional system that at best was a half-way house to liberalism. The middle-class liberals, defeated in 1848 and again in 1866, were presented with the long-coveted prize of national unity; dissatisfied bourgeois were given satisfaction by the establishment of a free economy in the late 1860's. The *Rechtsstaat* protected their rights. Bismarck's democratically elected Reichstag offered the representatives of the nation carefully circumscribed powers and gave Germany the prestige of belonging to the ranks of constitutional, pseudo-parliamentary states. But it was Bismarck's intention that the monarchical authority should remain inviolate—and with it, the traditional prerogatives of the Crown. The German middle classes came to accommodate themselves to the system, some faster, some slower, but most of them dimly aware that the Bismarckian system protected them against threatened upheavals from below. Bismarck expected that the hitherto dominant classes would continue their sway and that the habits of deference on the one side and of *noblesse oblige* on the other would moderate or disguise excessive class egoism. Bismarck clung to the realities of power but made ample room for the liberals to nurture illusions about their own future place in the governing of Germany.

In less than a decade, however, the Bismarckian system ran into trouble. The different groups refused to play according to Bismarck's script, and an economic crisis of unprecedented severity sharpened the various antagonisms. The government's first target had been the civil power of the Catholic Church, but the *Kulturkampf* ended with the Church intact, the Center strengthened, and the Catholics alerted. In fact, Catholics and socialists seemed to flourish in opposition to Bismarck's policies; the *Bürgertum* was split between doctrinaire free traders and liberals on the one hand, and industrialists clamoring for state protection on the other. By the end of the 1870's, Bismarck, half-pushing and half-pushed, reached out for a new alignment, so different from the past that it has sometimes been called the second founding of the Reich. The liberal façade of the preceding decade was abandoned, as was free trade. A new coalition of Junkers and industrialists was put together, a new program of anti-socialist repression was adopted, and the regime acquired a harsher tone, even as Bismarck himself became more rigid and embittered.

Imperial Germany has been depicted in many ways: conservative, authoritarian, Bonapartist. It seems to me that the character of Imperial Germany after 1878 can best be caught in the term "illiberal."[4] By illiberalism I mean not only the structure of the political regime, suffrage restrictions, or class chicanery, but a state of mind. For just as liberalism bespeaks a state of mind, so does its negation. Illiberalism first of all constituted a commitment in mind and policy against any further concession to democracy, even at the price of one's political independence. Any concession in any realm might undermine the authority, prestige, and status of the entire system.

---

4. I am using the term as the dictionary defines it: "Not befitting a free man . . . not generous in respect to the opinions, rights, or liberties of others; narrow-minded." *The Shorter Oxford English Dictionary* (3rd edn., Oxford, 1967), Vol. I, p. 956.

If need be, existing concessions would be revoked; Bismarck himself lived with the thought that a *coup d'état*, a jettisoning of his own constitution, might be his only escape.[5]

Every country has its illiberal moments; every class or person, thwarted or threatened by a rising opponent, is tempted by an illiberal stance. Anyone pushed against the wall is likely to react with an erratic vehemence. As George F. Kennan once put it, in a different context, in 1947: "The fact of the matter is that there is a little bit of the totalitarian buried somewhere, way down deep, in each and every one of us. It is only the cheerful light of confidence and security which keeps this evil genius down at the usual helpless and invisible depth. If confidence and security were to disappear, don't think that he would not be waiting to take their place."[6] There is certainly a bit of the illiberal in each of us, but it is my contention that German society, far from keeping down the illiberal impulse, fostered it and formed it into a habitual response.

The amazing quality of German illiberalism was its pervasiveness. The political system may have formally imposed it, the class antagonisms may have sharpened it, the revered army may have embodied it, the schools and universities may have taught it, but it had evolved for a long time and was part of a cultural style. At every juncture in his career, a German would learn illiberal attitudes or see illiberal models in positions of authority: there were few, if any, accepted models of playfulness or tolerant dissent. Perhaps there was something symptomatic about German students who by dueling earned visible certificates of courage—so that for all later time they did not have to prove themselves in the field of civic courage.

---

5. Michael Stürmer argues this point in his article "Staatsstreichgedanken im Bismarckreich," *Historische Zeitschrift,* Vol. CCIX, No. 3 (Dec., 1969), pp. 566–615; see also the older treatment by Egmont Zechlin, *Staatsstreichpläne Bismarcks und Wilhelms II. 1890–1894* (Stuttgart and Berlin, 1929).

6. George F. Kennan, *Memoirs 1925–1950* (Boston, 1967), p. 319.

I am, of course, describing what might be called an ideal type, a person with a particular way of looking at the world, with certain psychological characteristics. I believe this type was most prevalent among the upper and educated classes of Northern Germany. The type had clear virtues as well, and the North German tended to look down on his new compatriots in the South, who, he thought, lacked what he would have called tough rectitude—and what I have called illiberal. The illiberal German felt threatened by the freer style of life in the South just as the Southerners were often made uncomfortable by their strident powerful neighbors of the North. It was the latter who were, in Nietzsche's phrase, *"reichsdeutsch"* and who felt themselves to be models for the New German.

German illiberalism also embodied the old virtues of obedience and the uneasy adulation of authority: it embodied the new faith in nationalism and the supreme value of the nation state. It signified the acceptance of a kind of civic nonage.

That nonage was a part of Germany's historic development. The German people never staged a successful revolution, they never once had the experience of successfully defying authority —an experience that presumably strengthens the self-confidence of an individual or a people. In Germany, revolutions came from above, changes were decreed by the dynasty or the bureaucracy: "From Bismarck to Adenauer, the Germans [in contrast to the French] have always sought a father, indeed it appears as if the German conception of the state is generally patterned after the model of the family."[7]

The practice of illiberalism reflected and reinforced an

---

7. Wolfgang Sauer, "Das Problem des deutschen Nationalstaates," in *Moderne deutsche Sozialgeschichte,* ed. by Hans-Ulrich Wehler (Cologne and Berlin, 1966), p. 408. See also Rudolf Stadelmann, *Deutschland und Westeuropa. Drei Aufsätze* (Schloss Laupheim, Württemberg, 1948).

illiberal ethos. The ruling classes disdained the liberal habits of tolerance, dissent, debate, openness as well as the politics of liberalism. They were afraid of opposition; they lacked, in Bagehot's phrase, the nerve for open discussion. The idea of a loyal opposition was as alien to Bismarck and William II as it had been to the Stuarts. The ruling classes felt strong enough only for an inflexible defense of the status quo at home and for an ever greater expansion of national power abroad.

Their rhetoric of strength and heroism disguised their sense of weakness. German elites were under all kinds of pressure: the Junker class was under economic pressure; the middle classes under pressure from below; and the country, they both felt, was threatened from abroad. Grace under pressure, as Hemingway defined courage, was not a notable trait of an illiberal society.

The German elites often concealed their true motives even from themselves. They talked ideals and began to forget that they also meant material interests. Material issues are negotiable, but if one thinks that every issue involves principle or status, accommodation is far more difficult.

Of course, illiberal attitudes served class interests—just as liberal attitudes at times served class interests in France and England. The fact that agrarians and industrialists sought to defend their interests is not extraordinary. What is extraordinary is that they should cling to an illiberal structure, embrace an illiberal stance, live in an illiberal political milieu—without realizing the likely costs. They did not venture into the kind of voluntary, civic activity that attracted their English or American counterparts. Civic initiative takes practice, and German society never fostered it. Most Germans looked to the state for guidance and initiative.

Conservatives have been traditionally praised for their realism; the German elite were so prone to surrender to illusions, to a kind of negative utopianism, that for this reason alone it would be hard to call them conservative. They sought to rely on bureaucratic rule, if possible, and on repression, if necessary. Their margin of confidence was slim; there was always a latent readiness to rely on force. Most Germans cherished an extraordinary admiration for power, especially military power. Puttkamer's system epitomized political illiberalism as did the *Vaterlandspartei* during the war; Heinrich Mann's *Little Superman* caricatures the illiberality of the whole culture.

After 1878, Bismarck's angered authoritarianism and the defensive alliance of agrarian and industrial classes gave the new Reich a cramped, frantic atmosphere. After 1890, William exuded confidence—to hide still greater insecurity. Basically, the Bismarckian system, at its inception still an ingenious improvisation, consonant with the fundamental realities of class and culture, became less and less viable in a changing social milieu. But what Ralf Dahrendorf has called the cartel of anxiety clung to its power and position; it wanted to defend everything—not out of greed, but out of fear. The members of the cartel regarded their political bastions—the Prussian suffrage system, for example, or the government's independence of the Reichstag—as the necessary outposts for *all* their attributes of power. Any change might jeopardize their economic power or social pre-eminence. They were afraid of change and conflict—and denied the need for either. From crisis to crisis, the political options narrowed, the state-of-siege mentality increased. Illiberal Germans heaped abuse on parliamentary institutions, on debate, compromise, tolerance, and reason. But in the absence of debate, of trust that opponents will observe the rules of the game, myths and illusions gain widespread credence.

Unreflectively, people came to think in the categories of friends and foes; as I point out in the second essay, Bismarck himself set the example. He once warned a colleague in parliament that he would go his own way: "Whoever goes with him is his friend, whoever goes against him is his enemy—to the point of annihilation."[8] Even his recollections are full of divisive bitterness—unlike de Gaulle, who in his memoirs also distorts history, but does so in order to create the impression that the French had always been essentially united, when patently they were not.[9] To think that the world consisted of either friends or foes made it easier to believe in force as an alternative to persuasion or debate. The pattern of illiberal self-defense was set in the 1880's and resorted to time and again thereafter. The German proletariat was forced to form a state within a state—not so much enticed by Marx as rebuffed by Bismarck.

Indeed, the German elite steadily exacerbated the class conflict they wished to overcome. For decades, the Left and the Right in German politics taunted each other; the specter that was haunting Europe, as proclaimed by Marx, was half believed in by the upper classes, and they invoked that specter to build still stronger political and ideological defenses against "the red danger." The Left saw its worst suspicions confirmed, and German socialists lived in too illiberal a climate to be safely revisionist and in too cohesive a society to be successfully revolutionary. They too developed a bureaucratic middle; they partially inspired, they wholeheartedly opposed, and they occasionally unconsciously copied the illiberalism of the upper classes.[10] German socialism produced no Jaurès, and

8. Hermann Oncken, *Rudolf von Bennigsen. Ein deutscher liberaler Politiker* (Stuttgart and Berlin, 1910), Vol. II, pp. 382–3.

9. Stanley Hoffmann, *"Les mémoires d'espoir," Esprit*, Vol. 38, No. 12 (Dec., 1970), p. 908.

10. German radicals have never been free of the illiberal contempt for democracy. Today's radical students, having coined the epithet *"Scheissliberal"* for their opponents, have the satisfaction of knowing that they have mobilized excremental language in the ancient Germanic tradition of illiberalism. The present crisis of German universities shows that illiberalism is still strongly entrenched in some sectors of German society. During the

yet within the socialist movement there was so much that was intensely patriotic, that longed for genuine acceptance and a dignified life in a Reich that would be a little more egalitarian and fraternal than Imperial Germany ever was. But the upper classes, frozen in fear and cramped in their egoism, did not seize the possibilities of reform and collaboration. Instead of building bridges, they built moats. German illiberals were incapable of bringing about "an age of equipoise," or a system where the privileged classes would actively promote the betterment of the less privileged.[11]

As socialism grew stronger before the war, so did the suspicions of the upper classes. Militarist excesses, like the Zabern affair on the other hand, confirmed the suspicions of democrats and socialists. As domestic tensions rose before 1914, as the German people—to Max Weber's dismay—still received no political education, few people saw a peaceful escape from the impasse ahead.

But men like Max Weber pointed to the compensatory qualities of life in Imperial Germany. The illiberal spirit that marked politics permeated schools and offices, family life and

---

summer of 1971, on behalf of the O.E.C.D., I visited many German universities and spoke with hundreds of university members. Much of what I saw and feared was epitomized for me by the remark of a top-ranking administrator in a deeply divided university: "There is no compromise possible on the fundamental issues of university politics and reforms. . . . We have no middle at this university, and that's good." Needless to say, that kind of illiberalism is contagious and Germans still seem highly susceptible to it. See my "Reflections on the International Student Movement," *The American Scholar*, Vol. 40, No. 1 (winter, 1970), pp. 123–37. At this time, when universities are facing similar challenges in many Western countries, it would be interesting to study how the traditions of a country's political culture help to shape its particular response to a common crisis.

11. The reference is to W. L. Burn, *The Age of Equipoise, A Study of the Mid-Victorian Generation* (New York, 1965). A. P. Thornton argues that, "In all the movements of liberal reform in Great Britain the same process can be found: members of a privileged class working to have their privileges abolished or extended to others." A. P. Thornton, *The Imperial Idea and Its Enemies, A Study in British Power* (London, 1959), pp. 355–6.

student fraternities. But illiberalism also put a high premium on cultural pre-eminence, on a kind of intellectual elitism. Academic life and scientific genius flourished, and Germans had many reasons to be proud of their place in the world, of their affluence, of their material success. In their homes, illiberalism was often attenuated by ties of exceptional loyalty and friendship, by a kind of domestic sentimentality, that softened much of the still strong authoritarianism of parents over children and of husbands over wives. Whatever shortcomings some *Bürger* detected in their political system, German illiberalism was still freedom itself when compared to Russian autocracy—and stability itself when compared to French liberalism, with its recurrent scandals and inefficiencies. In the non-political realm, most upper-class Germans were satisfied—and unaware that the political system that protected them at home also deeply endangered them abroad.[12]

The domestic tensions of an illiberal regime had profound repercussions on German foreign policy as well. It is my contention that the conditions of illiberalism at home prescribed an aggressive stance in German policy abroad and that the illiberal style at home bred a similar style in the conduct of foreign policy so that, quite aside from the substantive antagonism that Germany would inevitably have encountered, her mode of operation enhanced her dangers and contributed to the coming of the Great War. In short, illiberalism distorted both the style and substance of German foreign policy—a

12. Sympathetic foreigners tended to see only the pleasant side of things, as, for example, the English historian, G. P. Gooch, who spent three months in Berlin in 1895: "I had begun to get the feel of the country, to learn how Germans looked at the world, to realize their energy and thoroughness, to note their pride in their new-found unity, their delight in their growing prosperity, their confidence in their embattled strength, their worship of efficiency, their zeal for education, their respect for learning, their strange indifference to politics and tacit acceptance of authoritarian rule. . . . If in *Wissenschaft* the Germans were in the van, in political maturity they lagged far behind." G. P. Gooch, *Under Six Reigns* (London, 1958), pp. 39, 36.

contention that is amplified in my essay on Bethmann Hollweg.

In the decade of unification Bismarck had resorted to the old pattern of achieving unity at home by waging war abroad; in the following decades he painted lurid pictures of the enemies that threatened the Reich from within and without, and by such means rallied support behind his rule. He was careful, however, not to offend the real interests of other powers. His successors were more reckless. To be sure, their task was bound to be more difficult. By having become the dominant nation in Europe, Germany was necessarily exposed to multiple dangers. The dynamic of the European state system always worked against the aspiring, potentially hegemonial power; the competitiveness of world-wide imperialism heightened the risks.

German statesmen would have needed the greatest skill, the greatest restraint in order to protect and promote German interests peacefully. Instead, the record of prewar diplomacy was lamentable. On the eve of the Great War, Bethmann Hollweg blamed Germany's precarious position on the previous errors in simultaneously affronting Russia in Turkey, France in Morocco, and England on the seas: "challenge everybody, put yourself in everybody's path, and actually weaken no one in this fashion. Reason: aimlessness, the need for little prestige successes and solicitude for every current of public opinion. The 'national' parties with their racket [*Radau*] about foreign policy want to preserve and strengthen their party position."[13] German diplomats had to contend with domestic pressures, as did the diplomats of other great powers. But in addition to normal greed, ordinary class interest, and violent chauvinism, they had the further burden of defending a constitutional regime that was becoming increasingly unpopular. In some ways the Bismarckian system offered a splendid shelter of defense against a rising tide of opposition, but it

13. See below, p. 93.

also proved an easy target. By 1912, the Bismarckian system had become an albatross.

As I suggest in my essays on Bethmann Hollweg and on the Fritz Fischer controversy, fear more than lust for aggrandizement was the principal motive of German policy. But fear can lead to aggrandizement, and aggrandizement can sometimes be rationalized by fear.[14] What Hobbes thought "a general inclination of all mankind" has particular bearing on German diplomacy before 1914: "a perpetual and restless desire of Power after power, that ceaseth only in Death. And the cause of this, is . . . because [a man] cannot assure the power and means to live well, which he hath present, without the acquisition of more."[15] And that "restless desire" appeared to contemporaries as essentially defensive because they believed every forward thrust necessary to protect previous gain. Illiberalism permeated this style of diplomacy. The uncertain overestimation of one's putative opponent, the fear of encirclement, the national claustrophobia, the preference for bullying, the suspicion of compromise—all of these bespoke attitudes characteristic of an illiberal society.

Waldemar Besson recently wrote that after 1890 the Germans ceased to be "satisfied with what they have, and their neighbors consider them trouble-makers par excellence. A profound misunderstanding of their own situation gains ground

14. It is perhaps unnecessary to point out again that there are analogies to be found in the history of other countries. Louis J. Halle has argued that, "from the beginning in the ninth century, and even today, the prime driving force in Russia has been fear. Fear, rather than ambition, is the principal reason for the organization and expansion of the Russian society. Fear, rather than ambition in itself, has been the great driving force. The Russians as we know them today have experienced ten centuries of constant, mortal fear. This has not been a disarming experience. It has not been an experience calculated to produce a simple, open, innocent, and guileless society." Louis J. Halle, *The Cold War as History* (New York and Evanston, 1967), p. 12.
15. Thomas Hobbes, *Leviathan*, Part I, Chapter XI.

among Germans."[16] It is this dissatisfaction mixed with a false self-assessment that Besson described as the continuity of error in half a century of German diplomacy. This continuity of error and of style reflected the political culture at home. Illiberalism heightened the fitful recklessness of German foreign policy, helped to precipitate the Great War, and shaped Germany's disastrous policy in it—until the very external policy that was intended to save the illiberal society brought about its seeming destruction through the defeat of November 1918.

An illiberal regime had been established in Germany under the best of circumstances—and failed. A liberal regime was established in 1918 under the worst of circumstances—and failed. The prewar regime had fostered illusions that bedeviled Weimar. Edmund Burke once referred to "pleasing illusions, which made power gentle and obedience liberal."[17] Germany's ruling elites harbored far from pleasing illusions; they saw themselves always blameless and patriotic, threatened everywhere by corrupted workers, corrosive Jews, and envious foreigners. Few ruling classes could have been so blind to their true motives as were the Germans; few so misused the rhetoric of patriotism. *Their* illusions made power brutal and obedience harsh. The so-called November Revolution put in jeopardy the material interests of the upper classes; it threatened as well the deference that for so long had been paid them. Their illusions turned into ever more embittered fantasies. Weimar had to contend not only with the legacy of defeat and an exacerbated class struggle but with the outraged traditions of the past. The illiberalism of the past was driven frantic by seeming impotence and by a suspicion that the upper classes had themselves betrayed their Emperor. Some men of the old

16. Waldemar Besson, *Die Aussenpolitik der Bundesrepublik: Erfahrungen und Massstäbe* (Munich, 1970), p. 44.

17. Edmund Burke, *Reflections on the Revolution in France* (Baltimore, Md., 1968), p. 171.

Right turned into active plotters for a counter-revolution, as my essay on Adenauer demonstrates. But the bulk of respectable Germans, reared in illiberalism, remained frozen in more or less passive antipathy to the Republic. In 1919, Albert Einstein complained that "against the inborn servant soul [*Knechtsseele*] no revolution can help."[18] The traditions of the past obstructed all of Weimar's efforts to deal with the harsh exigencies of its own time. Heinrich Brüning, whose Chancellorship proved to be the hinge of Nazism, confirmed the persistence of prewar illiberalism when in his memoirs he boasted: "We were a transitional generation, full of contempt for the dominant materialism left over from classical liberalism."[19]

Hitler turned Weimar's debility into his triumph: his radical fanaticism transcended the illiberal tradition, but he could still appeal to that older tradition. He was the embodiment of what was vilest and most paranoid in the illiberal mind—with all the rage added of someone who was both *déclassé* and foreign. But he could speak in many tongues and, after Germany's collapse, he could once again offer the ancient promises of unity at home and national greatness abroad. Fear, insecurity, yearning for power, massive unreason, and hidden class interest converged to bring him to power. A weary people was seduced as well as terrorized into submission. To his supporters he appeared as the ruthless radical that he was; to respectable and frightened Germans he appeared as the uncouth, even brutal, champion of their threatened values.[20]

18. *Albert Einstein Hedwig und Max Born Briefwechsel 1916–1955*, with notes by Max Born (Munich, 1969), p. 39.

19. Heinrich Brüning, *Memoiren 1918–1934* (Stuttgart, 1970), p. 17.

20. Hitler's appeal to both young and old was particularly evident in the response of the universities. By 1930, National Socialist students emerged as the victors in university elections. "Students, like other middle-class youths, were consistently more susceptible to National Socialist propaganda than their elders. . . . The tactics of the storm troopers were applied to the universities." In October 1932, a famous German philosopher, Eduard Spranger, objected to any censuring of National Socialist rowdies among the

Heir and manipulator of illiberal traditions, Hitler perverted even those, and in the end turned his fury not only against traditional enemies but against the illiberal elites themselves. Under Hitler, Germany's illiberalism fed a hideous conflagration of many causes, and when that fire was finally extinguished, many people hoped that illiberalism had perished with it.

Preoccupation with a past so complex and so important needs no particular justification. It may be that the accident of German birth gave me an added incentive to work in this extraordinary field. It certainly left me with strong memories. I was seven when Hitler came to power; for the next five years I lived under the two faces of Fascism. As the victims of Nazi terror furtively came to my father's office as patients, I felt something of the omnipresent fear, the ravages of covert terror; in school I saw the smiling face of Nazism, as fellow students reveled in their uniforms, sang their songs, and prattled their litany of love and hate. I sensed their exultation and felt their cruelty. I remember the shadows of terror, and I remember the public face of Fascism, exuding pride of power. The Nazi presence—the sea of flags and uniforms—was everywhere. And so was the latent fear: one lived at the mercy of a merciless regime. I experienced the ambiguities of Fascism long before I understood the word. In many ways it was a privileged childhood, crowned by the still remembered sense of freedom I felt when I landed in America as a twelve-year-old.

---

young, because he thought "the national movement among the students still genuine at the core, only undisciplined in its form." When the National Socialists purged the universities of Jews and alleged Leftists, there was hardly a murmur of protest: "Many a scholar's behavior in the face of these risks [such as loss of position or ostracism] contrasted sharply with the otherworldly idealism he had so often preached to others. Gone were the heroic poses which had earlier been taken against the tolerant authorities of 'the rabble state.' An ambiguous passivity took their place." Fritz K. Ringer, *The Decline of the German Mandarins. The German Academic Community, 1890–1933* (Cambridge, Mass., 1969), pp. 436–7, 439, 443.

The present collection of essays reflects my interest in the German past, as that interest has evolved over the past seventeen years. I found the essay a congenial form because, unlike the monograph, it allows for a personal and tentative note. Most of these essays are tentative, and some are personal. A few were written for specialists; most were originally intended as lectures, and something of the informality of these occasions may have survived successive revisions.

As a group, the essays deal with two overlapping themes: the emergence of political illiberalism in modern Germany and the catastrophe that resulted from the collision of German power with the interests of other European states. Of the centrality of German history I have already spoken; nor is it necessary to argue the importance of the First World War. Some events, as they recede in time, shrink in significance; the First World War stands out in undiminished horror and importance. It was an earthquake that weakened or destroyed old societies and that enabled new forces to assert themselves under often barren and precarious conditions. It brought forth the programmed terror that men have intermittently suffered since—and in part because of—the war. The two themes of this book, then, touch on the fundamentals of our own lives.

If the book has a unity, it is not so much the unity of subject as of intent. These essays were written from the same perspective, and they should reflect the same style of inquiry. They all represent the same tentative approach to history, and the remarks that follow are not intended to define a method but to suggest what I think were the premises of my work. These essays attest a particular interest in the style and spirit of politics rather than in the structure or substance of politics. They seek to examine specific moments in the careers of Bismarck, Bethmann Hollweg, and Adenauer in order to discover something about the interplay of personal motives, historical traditions, and political pressures. They deal as well with characteristic German attitudes toward politics.

For politics constitutes more than the structure of government or of parties; it is more than the clash of economic or class interests. Politics is also a matter of milieu, of ideas, of attitudes, of styles of thought and conduct. As I tried to show in *The Politics of Cultural Despair,* a great yearning for national regeneration and for an all-powerful Caesar existed already in Imperial Germany; the translation of this yearning into an active political force required a particular set of historical circumstances. Moods, feelings, and ideas do change the world; they are not the sudden creations of some mythical wirepullers. How they change the world, and in combination with what other circumstances and interests, is a central and complex subject for the historian.

It is important, therefore, to know what Germans thought about parliament—as well as what they did in parliament. It is necessary to remember that the army was not only a military machine but the embodiment of certain conscious and unconscious values. Gerhard Ritter has written a magisterial history of German militarism; Eckart Kehr analyzed the material and class interests behind particular institutions or innovations of the army. In his surrealistic novel, *The Sleepwalkers*, Hermann Broch says something about the psychological uses of the uniform in Imperial Germany. The historian must be alive to all manner of clues. The conventional divisions of historical inquiry inhibit rather than promote such awareness.

My interests accordingly led me away from various conventions and abstractions: I do not think that the study of the domestic and foreign affairs of a country can be intelligently separated; I believe that Élie Halévy was one of the first to point this out, as I argue in my essay on his work. I doubt that the history of Germany can be understood without constant reference to its European context. I believe that for the historian a nation's literary imagination is as revealing a source as are its political controversies or its economic statistics. Much history is written as if there were some validity or heuristic value to supposing that the abstractions of "economic man" or "political man" existed in reality. Men rarely act according to the dictates of a single realm; for that they are too much a bundle of past experiences, of shifting aspirations and fears, of political ideas, of material interests and social ambitions. Men live simultaneously in the private and the public realms, and their several roles constitute the drama of their lives. All of this is embarrassingly obvious—in theory; it is difficult for the historian to convert into practice.

Life is messier than historians allow for. Men react to particular situations in the light of their own complicated past; they are often unaware of the tangled motives that determined a particular decision. As James Joll recently wrote: "When political leaders are faced with the necessity of making decisions the outcome of which they cannot foresee, in crises which they do not wholly understand, they fall back on their own instinctive reactions, traditions and modes of behavior. Each of them has certain beliefs, rules or objectives which are taken for granted; and one of the limitations of documentary evidence is that few people bother to write down, especially in moments of crisis, things which they take for granted. Yet if we are to understand their motives, we must somehow try to find out what, as we say, 'goes without saying.' "[21] And even Marx wrote, of the summer of 1848 in France: "This epoch is characterized . . . not by the resolutions of the National Assembly, but by the grounds advanced for these resolutions: not by the thing but by the phrase; not by the phrase but by the accent and the gesture which enliven the phrase."[22]

Concern with the accent and gesture of politics has led me to touch on the non-rational elements of the German past. Is

21. James Joll, *1914. The Unspoken Assumptions*, an inaugural lecture (London, 1968), p. 6.
22. Karl Marx, *The Class Struggles in France, 1848–1850*, in *Karl Marx and Frederick Engels. Selected Works* (Moscow, 1951), Vol. I, pp. 184–5.

not the record of German history over the last century a clear argument against the adequacy of the older conception of politics as essentially the rational pursuit of rational and usually material ends? This type of politics exists, but it requires professional or ideological blinkers not to see how various fears and anxieties swept over German politics, how various resentments and passions suddenly erupted. German history can be read as a lesson in the symbolic and projective side of modern politics.[23]

Historians are rarely without blinkers, and German historians have had particular difficulties in their vision of the past. A century of broken history has had its impact on historical writing; changing loyalties led to changes in genre as well. For decades, a patriotic professoriate wrote "national-liberal" history, i.e., history that would uphold Bismarckian principles or the ideals of an illiberal Germany. Hence historians wrote about statecraft and institutions and implied that their subjects were insulated from the realities of economic or class struggles. After 1918, historians broadened their perspective to include intellectual history, without essentially changing their political bias. The historiography of that older genre had considerable merit; as a young historian recently wrote of one aspect of it: "In a peculiar way, the brilliance and poverty of history as a science appears before our eyes in the transformations of the Bismarck-interpretation."[24] The historiographical effusions of the Nazi period

23. No wonder that a modern political scientist concludes: "To a large extent the psycho-cultural study of politics has its origin in German experience. Many of the classic works on the non-political roots of political attitudes—works that delved into psychological and social variables—were written by men trying to answer questions raised by German National Socialism." Sidney Verba, "Germany: The Remaking of Political Culture," in *Political Culture and Political Development*, ed. by Lucian W. Pye and Sidney Verba (Princeton, 1969), p. 131.

24. *Bismarck und die preussisch-deutsche Politik 1871–1890*, ed. by Michael Stürmer (Munich, 1970), p. 25.

were not so much coerced from above as volunteered from below; earlier traditions could readily be bent to Nazi requirements. The real break in German historiography—as in so much of German life—came after Hitler. A new generation has foresworn the national-liberal traditions; a different political outlook has favored the development of a new genre. Historians have at last begun to study economic and social forces, and the internal history of the Second Reich is now being written.

But German historiography retains a peculiar inclination to move from one absolute to its opposite. It has a proclivity for "either-or" positions—mirroring perhaps a similar inclination in German culture. For a long time German historians erroneously believed in *Der Primat der Aussenpolitik*; the younger generation now insists on a virtual *Primat der Innenpolitik*— so much so that, in 1970, Waldemar Besson half seriously apologized for still writing about foreign policy as if it existed.[25] There have been other reversals of perspective as well. Earlier historians argued that ideas were the stuff of history, later historians implicitly suggest that ideas are but the function of the material substructure. Historians once argued Germany's innocence in 1914, and their successors now posit her guilt. The either-or quality persists, great systems are still either accepted or turned on their head, and in this fierce battle of abstractions—with clear political interest involved—the multifarious complexity of life often escapes, or at least the nuances of style are brushed aside as frills or "mere" disguises. Earlier historians who thought that history was all a matter of wars and statecraft and present historians who think that the determinants of history are class relations or material interests recall Andrew Undershaft, Major Barbara's father, who, accused of having no religion, indignantly denied such an imputation and defined his credo: "There are

25. Waldemar Besson, *op. cit.*, p. 16.

two things necessary to Salvation. Money and gunpowder."
There have always been crypto-Undershafts among historians.
These generalities have had a direct bearing on my work. If
anyone should have approximated Undershaft or fitted the abstraction "economic man," it should have been Bismarck's
banker Bleichröder. Germany's richest man should presumably
have followed the promptings of his material interests. Earlier
generations of historians denied Bleichröder's importance. How
could Bismarck have been anything but repelled by the Jewish-
materialistic machinations of this plutocrat? Contemporary
historians tend to see Bleichröder and his fellow entrepreneurs
as economic men and overlook German ambivalence to wealth
and capitalism. In Bleichröder's lifetime, the United States and
Germany were industrial countries par excellence, but their
ethos regarding business and capitalism was fundamentally
different, and that difference had a marked impact on their
political developments as well. Bismarck had a firm grasp of
money—whatever subterfuges others might find for their appetites. Bleichröder, too, sought wealth—that was his business—
but his struggle for status, for acceptance, indeed for identity
was an equally important element in his career. In the thousands of letters and documents I have unearthed in preparing
a biography of Bleichröder, I found many surprises—none
perhaps more indicative of the style of German politics than
Bleichröder's letter to William I, imploring the monarch to rein-
state Bleichröder's son as an officer in the reserves, despite a
terrible lapse of conduct. Without this royal act of clemency,
Bleichröder intimated, he would have to leave his native country, which he loved and served so well.

If anyone should have conformed to the abstraction of "political man" who operates according to the dictates of *raison d'état,*
it should have been Bethmann Hollweg, Imperial Chancellor, as
he was weighing decisions of war and peace in the weeks between Sarajevo and the outbreak of the war. It is a remarkable

abstraction of historians to depict statesmen as if they were political calculators who had checked their psyche and their past, their upbringing, their aspirations, their unspoken assumptions in the vestibules of their offices. A glimpse of Bethmann Hollweg, through the eyes of his confidant, dispels such simplicities. Bethmann's fatalism and his fears, his ambivalent feelings about the military, his impressions of the present domestic scene and the likely prospect of the international future—all of these factors shaped his decisions during and after the July crisis.

By the nature of their training and the character of the available evidence, historians are ill-prepared to deal with these peripheral considerations. But they need not deny them. They need not pretend that these elements of individual or mass psychology are the trivia of history or the function of something deeper that they call class or material interest.

Different political styles and sudden flights of national passions may even illuminate the complexities of international relations. Consider, for example, the fateful estrangement between Germany and England that began in the Wilhelmine period and lasted beyond 1945. Were the issues only substantive, was it only a matter of commercial competition, imperialist rivalry, struggle for hegemony? Did not the style of the two nations exacerbate grievances and feed suspicions? German alternation between playing the bully and the injured innocent and the British ideal of unflappability—differences like these exist among nations as among men, and they matter. As late as 1926, Sir Austen Chamberlain, committed to returning Germany to a position of equality, noted with exasperation that a new German demand was *"echt deutsch*—in other words, very bad diplomacy. The Prussian must pull off his Jack-boots before the new world will be comfortable to him."[26]

26. *Documents in British Foreign Policy, 1919–1939*, ed. by W. N. Medlicott *et al.*, Series IA (London, 1968), Vol. II, No. 181, p. 321.

One of the great intangible difficulties for German diplomats has been that the world has never felt comfortable to them—in jackboots or out. One could add that the English world never tried to make them comfortable.

Nor is class conflict solely a matter of conflicting interests. The importance of money and class is beyond dispute. Before Marx, novelists like Stendhal and Balzac analyzed class relations and described class exploitation. After their work, class should have been central to any understanding of modern society. Marx attributed to a simpler definition of class a cruder impact on history: the world was suddenly reduced to class relations, men thought and acted within the context of their material interests—and that context can be defined narrowly or broadly, to suit polemical or philosophical intent. Marx dogmatized a truth that others had intuited; his insistence, however, that ideas and interests are not dissociated has had a profound effect on historiography. Class relations have their milieu as well, and different societies devise different ways of exploitation. By slighting the non-material grievances of the lower classes, historians have often belittled their sufferings. Certain attitudes of the upper classes can be as galling to their putative inferiors as their grasping ways. The German bourgeoisie was peculiarly adept at disguising the realities of the class struggle; they saw themselves as the bastions of *Bildung,* or culture, hence with a special dispensation for *Besitz,* or property. A particular stance of bourgeois denial of bourgeois realities I have called *Vulgäridealismus,* a metaphysic of snobbery, and sought to evoke thereby the manner by which Germans could idealize their material interests—to the still greater injury of those below them.

The Germans have been superbly rational in their laboratories and industrial organizations. Their vision of politics and society, however, was blurred by clouds of evil fantasy. The role of myths in the German past is striking. From the 1870's on, successive conspirational theories poisoned German life: The Jew as sinister agent of national decomposition, England and France as plotters of encirclement, the Bolshevik conspiracy, November criminals who stabbed Germany in the back, and finally the great outcry against the Weimar "system" as the embodiment of treason and corruption. Was Germany peculiarly susceptible to such paranoid simplifications? Can one understand German history of the last century without paying particular attention to the element of fear, of *Angst*? Whence this vulnerability to an emotion so alien to the virtues of heroism and courage on which Germans were nurtured? The prevalence of fear had many causes; no one would assert that these emotions were autonomous, unrelated to the great upheavals of economic change and depression, class antagonisms, or international conflict. But it is wrong to say that they were simply manipulated or mobilized by embittered capitalists, as some of the cruder theories would have it.[27]

Not long ago, a German literary historian noted that "historians are not interested enough in psychology, and psycholo-

---

27. Present-day interpreters would do well to ponder Franz Neumann's great essay on "Angst und Politik." I remember being present at a memorable occasion in 1954, at the Free University of Berlin, when he first delivered that lecture. Soaring beyond his brilliant *Behemoth* and its austere Marxist analysis, he insisted that, "Anxiety is, or ought to be, a central problem of the sciences. . . . Germany of 1930–33 was the land of alienation and anxiety. . . . But how was the people to be integrated, despite all cleavages of class, party, religion? Only through hatred of an enemy. . . . It would be a mistake to construe a connection between the socio-economic status of a person and his antisemitism; that is, to claim that the academically educated person is more immune than the uneducated, or the poorly paid more immune than the better paid." I sensed then that here was being presented a new vision of politics—with a range of questions that went far beyond the role of monopoly capitalism. Neumann's death a few weeks later took away a man of uncommon intellect and courage, and no one elaborated his new beginnings. Franz Neumann, "Anxiety and Politics," in *The Democratic and the Authoritarian State, Essays in Political and Legal Theory*, ed. and with a preface by Herbert Marcuse (Glencoe, Ill., 1957), pp. 270, 287.

gists are not interested in history."[28] Most historians have always been psychologists of sorts; it is impossible to interpret human behavior without some psychological acumen. There are, however, large areas of human and social behavior that historians have shunned, partly because they realize the inadequacies of their evidence and of their own professional knowledge of certain types of behavior. But they should at least acknowledge the presence of forces outside the traditional purview of history. Until recently, historians have slighted the symbolic side of politics, but it is precisely in the imagery and rhetoric of politics that some of the irrational elements find their clearest embodiment. Weimar was dissolved in a frenzy of raw emotions, whipped up again and again by rallies, parades, incantations, and by an uncanny leader who in the final and most gruesome outburst of illiberal passion identified himself with deeply rooted traditions of the past and swept off their feet those anxious for redemption, while blinding would-be opponents with the radiance of resurrected symbols. National symbols had been important in quieter times as well; one thinks of the ritualized Sedan celebrations, of Weimar's deeply divisive struggle over the national flag, which is dealt with in my essay on Adenauer.

A history of symbols and gestures in modern Germany could be written, a kind of iconography of politics, beginning with Bismarck's masquerading in his uniform and ending perhaps with Willy Brandt's kneeling in symbolic contrition at the ghetto gates of Warsaw. Hitler exemplified the projective quality of modern politics. For decades all manner of resentments had pervaded Germany's political culture. Hitler, suffering these resentments himself and sensing them in others,

28. Richard Alewyn made this observation, and it is quoted in *Die politische und gesellschaftliche Rolle der Angst,* ed. with an introduction by Heinz Wiesbrock ("Politische Psychologie," Vol. 6; Frankfurt, 1967), p. 10, *n.* 17.

demonstrated how politics could serve as an escape from boredom, from failure, from self. Nor did this type of politics disappear with the end of the Third Reich. It remains with us, at least potentially, and we see it still in familiar and unfamiliar places.

Other countries have experienced similar movements. Richard Hofstadter analyzed "The Paranoid Style in American Politics," and did so keeping in mind the experience of other countries and the questions of other disciplines. Historians generally have come to understand that, in his phrase, the perspectives of the social sciences add "to the speculative richness of history."[29] For me as for many of my generation, Hofstadter's own work exemplified the possibilities of history for our time. His was the greatest influence on me, and an inadequate acknowledgment of it can be seen in my adoption of the terms milieu and political culture, to which he gave unique substance.

Modes of historical interpretation change, especially in free societies and at moments of political upheaval. My own involvement in the Fritz Fischer controversy on the origins of the First World War showed me anew that the political passions and conflicts of the present sweep over the past as well. The past grows with the present. Historians view past and present in some sort of simultaneous vision. Some of them believe that an informed picture of the past may shed some light on the unfolding future—or at least they know that a mythical past ill instructs the present. And however much we are committed to the scrupulous reconstruction of the past for its own sake, some of us may at times cherish the hope that our efforts will provide some guidance to the present as well.

29. Richard Hofstadter, "History and the Social Sciences," in Fritz Stern, ed., *The Varieties of History* (Cleveland and New York, 1956, 1962), p. 364. See also his *The Paranoid Style in American Politics and Other Essays* (New York, 1965), esp. pp. vii–xiv and 3–40.

. . .

The German past has acquired a special relevance to the American present. In our first encounter with the tragedy of power, we seem to hear echoes of earlier disasters.

Anyone listening to our intellectual life will know that German has suddenly become the accepted language of crisis politics. In our moments of outrage or perplexity, we talk of storm troopers and Reichstag fires, of concentration camps and genocide, of Munich, Auschwitz, Lidice, of book-burning and Gestapos. Beyond these labels lies the dim, collective memory of the ultimate crime of the Nazis, and activists of whatever persuasion often condone their revolutionary pranks by pretending they are exorcising the ghost of six million Jews who, they say, allowed themselves to be marched to their deaths. The young sometimes see their elders as accomplices or perpetuators of earlier crimes, and they confound a moment of repression with the long night of totalitarianism; the older generation, in turn, see in youthful militancy the pacemakers of a fascist backlash. Advocates of the Vietnamese war have for years deluded themselves and others by invoking Munich and the failure of appeasement to justify their persistent error. Out of respect for the dead, we should adopt a moratorium on facile analogies with unique suffering; the memory of that past should not be dissipated by mindless invectives.

The analogies with Germany, however, bespeak both polemical intent and genuine unease. America is and feels herself to be in crisis, and the question "Is America destined to go authoritarian?" no longer seems safely absurd. We once thought ourselves the saviors of the Western world; our detractors today think us the terror of that world. In the last decade, we have lost more moral self-confidence and credibility than most nations accumulate in their history. Amidst all this uncertainty and self-doubt is there nothing that the German experience can tell us?

Some years ago, Henry Kissinger wrote that America had not experienced tragedy and implied that we needed to learn from the experience of others.[30] We have lost that innocence in the horror of Vietnam, but we can still ponder the fate of other countries. The United States owes its present position as the world's pre-eminent nation to the reckless squandering of German power in the first half of the century. In some ways, our very position in the world is a reminder of how Germany had become the foremost country of Europe and had pursued power with ever greater arrogance and self-deception. In the successive bids for hegemonial power, the Germans showed that the pursuit of power demands realism and promotes delusion, that a nation new on the world stage is apt to misunderstand and disregard the motives and interests of other nations, while deluding herself about her own motives. German politics also reminds us that domestic tensions put foreign relations in jeopardy and that an unstable and uncertain nation is likely to pursue an erratic and at the same time uncompromising policy abroad. It warns us that unresolved domestic conflicts can predispose a nation's leaders to pursue a forward policy abroad, to accept the risks of war—and to find that foreign wars exacerbate the very conflicts they were intended to defuse. The role of super-patriots in the German past has been dismal; German politics gives little comfort to those who would put their confidence in military expertise: the German and indeed the European record during the First World War bespeak bankruptcy as the military seek to cope with new types of warfare and new political challenges. The list of warnings could be extended. I believe that Germany's encounter with imperial power before 1918 may be more relevant to America today than

30. Henry A. Kissinger, *Nuclear Weapons and Foreign Policy* (New York, 1957), p. 426.

the more often invoked and more obvious lessons of Weimar. It was before 1918 that a seemingly moderate Germany experienced the dangers and temptations of imperial power.

The lessons of Weimar seem clear and less applicable. Weimar did present a terrifying picture of the dialectics of radical politics. The extremes of Right and Left tacitly collaborated against an undistinguished, fearful middle. Weimar exemplified for all times the precariousness of freedom—how easily free institutions are subverted, how readily diverse groups and classes forsake liberal institutions, how few people rally to the defense of imperfect freedom while the many pursue the phantoms of revolution or national regeneration. Weimar also reminds us that anxiety and unreason are political elements and that non-material grievances can have a sudden and dramatic effect on a nation's politics. But analogies to Weimar suffer from the simple fallacy that Weimar was merely an epilogue in disaster; as I have argued before, Weimar's weakness was itself the outcome of the earlier illiberal traditions.

The differences between America and Weimar are fundamental. The American political tradition *is* different from the traditions of German illiberalism, though there is no guarantee that liberalism today will find the needed resiliency and courage in order once again to adapt an old system to new demands. The German elites thought that foreign adventurism and domestic repression would work; they were wrong. Troubled and riven as our society is, tempting as repression might be to an alarmingly large segment of the population, the country today still has traditions and institutions that offer formidable barriers to authoritarianism. To exaggerate dangers is no better than to deny them. We are today in the midst of protest and dissent that Germany never experienced in her century of statehood—and that few, if any, European states encountered during a war.

These are generalities. History offers no specific lessons. Our task is not to keep America from becoming Weimar; perhaps our task is to keep America from irredeemably betraying herself. As she staggers onto a path of power and responsibility from which no nation has returned unharmed, and does so under conditions more precarious and more decisive than any other nation ever faced, her greatest asset may be her liberal tradition, however imperfectly embodied and however often challenged. The stakes are immense. In an idiom that is characteristically American: The buck stops here—with us. For everybody.

Part One

The Illiberal Society

The Political Consequences of the Unpolitical German

This piece marked my first effort to deal with the political
culture of illiberal Germany. In it, I sought to deal with
the self-image of the German *Bürger,* with the cultural
rationalizations for his political behavior. It pointed to the
allegedly unpolitical stance of upper-class Germans as
one element of continuity in German history and ques-
tioned the then still popular notion that "bad" Germans
trounced "good" Germans. Although no longer satisfied
with some of the formulations in this essay, I still believe
that my notion of *Vulgäridealismus* is sound, that my discussion of the self-deception Germans practiced has some
bearing on the nature of German class antagonisms and
German imperialist ideology, and that my emphasis on the
political fatality of a certain kind of idealism may be
useful for an understanding of various mass movements—
not necessarily restricted to those of the German past.

I would tackle the problem of political self-awareness
differently today. The piece stands, however, as an early
exploration of a difficult theme; as such it received some
attention. Specialized studies have since appeared, particularly on the outlook of the German professoriate. These
tend to sustain my general conclusions. Minor changes in

the text would have proved useless and, accordingly, the essay is here reprinted as it first appeared in 1960 in the now defunct magazine *History*. It was originally delivered as an address to a general session of the Pacific Branch meeting of the American Historical Association in December 1957.

For many decades, the course of German politics has puzzled and, at times, terrified the nations of the Western world. How could the Germans, a people of such intellectual eminence and moral intent, endure the blundering authoritarianism of the Empire, the divisiveness of Weimar, the tyranny of Hitler? Why was Germany without a stable political tradition, why had it failed to adopt successfully the political institutions that had become the norms of Western political culture? A frequent answer was that there were two Germanies, the Germany of the educated citizenry, peaceful and potentially democratic, and the official, aggressive Germany, governed by a handful of men. The classic expression of this faith in the other Germany was Wilson's refusal, in October 1918, to deal with the Kaiser's government; he would deal with a democratic Germany or none at all. This idea of the two Germanies—the majority held captive by a small minority—dominated Western historical thinking as well. It encouraged historians to hunt up villains, to fasten on specific groups or minority interests that may have inhibited Germany's natural bent toward the West.

This view presupposed a far sharper division within Germany than in fact existed; it overlooked the many ways in which the German elite had accommodated itself to its political nonage and had benefited from it. Before 1918 and after 1933, the German *Bürger* did not feel thwarted or enchained; they thought themselves free. Their acquiescence in different political regimes suggests that there was but one Germany, in which the different forces were inextricably mingled. To gain the proper perspective on this Germany the historian must examine German society not at points of obvious divergence or extremity, such as Nazi Germany, but in periods of apparent normality and quietude. Nor should he concentrate exclusively on some tenacious groups, such as the German army or the much-maligned Junkers. It is not the "bad Germans" that are unique—every Western nation has had its reactionary die-hards, its racists and hypernationalists, its imperialists and fascists—but the "good Germans," the several generations of peaceful and splendidly educated, seemingly Western men. It is to them, to their worship of culture and their depreciation of politics, to their sentiments and ideals, that I shall want to turn.

For a century or more the German term *"Kultur"* had a reverential connotation that the simple English word "culture" cannot render. It was invested with the awe and reverence that Germans felt, or thought they should feel, for the diverse creations of the spirit, for the mystery of the arts that to so many possessed a voice as tender and as powerful as religion itself. This idealization of culture inspired and guided the great intellectual and scientific achievements of modern Germany; German learning had a great influence on the life of other peoples —as American universities so clearly exemplify. But the ideal of culture, once embodied in institutions, became more and more a passive appreciation of past creativity, and in time it degenerated into little more than the ritualistic repetition of phrases and pieties. Far more important than the decline was the impact that this veneration of culture had on German society, on politics, religion, and on what may be called the national self-image. As I will try to show, it fostered several political prejudices and positions, none favorable to the development of a democratic society or even to the growth of a cohesive nation. It hastened the rapid and peculiar secularization of Protestant Germany and served as a rationalization for a good deal of political and social irresponsibility and iniquity. There is pathos in the fact that the Germans used their greatest achievement, their culture, to augment and excuse their greatest failure, their politics.

The exaltation of culture, the veneration and perfection of learning, had its origins in German Idealism, that extraordinary outburst of artistic and intellectual creativity from 1770 to 1830. Diverse, even antithetical, though the several strands of German Idealism were—*Sturm und Drang*, classicism, romanticism, and idealistic philosophy proper—together they formed the intellectual basis of modern German society. Germany's cultural awakening coincided with the democratic revolution of the Western world; the revolution overwhelmed Germany in its most inexorable and ruthless guise, in Napoleon, and it is no wonder that German Idealism, which had earlier been in such close dependence on the West, in time absorbed a sharp anti-Western and anti-French strain. It has been said that Idealism was Germany's equivalent of the French Revolution, and in some ways at least, Idealism did become a substitute for and a defense against the Revolution. German nationalism, inflamed by Napoleon's triumphs, turned against the political ideals and achievements of the French Revolution. What was exalted by German nationalism was the cultural achievement and destiny of the Germans, their peculiar gifts for poetry, truth, and music. Consequently German nationalism was less concerned with the political destiny of the Germans, with their practical rights and liberties as citizens.

I shall not analyze Idealist philosophy nor trace the impact of specific ideas or philosophic systems on German thought, in the manner, say, of John Dewey's *German Philosophy and*

Politics, or of other polemical essays in intellectual history.
I am concerned with the effect of Idealism on a level below
that of formal philosophy and pure ideas. The German *Bürger,*
however superbly educated, did not grapple with the precise
ideas of Kant or Hegel or even Goethe, but some of the ideas,
condensed into a few pat phrases, did mold and perpetuate a
vague, elusive, but important *Lebensgefühl,* a cultural stance,
a style of life. It is with the political consequences of these
elusive attitudes, with the intellectual or aesthetic presuppositions of politics rarely articulated because so habitual and common, that I want to deal.

Historians have seldom studied this layer of German culture,
partly, no doubt, because they took at face value the historical
cliché that the German *Bürger* was unpolitical, hence, for the
political historian, an object of pity, not of study. Yet the
allegedly unpolitical stance of a highly influential class with
strong cultural prejudices deserves the closest scrutiny; in it
one may find an obstinate condition of Germany's political
failure. The self-consciously unpolitical strain in German life
has had a profound, and on the whole, an injurious impact on
German politics.

It was not accidental that Prussia began its intense institutional concern with culture—the establishment of new universities and the improvement of old ones—at the time of its
unprecedented humiliation at the hands of Napoleon. "The
state," said Frederick William III, "must replace by spiritual
forces what it lost in material strength." Here was the characteristic confusion of spirit and power, and the inchoate assumption that culture could substitute for power. From then on the
moral indispensability of education became an article of faith:
the self-fulfillment of the individual required the humanistic
cultivation of the mind. Under Wilhelm von Humboldt, the
Prussian school system was reformed, the ideal of a general
education—*allgemeine Bildung*—was embodied, perhaps im-

prisoned, in those bastions of learning, the German *gymnasia.*[1]

This educational system, with its recruitment and rewards, its gradations and pretensions, was of singular importance in a society that was still far from open, in a society where Guizot's *"enrichissez-vous"* would have been a senseless admonition. Intellectually, the schools sought to prepare the universal man, but not the public-minded citizen; here students gathered their knowledge of the classics, of Christianity, of the Enlightenment, and of Idealism—knowledge often mechanically acquired, but all precious and all conspicuously displayed. The earnest belief in the indispensability of this kind of intellectual and aesthetic education was given practical value as well: the rewards of higher education were enormous and in an economically backward society they continued to be the most important means of climbing the social ladder. An academic degree was a prerequisite for most positions of status and prestige, and in the early nineteenth century, the academician or civil servant of humble origin was by no means exceptional. Higher education, moreover, granted the student partial exemption from military service—no mean incentive to culture.

This exaltation of culture had a still more penetrating effect on German society: for the educated classes, especially in Protestant Germany, it brought about the gradual secularization of religion through culture, the substitution in a sense of one for the other. This process, obviously so comprehensive and complex that I can do no more than hint at it, involved the approximation of religion, more accurately of Protestantism, to culture and metaphysics, by stripping religion of the super-

1. The austere intellectualism of the schools and the authoritarianism of the teachers, the remoteness from the workaday world, the absence of sports, helped to mold the typical scholar of the nineteenth century; but at times these also led to sudden outbreaks of youth irrationalism and anti-intellectualism, of which the Youth Movement before 1914 was the most famous example.

natural and the mysterious, of sin and redemption, reducing it to an ethical essence, to a universal core that was immune to higher biblical criticism. It involved as well the elevation of the aesthetic and intellectual aspects of culture; of philosophy, literature, and art, to be the supreme revelations of the human spirit, and the substitution of the moral commands of German Idealism, of Kant in particular, for older universal and religious commands. The *reductio ad absurdum* of this culture-worship must surely have been the proposal of one German historian that the works of Goethe should be added to the other books of Divine Revelation.

With this veneration of culture there emerged another ideal, a universally accepted tenet of Idealism that persisted as the talisman of the educated classes: the belief in the perfectibility of the aesthetic or rational faculties of the individual, quite independently of political conditions. The inner freedom that Luther preached became secularized, but the state itself, while it must not actively inhibit the pursuit of knowledge, could do little to infringe on the highest good, the unfolding of the personality. To be sure, there were important variations of this belief: the Kantians had a very different sense of the individual's self-fulfillment from the Romantics or from those who cherished Goethe's and Schiller's image of the *Genie*—of the demonic, asocial genius who in a different guise appears in Hegel's irresistible world-historical figure. This admiration of the self-fulfillment of the individual, in the strictly private sphere, through learning but without good works, proved yet another link between Protestantism and German Idealism. It was in Schleiermacher that the two strains most clearly mingled, and after him this essentially humanistic belief was wrapped in a religious mystique as well. The cultured man, by and large, ceased to be a church man, and his so-called religion of Idealism contributed, as the great Catholic historian Franz Schnabel points out, to the utter secularization of the academically trained classes in Protestant Germany.[2]

This type of individualism had nothing egalitarian about it; here was not the Christian belief in the equality of souls and sinners nor the beneficial abstraction about a natural man who was created equal "and endowed with inalienable rights to life, liberty, and the pursuit of happiness." This individualism had a distinct aesthetic-aristocratic bent and could, indeed quickly did, degenerate into a cult of the personality. Only the exceptional individual, the great personality, could attain the self-fulfillment, the self-mastery that Idealism prescribed.

This veneration of culture and personality, which became one of the principal pieties of nineteenth-century Germany, was neither exclusively German nor in itself culpable. The man of culture has often disdained the grubbiness of politics, has usually been remote from the lower classes. But a difference persisted, a difference well brought out in Matthew Arnold's *Culture and Anarchy*, a book which one would expect to be closely akin to the German ideal. "Culture has one great passion, the passion for sweetness and light. It has one even yet greater! The passion for making them prevail . . . and it knows that the sweetness and light of the few must be imperfect until the raw and unkindled masses of humanity are touched with sweetness and light." The German academically trained person lacked the passion to make it prevail.[3] He often felt that the

2. It is significant that in the nineteenth century the formally Protestant groups played the pre-eminent role in German intellectual life, even as the Protestant Church steadily declined. Catholicism, on the other hand, had less impact on intellectual life, and suffered less from the loss of faith in the last century.

3. In 1867, young William James met and reported on this strange, admirable being, the German professor. (It was Wilhelm Dilthey whom he so described, a man far less remote from reality than most of his colleagues.) "He is the first man I have ever met of a class, which must be common here, of men to whom learning has become as natural as breathing. A learned man at home is in a measure isolated; his study is carried on in private, at

passive enjoyment of culture sufficed, that culture could be tended in almost any society and, finally, that almost any regime or social injustice could be rationalized or glorified, by reference to German culture. It was not only that spirit and politics were divorced, as the Germans have always maintained, half proudly and half regretfully; it is that spirit often became a cloak for the politics of callousness and irresponsibility.[4]

To be sure, in the early nineteenth century, this veneration of culture and personality coincided with the dominant political aspiration. In Humboldt's mind and time, this *Humanitätsideal* served as a spur to the creation of a liberal society. Indeed, in the pre-1948 movement, most academics sought to translate the inner freedom of man into external freedom as well, and the liberals of those days fought the establishment, the court,

---

reserved hours. To the public he appears as a citizen and neighbor, etc., and they know at most *about* him that he is addicted to this or that study; his intellectual occupation always has something of a put-on character, and remains external at least to some part of his being. Whereas this cuss seemed to me to be nothing if not a professor . . . as if he were able to stand towards the rest of society *merely* in the relation of a man learned in this or that branch—and never for a moment forget the interests or put off the instincts of his specialty. If he should meet people or circumstances that could in no measure be dealt with on that ground, he would pass on and ignore them, instead of being obliged, like an American, to sink for the time the specialty." *The Letters of William James*, ed. by Henry James (2nd edn., Boston, 1926), Vol. I, pp. 110–11.

4. It is noteworthy that Germans have traditionally exalted those self-images that attested their non-political, or individualistic, nature. The much-revered image of Tacitus' primitive German, that self-reliant, robust, and incorruptible barbarian, fighting against the decadent and overcivilized Romans, hardly fostered the political virtues. In the sixteenth century, the legend of the German *Michel* or of the *Dummer Michel*, the clumsy, charitable boor, sprang up, and by the nineteenth century the stupid *Michel* was widely and fondly caricatured as the typical German "with his excessive benevolence and political immaturity." Again, the revival of the Siegfried myth: the unsuspecting, naïve hero cut down by the scheming villainous Hagen. The Germans have ever doubted their political capacities, and their outstanding rulers, from Frederick II to Hitler, and perhaps beyond, have rarely troubled to disguise their contempt for their people's political sense. The German pantheon, resplendent with poets, thinkers, and warriors, contains few, if any, statesmen—a consequence of Germany's political history.

the nobility, and the church as obscurantist or tyrannical institutions that inhibited the growth of the free individual. However diverse the liberals' programs, they all demanded the legal freedom of the person, i.e., his protection from every form of public arbitrariness, his liberation from economic and social disabilities, and his spiritual freedom, i.e., his right to hold, exchange, and propagate dissenting beliefs. It was only regarding the capstone of the free society—the right to self-government, the erection, in other words, of a representative or parliamentary system—that intellectual opinion was divided, and here I would suggest that the drive to self-government was blunted by the prevalent depreciation of political life.[5]

It was in the decisive decades between the failure of 1848 and the national successes of Bismarck that the political implications of unpolitical Idealism emerged more clearly. For it was in those decades of quickened political life that several strains of German liberalism capitulated before Bismarck and his national goals, in effect abandoned, or indefinitely postponed, the demands for political self-government. But it was the way in which they renounced their ideals that indicates the critical importance of the Idea of Culture. When, in 1864, the

5. The political views of liberalism have recently been analyzed in Leonard Krieger's masterly work, *The German Idea of Freedom: A History of a Political Tradition* (Boston, 1957). Beginning with the Old Regime and concentrating on the major figures of German liberalism, he traces the peculiar doctrinal development of German liberalism, the continuing efforts to associate the idea of freedom with existing political institutions, to render compatible freedom and the authoritarian state. During the nineteenth century, in the mind of the educated man, this idea of freedom became qualified, I think, by the ideal of culture, which transcended the political divisions, and permeated liberals as well as conservatives, making the former more conservative and the latter more self-righteous. Although most bibliographical references are omitted from this essay, I want to call the reader's attention to Hajo Holborn's article, "Der deutsche Idealismus in sozialgeschichtlicher Beleuchtung," which is central to this theme and from which I learned a great deal. *Historische Zeitschrift*, Vol. CLXXIV (Oct., 1952), pp. 359–84. (Now available in English: Hajo Holborn, *Germany and Europe, Historical Essays* [Garden City, N.Y., 1970], pp. 1–32.)

German liberals lost heart in their own course, which for once had massive popular strength behind it, they neither accepted nor rejected Bismarck's practical dictum, that blood and iron must decide the great questions of the day; they were not content to say that this was a necessary sacrifice for the fulfillment of higher national goals. Rather, they repudiated politics altogether, and asserted that politics—as the then novel term *"Realpolitik"* implied—was necessarily divorced from the realm of ideals and morals, that spirit and power were distinct, though not necessarily antithetical.

Hermann Baumgarten, a liberal historian and Max Weber's uncle, became the leading apologist of this retreat from politics: "The *Bürger* is meant to work, not to rule, and a statesman's primary task is to rule." Referring specifically to the *Bürger's* heritage of Idealism, he concluded that in one sense he was too good for politics and in another not good enough. What better example of this than the immediate past: "We have had the unprecedented experience that our victory would have been a disaster while our defeat has been an immense blessing." Bismarck had to be accepted, for he was the master of the practical realm, and in that acceptance emerged full-blown the unpolitical German, the good German who would tolerate and acquiesce in political imperfection, even turpitude, as long as his escape into Idealism was not blocked by the public authority of the state. They were willing to render unto Caesar what was Caesar's and unto Culture what was Culture's.

But some liberals were not content with the retreat from politics, this escape to Idealism. Treitschke, for example, took quite a different position; far from retreating to culture, he provided Bismarck's *Realpolitik* with a spiritual justification, a moral veneer. The decline of Protestantism and the exaltation of culture had gone hand in hand; Treitschke, born into an austere Protestant family, gradually embraced the religion of Idealism, and invested Bismarck's new state with the same passion and absolute moral righteousness that previously had belonged to religion.[6] What Treitschke did rhapsodically, thousands of Germans, organized in the National Liberal Party, did prosaically: they idealized, in Max Weber's phrase, they ethicized, Bismarck's achievement of power. Some eighty years later, Friedrich Meinecke said of the liberal transformation of this period: "Specifically German . . . was the tendency to elevate something primarily practical into a universal worldview theory."

The new Empire was intensely practical. The quaint and quiet nation of poets and thinkers survived only in the nostalgia of the educated classes. After 1871, the material conditions of Germany, though not her politics nor her spirit, rapidly approximated those of the West. For centuries politically divided, Germany was now a nation state, as were her Western neighbors; for centuries economically backward, Germany, in her first economic miracle, bounded ahead, surpassed France, challenged Britain, and became the leading industrial nation of the continent; for centuries a weak state, she now became a great military power, a power that by its existence in the heart of Europe posed a threat to Europe. How prophetic was the British M.P. who, after the battle of Sedan, said: "Europe has lost a mistress and gained a master." But the master's house was divided against itself. Bismarck's semi-absolutistic regime, with its democratic appearances and feudal reality, postponed and embittered the conflict between the aspirations of the democratic forces and the privileges of the nobility and its newly won allies, the captains of industry. Bismarck's political system intensified the class antagonisms, and the newly united nation became socially more divided.

The response of the academic classes to the new Germany

6. For Treitschke the state was "the most supremely real person, in the literal sense of the word, that exists." For a worshipper of personality, this Hegelian identification meant a still higher aesthetic value for the state.

was diverse. We have already noted the devastating impact of Bismarck's success on many liberals; no wonder Mommsen charged that Bismarck had broken the moral backbone of the nation and Nietzsche thundered that military victory must not be confused with cultural vitality. After 1871, a small part of the academic class remained critical of Imperial Germany even in the face of success and still hoped that Germany would adopt the political institutions of the West. A larger group retired to what came to be called the unpolitical realm, reconciled to their political impotence. A still larger group idealized the existing Germany and its imperialist ambitions and avowed that German culture, superior to that of the West, justified German power as well. Underlying all three positions, blunting the drive of the first and intensifying the jingoism of the last, was the cultured person's fear of the rapidly growing proletariat and his suspicion that culture and democracy, if not incompatible, were certainly opposed to each other. Without surrendering his unpolitical pretensions, the cultured German could, for the sake of his culture, support every conservative measure and oppose every radical move. *Bildung* became as much a conservative bulwark as *Besitz,* and both began to accept the refeudalization of German society. Years later, Friedrich Meinecke, himself an outstanding representative of the intellectual splendor and political fatality of German Idealism, summed up with unmistakable sympathy this fear of the good but unpolitical German:

> About the middle of the nineteenth century and later it was the high aim of German culture to preserve from this pressure [by the masses] and from its coarsening and deteriorating effect the sacred heritage of the Goethe period—an almost miraculous gift bestowed upon the German people—and at the same time to support what seemed vital and fruitful in the demands of the new masses.[7]

7. It is curious that intellectuals, and by no means only German intellec-

Certainly the preservation of culture and quality in the face of this coarsening intrusion—which since the 1870's the Germans have chosen to call the threat of Americanization—should engage our sympathetic interest. Critics in the West have argued a similar concern. Still, we must note that Germany's concern with culture became more and more inimical to the course of German politics itself and soon turned into strong resentment against the West.

At their best the prewar generation of German academics and professionals preserved and enriched the magnificent traditions of German learning. Although no longer the universalists of the early century, they had become erudite specialists, and the creativity of German as well as European thought in the prewar years attested the renewed vigor of that culture. Politically these men had become reluctant adherents of the Empire, often hoping that social reforms would resolve the prevailing antagonisms. The young Weber once likened the Germany of William II to an express train that was roaring ahead without an engineer; the image is apt. Proud of the progress and modernity of Germany, the academic elite of Germany was alarmed at its political ineptitude and troubled by a premonition of national disaster.

Some of them, unwittingly, hastened the coming of this disaster, for they became exuberant imperialists, justifying Germany's headlong rush into world politics by a kind of cultural Darwinism. Once more, brute force was gilded by idealistic invocations, by reference to Hegel and Fichte and the German Idealist tradition. Similar rationalizations had been propagated in Western countries; the difference, as Ludwig Dehio points out, was that the ideals of the Western powers, of

---

tuals, often exaggerate the precariousness of intellectual life and of human creativity, protesting that it is doomed to extinction because of the rising masses, because of affluence or poverty, philistinism or creeping conformity. Is the intellectual enterprise really so feeble and intellect so vulnerable or corruptible?

Spain during the Counter-Reformation, of revolutionary France
or liberal England, possessed a universal appeal, whereas the
"German mission" was parochial and unpersuasive. The Germans were searching for the identity of their mission, in a
sense for their own identity; the Kaiser's theatrics were a
pathetic instance of this search. To many Germans, with their
honest confusion of culture and religion, a superior culture was
as much a legitimate reason for ruling others as the Christian
missionary impulse had once been. Goethe, after all, was
almost as good as God—just as pushpin was always inferior to
poetry. The German intelligentsia came to believe that the
moral justification of expansion was a guarantee of political
success as well, and thus revealed anew the dangers of the
unpolitical mind.

The educated bourgeoisie still indulged in the incantations
of culture and personality; but material conditions had changed,
and these incantations became more and more spurious and
less and less disinterested. To pretend to be unpolitical at a
time of violent social change and unrest is in itself a support
of the existing order. Between 1871 and 1918 a new type of
idealism prevailed, one that, because of its wider diffusion and
subsequent debasement as well as in recognition of its remoteness and specious descent from the earlier Idealism, I would
like to call *Vulgäridealismus*.[8]

These ideals were still propagated in the schools, and many
more Germans were now receiving higher education. Already
in 1872, Nietzsche warned that the quality of humanistic
education was put in jeopardy by the steady increase in the number of students—a concern not unknown to us. Nietzsche diag-
nosed the debasing of these ideals as well. It was he who
arraigned the culture philistine, that passive consumer of culture who lacked all energy or independence. Still, the pious

8. I am, of course, patterning the phrase after the common German terms
"Vulgärmarxismus" and *"Vulgärliberalismus."*

elevation and conspicuous consumption of culture persisted, attesting sometimes an innocent delight in spirit, frequently representing a claim to an exclusive propietorship of culture. To carry one's learning lightly is an English phrase that has no German equivalent. The compulsory citation with which all public talks had to begin and end, the indispensable invocation of Goethe and Schiller, became the aesthetic paternoster of the German intelligentsia.

But why not leave the Germans to their pleasing and by no means unique admiration of culture? The answer must be that this Idealism became more and more of a political force, it became in fact the rhetoric with which the unpolitical German denounced the mass society, democracy, liberalism, modernity, indeed all the so-called importations from the West. Treitschke was perhaps the most popular representative of this strain of *Vulgäridealismus*. In the name of Germany's superior national culture he denounced English materialism and utilitarianism, Jewish corruption, socialist greed, and also the Germans themselves. He attacked universal suffrage, because "our Idealism has always been our strongest national asset; thus it is absolutely un-German to let stupidity and ignorance have the decisive voice." In this way the narrowest class interests could be ennobled and the most aggressive passions cloaked in the rhetoric of Idealism. Men of less bellicose inclinations than Treitschke's appealed to Germany's idealist tradition in order to denounce the forces of modernity and of the West. The deference to culture often bred a condescension for those who had been denied this aristocratic-aesthetic dispensation. Implicit in this attitude was a disdain for the culturally unpropertied and untitled, and *Vulgäridealismus* could also be defined as a learned attempt at a metaphysics of snobbery.[9]

9. For a satire of the Central European *Vulgäridealist* in the United States, see Jacques Barzun's description of Dr. Schlagobers, the "professional European." *God's Country and Mine, A Declaration of Love Spiced with a Few Harsh Words* (Boston, 1954), Chapter 2.

This vulgar idealism widened and sanctified the social divisions within Germany, yet thought itself unpolitical. It had no concern with practical matters and considered itself dogmatically opposed to realism, pragmatism, and above all to materialism. It is ironic that the German bourgeoisie often hid its massive materialism behind this idealism, while the socialists hid their passionate idealism behind a façade of scientific materialism. From their Olympian heights, high above the baser struggles, these idealists marshaled the forces of culture against anarchy, in the effort to defend the status quo against the presumption of the lower classes. It is these idealists that recall a remark that President Lowell of Harvard is said to have made: "I don't mind idealists; it is the unprincipled idealist that I find bad."

The tradition of idealism reached a tragic culmination in 1914, when at the beginning of Germany's most exacting collective effort, the unpolitical character of its people was glorified and institutionalized. The great exaltation of 1914 has been wrongly interpreted as proving Germany's militarism or chauvinism; actually it was the response of a nation that had for decades searched for "the moral equivalent to war" and now had found in war the equivalent of morality. The heroism and the national unity it had sought for so long had at last been attained. In August 1914, the Germans rejoiced, as they were released from the tensions of the armed peace at home and abroad. With joy they adjourned all politics for the duration; the enfeebled political regime, never so much in need of strengthening, was virtually dismantled, and in 1916 was altogether superseded by the disastrous dictatorship of Ludendorff and Hindenburg. Year by year the cost of this unpolitical rule became heavier, and her final defeat was in no small measure brought about by the selfish ineptitude of Germany's nonpolitical rulers.

It was during the war that the idealistic tradition was everywhere proclaimed as Germany's superior surrogate for politics. It became a self-conscious doctrine, and writers like Thomas Mann, Weber, Sombart, Troeltsch, and many other of the great German savants, pulled together the various strands of the idealism I have been describing. Immeasurably angered by the West's moralistic invocation of the universal ideals of freedom, and its slogans about Huns and barbarians, the German intellectuals hurled back a mighty declaration of cultural independence. With the wrath of a Fichte they proclaimed that the German ideals of culture and personality were far more elevated than the selfish, humdrum ideals and institutions of the West. Under provocation, and be it added, often under galling provocation, the German intellectuals developed the anti-Western implications of Idealism to a high pitch.[10]

A few examples of this wartime literature will suffice, important only because even in its exaggeration it was representative of German thought. Ernst Troeltsch, that superb and sensitive historian of the social teachings of the Christian churches, penned a restrained and moderate disputation against the

10. During the Second World War, when the realities of German atrocities far exceeded the worst fantasies of Allied propaganda during the First World War, the anti-German propaganda was far more subdued. Still, there were regrettable exceptions.

Not a spirited eccentric like Mr. A. J. P. Taylor, but the very sober historian Sir Llewelyn Woodward wrote, in 1942: "The Teutonic tribes had the standards of other barbarians; they were neither 'better' nor 'worse' than other human beings in this particular cultural stage. Their descendants in Germany have kept barbarian standards of value longer than their descendants in other areas of western Europe. . . . At a time when other countries were slowly outgrowing the 'barbarian' stage, Germany was the only state in western Europe in which, at the beginning of the twentieth century, there had been for two generations something like a large-scale retrogression in social and political standards of value. . . ." *Short Journey*, pp. 230–1. This seems rather an absurd interpretation of a people that before 1914 was tiresomely law-abiding, docile, and very much repressed. Before the first war, violence in German society was largely verbal—as witness the personal and political polemics, and perhaps the humor as well. Repression, social and sexual, is an important, obvious, but nevertheless neglected factor in pre-1914 society—as it was in the flamboyant rebellion against it in the 1920's.

West's claims that it was fighting for the universal ideals of progressive humanity. In his essay on the spirit of German culture, this unpolitical strain that I have sought to discuss reaches its clearest expression. Troeltsch seeks to examine "the true cultural antagonisms" between Germany and the West, antagonisms that conditioned the political differences as well. After dissecting British and French cultures, pointing to the materialism of the one and the purely formal democracy of the other, Troeltsch defined "German freedom which will never be purely political, but always linked with the idealistic concept of duty and the romantic concept of the individual." The spiritual-metaphysical essence of the Germans, diffused, as Troeltsch points out, through the educational system, inhibited the establishment of formal Western institutions. Because of the belief in personality "we Germans are above all a monarchical people." The social divisions of modern Germany needed an independent monarchy as a disinterested arbiter among the competing material interests: "No parliamentary majority can achieve that." The absence of a parliamentary regime "does not in the least impair personal freedom or human dignity . . . in many ways we feel freer and more independent than the citizens of the great democracy." By its thoughtful tone Troeltsch's essay stands out amidst the poisoned literature of the war. By that very token it deserves to be taken seriously, as a manifestation of something deeper than an ephemeral patriotic outburst.

Other writers worked the same theme, more extravagantly and more crudely. Thomas Mann's *Betrachtungen eines Unpolitischen* must rank as the most painful elaboration of the equation of Germany with idealism and of the German with the unpolitical. "The difference between spirit and politics subsumes the difference between culture and civilization, between soul and society, freedom and suffrage, art and literature; and culture, soul, freedom, art—that is Germanism [*Deutschtum*], and not civilization, society, suffrage, and literature." Mann concluded by accepting not only the existing monarchy but also the authoritarian state in any form, the *Obrigkeitsstaat,* which alone fits the German character. Here the reconciliation of freedom and authority had reached its most unpolitical, its most ethereal form, and a wartime utterance of Meinecke explained how this reconciliation was attained: "By cleansing the idea of the nation of everything political and infusing it instead with all the spiritual achievements that have been won, the national idea was raised to the sphere of religion and the eternal."

The rest is an epilogue in disaster. Many of the men who had proclaimed Germany's imperviousness to politics fathered the Weimar Constitution. Weber helped to draft it—it was he who sought to make the presidency a strong office, because the Germans, he thought, needed a strong authority. With others, Weber founded the Democratic Party, the only non-proletarian group that unreservedly supported Weimar, and the only party that lost in each election; it had begun in 1919 with 18 per cent of the vote, and ended in 1933 with .8 per cent. Despite Weber, Troeltsch, Rathenau, despite Meinecke's brave, if thoroughly unpassionate, rallying to the Republic, and despite Thomas Mann's belated recognition of the moral necessity of politics and the virtue of the Republic, the educated classes of Germany remained aloof from the Republic, seeing in it a shabby, shaky substitute for the imperial regime.[11]

What was the alternative for the university professors, the

11. The uneasy antagonism to the West remained as well. In 1925, in his well-known biography of Luther, Gerhard Ritter wrote: "In recent years it has been much disputed whether Luther belonged to the Middle Ages or 'the modern world.' To me the far more important question seems to be whether we ourselves belong to the modern world—or want to belong to it—if by that term one means primarily the spirit of Anglo-Saxon and Romance culture." *Luther, Gestalt und Symbol* (Munich, 1925), p. 154.

teachers, the clerics, and civil servants?[12] Many retreated once more to an unpolitical idealism, not as in previous generations to gild the existing regime by a transcendental ideal, but to condemn the existing Republic in the name of an unattainable, mystical ideal. In fact, the simple repudiation of the present was considered idealistic. The educated German went his way, unpolitical, usually utterly contemptuous of the Republic. That attitude itself was inimical to the survival of the Republic.

But a still greater fatality befell this unpolitical German. How was he to respond to the idealism of the nationalist assassins and the Hitler movement, groups clearly in rebellion against reality? In a very real sense, the Hitler movement was idealistic, and that was the condition of its success. Did it not inveigh against materialism and selfishness, defy reality, promise the end of fratricidal conflict and the establishment of social harmony, of unity and leadership, power and confidence? To make it appear that his party's nihilism was really idealism, its resentful and cowardly brutality virile strength— that was Hitler's great propagandistic success. The unpolitical, the educated German hesitated. It was not the few men of culture that joined the party before 1933 that promoted Hitler's success, but the many that failed to oppose him, failed not out of fear, but out of uncertainty lest this be the untamed Caesar, the real Germanic savior. His anti-Western tirades, his

12. As one illustration of the anti-republican mood, consider Meinecke's attempt, in 1926, together with some colleagues, to organize a few university professors who would be willing to accept the Constitution, either because they thought the Republic an unfortunate necessity or because they were republicans by persuasion. Meinecke explained his intention: "What a misfortune that for our students the present political order is poisoned—not always directly, for few people dare more than an occasional malicious interjection—but indirectly through the whole political attitude of their teachers." He disavowed the founding of a republican group: "For we would only form a rigidly contained minority group that would be rendered ineffectual by all the means of social boycott." *Die deutschen Universitäten und der heutige Staat* (Tübingen, 1926).

anti-Semitism, uncouth though they were, stirred memories of earlier, more genteel forms of idealistic anti-Semitism. And the way the Jews were mocking culture, were composing cheap three-penny operas, was really intolerable, the *Bürger* thought. If the educated classes floundered, how much more readily would the economically aggrieved, socially disinherited, flock to the Hitler movement. The idealistic appeal of the Nazis must be reckoned with. Dehio was right when he wrote of them and their immediate predecessors: "Idealism was linked to crime, and the nihilistic will to power prepared itself, quite without conscience, to annihilate Occidental ethics."

Even after 1933, many educated Germans were blind to this criminality of the Nazis. So constantly had they depreciated politics that the absence of a free political society troubled them little, if at all. A few were incarcerated, some emigrated, some joined the movement, many retired to the unpolitical sphere; it is no accident that after 1945 the educated Germans argued that their highest achievement had been an "inner emigration," a retirement within the self.[13] A handful of heroes rebounded from this inner emigration and, in a final gasp of genuine idealism, risked their lives in the revolt of the 20th of July. It, too, failed, and the savage vengeance that Hitler visited upon the plotters expressed his hatred for the educated, aristocratic Germans.

In 1946, when all seemed irretrievably lost to the Germans, Meinecke wrote one last summary of German history, conclud-

---

13. A German newspaper recently provided an unintentionally amusing illustration. When Hjalmar Schacht was forced out of the presidency of the Reichsbank in 1939, a few unpolitical bureaucrats tried to forestall the appointment of a Nazi, and hence sought to prevail on a young conservative colleague, Karl Blessing, to seek the job. His reply: "Dear friend, when I shave in the morning I have to look at myself in the mirror, and I have to be able to say: 'Blessing, you are a decent chap.' But under this regime, the currency cannot be protected, and hence I would not be a decent fellow if I took the post of president." *Die Zeit,* January 2, 1958. After the war, Blessing was president of the Bundesbank of the Federal Republic.

ing with an invocation to the German spirit. His final counsel
was:

> In every German city and larger village, therefore, we should like
> to see in the future a community of like-minded friends of culture
> which I should like best to call Goethe Communities. . . . The
> whole idea must start with individuals, with personalities, the
> special few who first build among themselves only one such
> Goethe community, and then let it develop, here in one form,
> there in another.

After their disastrous failure, the Germans were to read
Goethe to each other! Was Goethe once more to become the
acknowledged legislator of the Germans, was Germany's great
tradition once more invoked for a purpose that it could not
and was not intended to serve? The provisional answer over
the last decade would seem to be no.

The vague idealism of the unpolitical German seems not to
have survived Hitler's excesses, and there appears in progress
a gradual *embourgeoisement* of West German culture, a willingness to be pragmatic, realistic, prosperous. What so many
Germans for so long dreaded and denounced—the Americanization of German culture—seems now to be taking place,
quietly and fitfully, but to the apparent pleasure of the Germans and to the likely benefit of their still untested democratic
regime.

Money, Morals, and the Pillars of Society

Hemingway's remark that "there is a tendency when you really begin to learn something about a thing not to want to write about it but rather to keep on learning about it always" has a peculiar relevance to historians. The deeper we dig the more we find—and the narrower the bounds of our work tend to become. I now realize that the two invitations which prompted this essay and the preceding one gave me a chance to reflect widely on the kind of research I was pursuing and helped me to place the particular in the framework of the general. Just as the preceding essay developed some of the major themes of *The Politics of Cultural Despair,* published a few years later, so, in this essay, I try to clarify some of the broader aspects of my forthcoming study on Bleichröder. In a sense, this essay tries to explore German attitudes toward money, in much the same way as the earlier essay discussed German attitudes toward politics. I wanted to sketch the crisis of values created by the impact of capitalism and the crash of 1873 and to relate that crisis to the political milieu of the new nation. Originally delivered as an address in December 1969 to the Modern European History section of the American Historical Association, this piece was subsequently revised and published in 1970, and is here reprinted without further changes.

Perhaps one of Europe's more remarkable achievements has been the creation of a flourishing bourgeois civilization that has never been free from the most penetrating bourgeois criticism. *"Épater le bourgeois"* was a great pastime of the last century, and the sport still seems to be alive. Ibsen's *Pillars of Society,* published in 1877, was a radical analysis of the moral pretensions and the moral burden of bourgeois society. The pillars of that society were rotten; the life of the protagonist was a lie violating his own nature and that of his fellow men. It is as if Ibsen had written a dramatic commentary on the *Communist Manifesto* without indulging in the comforting hope that a social revolution would create a new man in a newly virtuous society. In the play, salvation came through an improbable act of contrition and self-purgation; at his most revolutionary, Ibsen thought that the feminine slamming of doors sufficed for human improvement.

He had, however, written a powerful indictment of contemporary mores and had exposed the psychic cost of bourgeois striving. Subsequent years provided frequent substantiation of his charge that beneath the façade of prosperous respectability was teeming corruption, produced by the lure of wealth and power. Old virtues—probably always more honored in the breach than the observance—disappeared in all but name; empty labels remained, reminding the world that a new code had yet to be formulated. Unbridled capitalism offered immense advance and taunted people with ever-new temptations. Out of greed, men cheated and cajoled, robbed those below them of their just rewards, injured and despised them.

Ibsen situated his conflict between pretense and reality in a Norwegian seaport, as it was gradually being subverted by modern forces. The same discrepancy and the same growing sense of unease and corruption prevailed in Bismarck's new Reich. For a people that had long been exceedingly sentimental about its moral virtues, the dim realization of a transformation of values was painful indeed.

Initially, the mood of Imperial Germany was jubilant. The dream of decades had come true on the battlefields of France. Treitschke celebrated that war as a "blessed fate. For truly only such a prodigious event, such an act of violence, so brutal and so insolent that it had to wake even the dullest conscience, would have been able to lead the south back to the great fatherland."[1] God had punished the decadent French and rewarded virile, honest Germans by an imperial crown, won in the very seat of ancient *gloire,* in Versailles, whence Germany had been kept divided. Or so legend adorned victory—for outward façade was sustained by internal legend and by an exaltation of German victory that seemed designed to compensate Germany for its almost uninterrupted experience of defeat. The exaltation of 1871 marked the climax of an ancient tradition— a particularly crass and ugly climax. It was a kind of national intoxication; it was unrestrained hubris. In our century, victory has been too costly to permit exaltation; no great power is likely ever again to have that experience.

Glittering façade, noisy exaltation, and solid achievement persuaded historians—particularly German historians—that the early decades of the Second Empire were one of the great periods of German history. Certainly Germany rose to the pinnacle of her European power—and thanks to Bismarck's skills, did so without provoking another war. The internal scene, however, was more somber: the new nation came to suffer from

1. Heinrich von Treitschke, *Historische und Politische Aufsätze,* Vol. III (4th edn., Leipzig, 1871), p. 612.

new conflicts and uncertainties, disappointments and psychic discontents.

The exaltation of victory was followed within two years by a financial crash of unprecedented scope, triggered to some extent by reckless overconfidence and fraudulence. The crash of 1873 revealed the emergent transformation of values: a new capitalistic ethos was in the ascendancy. But the crash, quickly translated into moral terms, produced a shock in German public consciousness that in turn inspired the repudiation of economic liberalism and the rise of new antagonisms. In the political realm, too, crisis and scandals emerged. The triumph of unification was followed by gradual disenchantment with the political life of the new nation. The German people suffered not only from a quick reversal of mood but from an attendant crisis of self-assessment and self-understanding. The old, peculiarly German, question, "What is German?" assumed new urgency.

I would like to deal with two related facets of the internal weakness of the new nation. First, I want to suggest that the rise of industrial capitalism brought about a fundamental crisis of moral conscience. The members of the Junker class in particular found it hard to reconcile their old values with the sudden necessity to adapt to a new kind of economy. At the very time when Bismarck seemed to have preserved their political pre-eminence, a new economic system put in jeopardy their material power and challenged the moral priorities by which they had justified that pre-eminence. Their role in the crash of 1873 and in its aftermath served as a focus of that moral crisis.

Second, I should like to show that in the long run Bismarck's style—quite aside from his policies—came to have a disastrous impact on the political culture and public morale of the new nation. Far from fostering participation, he gradually became an autocrat who offered little leadership. Having played a central role in creating the new nation, he unwittingly played a central role in keeping it divided.

It was Germany's peculiar fate that the crisis precipitated by capitalism coincided with twenty years of Bismarckian rule. That the coming of capitalism brought moral and social dislocation was a common experience in the world; for better or for worse, Bismarck was *not* a common experience. The two experiences together shaped and obscured the political culture of the 1870's. The coinciding of the two illustrated Germany's middle position between the bourgeois-capitalistic world of Western Europe and the backward autocracies of Eastern Europe.

More than the achievement of national unification, the triumph of industrial capitalism changed the reality of German life, although awareness of this fact was partially disguised by the survival of an earlier code of private and public virtues. The material consequences of industrialization were clear-cut: the immense growth of German power, the demographic shifts, the impact on class antagonisms and on politics. We are less familiar with the psychological impact of capitalism on the Junker class with its long-cherished, contemptuous disdain for business and bourgeois life. A succinct statement of their predicament can be found in Friedrich Spielhagen's novel *Sturmflut,* which deals with the moral crisis and material temptations of the 1870's. Reminded that the aristocratic motto must always remain *noblesse oblige,* the Junker protagonist demurs, "because our condition has never been so precarious as it is today. In this, our leveling century, we have long been on the same plane, in the same dusty arena with the classes that rush on behind or against us—the very arena in which is fought out the struggle for survival; but sun and wind are unevenly divided. A multitude of means which the bourgeois class uses with the most incredible success is denied us because of *noblesse oblige.* Very nice: privilege we no longer have: God forbid. But unique duties [*Vorpflichten*]: we are supposed to defend our position in state and society and still preserve our moral qualities. This is all too often a difficult thing and sometimes it is impossible: it is nothing but the squaring of the circle."[2]

The rise of industrial capitalism was bound to create difficulties; the very speed with which it swept over Germany multiplied these difficulties. Offering a new way of life and a new means of gaining wealth and power, capitalism prescribed values radically different from previously held attitudes regarding the morality of money, the accumulation of wealth, and the propriety of unearned profits. This conflict of values was to some extent disguised because nineteenth-century Germans were perhaps particularly inhibited in honestly facing or discussing questions of money. In Western Europe, the upper classes also had begun with strong prejudices against the capitalist spirit, but they had had a much longer time and a more congenial political and religious milieu in which to make their compromises. Capitalism burst upon a Germany whose middle class had lost a revolution and whose Junkers still dominated politics and the public ethos. Capitalism took hold in Germany more rapidly than elsewhere, violating deeper prejudices and offering greater opportunities.

Three strands in Germany's cultural tradition militated against an easy acceptance of material values. First, there was the legacy of Luther's abhorrence of money as filthy lucre—a different attitude from that of Calvinists or Catholics. The most complicated attitude toward money occurred in regions where Lutheran pastors sought to keep alive this anti-capitalistic spirit. Second, and in the same regions, an unbroken feudal tradition proclaimed that manly virtues of honor and heroism were superior to and in conflict with material ambition. Birth

2. Friedrich Spielhagen, *Sturmflut,* in *Sämmtliche Werke,* Vol. XIII, Part I (6th edn., Leipzig, 1886), p. 47.

was more important than wealth, though Providence in its wisdom had decreed that the two should be joined by placing the Junker on his manorial estates. The Junker frowned on business and on most mercantile activities; to live off other people's misfortunes—his definition of money-lenders—was considered parasitical, as was the amassing of profit without work. He shared the common rural prejudice against clever city folk, against outsiders and Jews who carried on the kind of business that no Junker would touch—or could do without. The third strand was the German ideal of *Kultur* which came to be exalted and institutionalized in the nineteenth century. By its extravagant praise of *Bildung* and spirit, it clearly implied that any man dedicated to the higher things in life would have to be properly scornful of the baser things—of which money or business was a prime example. This third strand was distinctive to Germany and expressed something of the intellectual aspirations and political and material weakness of her middle classes.

German views concerning money described a difference in degree, not kind, as compared to those of other nations. A man's attitude toward money is never simple and never easy to establish. It is embedded in so many other values, it is so often encrusted by hypocrisy and disguised by subterfuges, that in the end the person himself is half-deluded. The problem is posed at the outset: does one talk about money, is one embarrassed by one's material interests? Changing attitudes toward money —and obviously I am using money as a shorthand for a more complicated set of questions—tell us a great deal about a society, a class, or an individual. Attitudes toward money often furnish an invaluable index of hypocrisy. Historians—perhaps because of their well-known indifference to money—have slighted some of these questions.

Evidence, of course, is hard to come by, but some historians may have neglected these questions because they assumed that modern men automatically follow the fiction of economic man and that anti-materialist rhetoric can be dismissed as mere rationalization. On the other hand, we know that modern mass movements of the Right and Left have exploited not only material grievances but also anti-materialist sentiments in society, and that certain cultural movements, such as the German Youth Movement, would be inexplicable without recognition of the anti-capitalist impulse behind them.

Men's attitude toward money is so enormously complicated because it expresses so much of their deeper selves. It fashions and reflects the direction of their lives; it encompasses their attitude toward work and pleasure, toward family and education, toward what is or ought to be the principal goal in a man's life. The pursuit of wealth can stand for drudgery and vanity, it can enslave a man to his workaday life, it can be a crushing experience. It can also beckon as an adventure, a romance, a leap to greatness. It can be a means or an end—but does it ever appear as a satisfying end? The ambivalence of financial success is illustrated by the conflict between Thomas and Christian Buddenbrook, between the tortured and repressed businessman and the idle, self-indulgent brother whose very existence taunts and threatens the successful Thomas. One's attitude toward money bespeaks an inclination to abide by prevailing norms or to rebel against them, to accept one's ticket or to seek another.

The prejudice against money-making is often as great as the love of it, and the contradiction fosters doubt and hypocrisy. Has the notion that money is the root of all evil—that preposterous exaggeration of the importance of the acquisitive instinct and of its relation to sin—ever *not* coexisted with rampant lust for wealth? Has the longing for the simple and austere life, the nostalgia for an Arcadian past, not been a cultural fact of extraordinary power? Money-grubbing and money-hating, the pursuit of wealth and the fear of wealth as a burden and a distraction—these attitudes express deep human and social ambivalences that can help us to understand the tangle of the past.

Some of these ambivalences are illustrated by the Junkers'

response to the capitalist challenge. In the relatively calm days of the early nineteenth century, they lived comfortably on and from their estates, and their habitual lack of cash was not particularly noticeable in a country that was generally poor and had made a virtue of sobriety. The Junker, however, had learned to become punctilious in the running of his estate; necessity had driven him to watch over his income. In fact, he had become remarkably adept at introducing new techniques that promised higher returns. For the rest, he felt or affected disdain for money, even for talk about money. His reluctance to intermarry with the commercial bourgeoisie suggests something of the tenacity of this prejudice. It left him without the material replenishment that his English counterpart had long since learned to accept graciously. The young Bismarck exemplified this indifference to money; although all his life assiduous in matters of finance, as a young man he affected scorn, and when trying to collect some outstanding debts from a friend, he apologized for his "Jewish kind of calculating character [*Berechnungswesen*]."[3]

Gradually the Junkers came into close contact with the new type of economy. In 1842, the industrialist Friedrich Harkort remarked that "the nobility feels that the railroad locomotive is the hearse in which feudalism will be carted off to the cemetery."[4] But the Junker was far too practical to indulge in any incipient Luddite sentiment. While most had to be dragged into the mysterious world of modern business, a few charged in, full of hope and greed. Neither the laggards nor the enthusiasts found the experience particularly inspiriting. Some began to participate in the highly speculative enterprise of railway construction—a real departure from their earlier code. The mag-

3. Bismarck, *Die gesammelten Werke,* Vol. XIV, Part I (2nd printing, Berlin, 1933), p. 179.

4. Quoted in Dietrich Eichholtz, *Junker und Bourgeoisie vor 1848 in der preussischen Eisenbahngeschichte* ([East] Berlin, 1962), p. 37.

nates of Silesia, never as reticent as their poorer, purer cousins in the older Prussian provinces, pointed the way. With the advent of a liberal economy, nobles and non-nobles became involved in joint-stock ventures.

By the late 1860's many succumbed to a scheme, at once symptomatic and disastrous, fathered by one of the great Jewish promoters of the time, Dr. Bethel Henry Strousberg. Having successfully built German railroads, Strousberg collected some fifty million talers for the construction of railways in Rumania. Foreshadowing later practice, he enticed great notables to decorate his board of directors, men like the Prince Putbus, the Duke of Ujest, and the Duke of Ratibor.[5] By 1870, the enterprise was on the brink of disaster, and Prussia's *Prominenz* and many ordinary people stood to lose all their investments. It took two bankers and the imperial government some ten years to retrieve these improvidently placed funds.[6]

5. Joseph Maria von Radowitz to Bismarck, March 10, 1871, in Acta betreffend Verhandlungen mit Rumänien, A.A. II, Rep. 6, No. 4205, Deutsches Zentralarchiv, Merseburg. See also Strousberg's self-justification, *Dr. Strousberg und sein Wirken von ihm selbst geschildert* (Berlin, 1876), pp. 337–88.

6. In 1879, Bismarck gave the French ambassador, the Comte de St. Vallier, a marvelously colorful account of the Strousberg affair. The European powers at the time were trying to force the Rumanian government to grant civic equality to its Jews, as it had promised at the Congress of Berlin. The Rumanians stalled, and Bismarck expressed his anger "at the crooks and savages . . . with a liveliness and brutal energy one often encounters in his assessments." The ambassador reported the conversation verbatim: "My other motive [for being anti-Rumanian] has to do with a more private matter which for us, however, has an urgent and distressing character; you are familiar with the Strousberg affair; you know what bloodletting it has inflicted on German capital; close to 200 million francs have been swallowed up in these Rumanian railways which yield nothing and the value of which is hardly one-tenth of the cost; our greatest lords and our bootblacks believed that Strousberg would present them with a gold mine and a great many risked the best part of what they possessed, believing the promises of this adventurer. All that is buried now in the Rumanian mud, and, one fine day, two dukes, one general who is an aide-de-camp, a half-dozen ladies-in-waiting, twice that many chamberlains, a hundred coffeehouse owners and all the cabmen of Berlin found themselves totally ruined. The Emperor took pity on the dukes, the aide-de-camp, the ladies-in-waiting, and the chamber-

In the euphoria of the day, the lessons of the Strousberg disaster went unheeded.[7] Instead, his pattern of promotion was widely emulated, and the victory of 1871 provided a heady atmosphere for still more promotion. The influx of the French

---

lains, and charged me with pulling them out of the trouble. I appealed to Bleichröder who, on condition of getting a title of nobility which as a Jew he valued, agreed to rescue the Duke of Ratibor, the Duke of Ujest, and General Count Lehndorf [*sic*]; two dukes and an aide-de-camp saved—frankly, that is worth the 'von' bestowed on the good Bleichröder. But the ladies-in-waiting, the cabmen, and the others were left drowning, and even Bleichröder's three Moses [whom he had dredged out of the water] were not so entirely saved but that they have to face each year some nice trial in which they are sued for two or three million marks which they cannot pay since their domains of Ratibor, Ujest, etc. are totally mortgaged in exchange for the Bleichröder guarantee. There is but one way for everybody to get out of this trouble and that is to try to sell the Rumanian railways. . . . [At present] the Rumanian government exploits the owners' misery with usurious barbarism; by annoyances, injustices, extortions, it wants to force them to abandon the railways to the government for a crust of bread . . . every day our German engineers and workers are being beaten, maltreated, imprisoned, cheated, robbed of everything, and we can do nothing to help them attain justice. That is why I just told you that I wished I could use naval ships as in Nicaragua to obtain satisfactions; but that is impossible, and neither do I have balloons [*aerostats*] to send in German troops." He urged the dukes to sell the railways, perhaps to Austria or Russia—for cash because to lend money to these great defaulters would be a mistake. The dukes thought that Bismarck might object to the Rumanian railways being sold to Russia, but he had reassured them "that it was a matter of indifference to me if the Rumanian railways and indeed all of Rumania should fall into Russian hands." The French ambassador warned the Quai d'Orsay that this was perhaps not quite so pleasant a prospect for France. Archives du Ministère des affaires étrangères, Correspondance Politique, Allemagne, Vol. XXVII, Feb. 26, 1879.

7. Ludwig Bamberger summed up the Strousberg fiasco with his usual anti-aristocratic bias: "Because charlatanry in all realms has no more credulous adherent than the aristocracy, financial wizards [like Strousberg] always manage to entrap many aristocrats who for their part are ready to contribute the radiance of their name to the sham gilding of an enterprise. In turn, they are rewarded from the first easily acquired profit of that enterprise. Strousberg understood perfectly how to fashion for himself such an aura out of the Prussian aristocracy; the aristocracy's still prevalent view that all financial business really encompasses fraud derives perhaps in part from its recollections [of Strousberg]." Ludwig Bamberger, *Erinnerungen*, ed. Paul Nathan (Berlin, 1899), p. 527.

indemnity—an unprecedented five billion francs—added material stimulus. A speculative fever suddenly gripped many Germans—and respected neither rank nor position. Hundreds of new enterprises were spawned, sometimes on flimsy foundations. An aroused public pounced on these creations and drove up the price of the shares—to the great profit of the original promoters, who were usually a group of financiers, including many Jewish financiers, and men of title. For a while, then, there were great profits, and more men were caught up in the frenzy. Prudence gave way to recklessness and occasional fraudulence, as more and more people thought that they could get rich fast.

The extent to which aristocrats were swept along by the same desire has not been properly recognized. For some, it was sheer greed; for others, it was tinged with what might be called professional necessity. The cost, not so much of living as of living in style, of maintaining status, had suddenly increased enormously. The burden fell most heavily on those impecunious Junkers in public service, whose still frugal salaries ill equipped them to survive in the fiercely competitive society of plutocratic Berlin. At the time of some unwelcome resignations from the government in 1879, Bismarck complained to the King: "Applications for ministerial posts are not very numerous in any case; the salary is too low compared to the external demands and only a *rich* man can be a minister without getting into financial difficulties."[8] Ideally, candidates should be rich,

8. Bismarck, *Die gesammelte Werke*, Vol. VI *c*, p. 156. German diplomats of the time were also underpaid and consistently received lower salaries than the representatives of other great powers. When Count Solms-Sonnenwalde, then Prussian minister in Dresden, wrote Bleichröder concerning the desirability of changing his investment portfolio, he added: "Forgive me, dear Baron, if I trouble you with so small a matter; but since the state cares so little about the improvement of the salaries of *Prussian* diplomats, while the Russian post here has been raised to 20,000 talers, I have to look out for other ways of augmenting my income." Count Solms to Bleichröder, March 9, 1875, Bleichröder Archive in possession of F. H. Brunner, a partner of Arn-

competent, and aristocratic: no wonder the supply was limited and the financial strain pervasive.

Hence the headlong rush into an unknown but infinitely alluring world; people sensed boundless opportunity and fought to take advantage of it. Financiers were besieged with requests and demands, and someone like Gerson Bleichröder had an exceptionally good vantage point from which to see how noble society, despite its anti-materialist ideology, sought instant wealth. His most celebrated client, Bismarck, was something of an exception; he was rather modest, almost old-fashioned, in his expectations. To be sure, he was deeply concerned about his finances. He always wanted more land and a higher return from it; he owned some stocks, but he shunned speculation and had some sense of what we call conflict of interest. He was closer to the old patriarchal Junker traditions than many of his Junker critics.[9]

Most others were less modest. Men wrote to Bleichröder in great secrecy, beseeching him not to reveal their correspondence. Among themselves they still sneered at money-making, especially Jewish money-making. But requests of the most extraordinary diversity poured in. Count Pückler, William's *Hofmarschall,* asked Bleichröder to make up some minor losses he had suffered on an investment. Bleichröder, he wrote, had assured him that a given stock would appreciate and had promised to compensate him for any loss if the stock were to fall. He now presented his claim. Count Pückler liked his profits without running any risks.[10] In 1878, one of the richest men in Germany, Count Henckel-Donnersmarck, begged Bleichröder, reputedly the richest man in Germany, to intercede with the

---

hold and S. Bleichroeder, New York. I would like to express my gratitude to Mr. Brunner for placing that archive at the disposal of Professor David S. Landes and myself. See also Rudolf Morsey, *Die oberste Reichsverwaltung unter Bismarck 1867–1890* (Münster, 1957), p. 113.

9. See Chapter 3.

10. Count Pückler to Bleichröder, Sept. 2, 1876, Bleichröder Archive.

government on his behalf. Donnersmarck thought the government the best potential buyer for some land he had bought six years earlier in Berlin's governmental quarter. Buyers were hard to find, even though he was prepared to sell at 30 per cent below his purchase price. "I am at your disposition for reciprocal services [*Gegendienste*]." Bleichröder duly intervened with Bismarck and with the commerce minister. There were many uses to Bleichröder's intimacy with Bismarck.[11]

Consider finally as one example among many, the case of Count Paul von Hatzfeldt, whose great talents led Bismarck to call him the best horse in his stable. Scion of an ancient family and son of the Countess Hatzfeldt, who as Lassalle's friend had imbibed some socialist ideas but not bequeathed them, Paul turned to speculation with a vengeance. From the battlefield in France he wrote to his wife that Germans are not so corrupt as Frenchmen, but "at the same time I must say that I should like to earn some money in some honest manner, and I am racking my brains to think of some way to do so. All one has to do is to get a good idea or to discover some good investment."[12] Hatzfeldt finally stumbled on yet another method: all one needed was a friendly banker. Between 1871 and 1873, Bleichröder placed Hatzfeldt on the board of two newly created companies; by these and other means he helped Hatzfeldt to a profit of about 100,000 talers in three years. But Hatzfeldt wanted more, and his letters to Bleichröder constitute a record of imaginative, mounting greed—a perfect symptom of the age. "Would it not be possible for me to try to get a railroad concession? You probably have many such projects before you and you could recommend one or the other of these. I would also count on your advice concerning the ways and means to go ahead with

11. Henckel-Donnersmarck to Bleichröder, Oct. 9 and 28, 1878, Bleichröder Archive.

12. *The Hatzfeldt Letters. Letters of Count Paul Hatzfeldt to his Wife, Written from the Head-Quarters of the King of Prussia 1870–1871*, trans. from the French by J. L. Bashford (London, 1905), p. 282.

the railroad. I fail to see why I could not succeed as well as Mr. von Kardof [*sic*] in this kind of enterprise, in which one can always anticipate a considerable advantage."[13] Wilhelm von Kardorff was a highly respected conservative politician who, as an associate of Bleichröder's, had participated in some important promotions. His mounting indebtedness was known to few people; Bleichröder, however, had to perform various salvaging operations.

Hatzfeldt did not get his railroad. Perhaps this saved his diplomatic career: excessive involvement in the promotional frenzy of the *Gründerjahre* would probably have hobbled it. As it is, that career had to overcome widespread gossip about his extravagant debts and his marital irregularities—and one might note in passing that the popular mind tended to link the two as twin failings of frivolous men. Hatzfeldt's debts, however, were but a particularly flagrant and highly publicized example of a common affliction among his fellow nobles.[14] Many of them suffered from the same combination of greed and indebtedness. The simple truth is that money had emerged as a central, though still unacknowledged, concern of Bismarck's contemporaries.

The novels of Theodor Fontane bear witness to this change in attitude. In his *Stechlin,* the old Junker muses that money is indeed the worst of all evils and that "men are in all things mendacious and dishonest, in money matters, too, and almost more than in matters of morals." The son, contemplating various injunctions about whom he, as a nobleman of the Mark Brandenburg, should marry and about how "money debases,"

13. Hatzfeldt to Bleichröder, Feb. 9, 1872, Bleichröder Archive.
14. And fellow diplomats. Count Harry von Arnim was deeply involved in stock market speculations at the very time when he was fighting for his political survival in the early 1870's. Bismarck suspected Arnim of delaying important negotiations with the French government in order to complete some market operations. Arnim's secretary at the Embassy, Friedrich von Holstein, also showed a lively interest in financial operations. Details will appear in my forthcoming work on Gerson Bleichröder.

thinks to himself, "But I know all this. As long as it is a great deal of money—then it can even be a Chinese woman. In the Mark, everything is a question of money because there is none around—money sanctifies person or cause."[15] In time, money sanctified even Jewish heiresses, as witness Bismarck's delicate remark about the desirability of Christian stallions breeding with Jewish mares, because, as he put it, "The money has to get back into circulation and [the crossbreeding] does not produce a bad race."[16]

Fontane also drew a memorable picture of middle-class hypocrisy. It was one of the paradoxes of German social history that as the Junkers became more realistic in their assessment of money, some of the bourgeoisie forsook their earlier realism, their pride in middle-class appreciation of money as exemplified by thrift, sobriety, and hard work, and began to affect disdain for money.[17] Fontane's Frau Jenny Treibel protests *ad nauseam*: "everything is worthless [*nichtig*]; but the most worthless

15. Theodore Fontane, *Der Stechlin* (Berlin, 1905), pp. 232 and 208. In Spielhagen's *Sturmflut*, some crafty promoters try to lure a count, heavily in debt, into the shadowy world of promotion. At different stages of submission, the count exclaims: "No, if I am to join the promoters, then it cannot be for a bagatelle. Then I want the coup to be a capital coup which will compensate me for the pangs of conscience that I will feel for having squarely violated the traditions of my family—a coup that will secure my future for all time." When he utters a last gasp of moral hesitation about people, especially ordinary people, getting rich fast, his tempter replies: "On the contrary, this should prove encouraging. If people without names, without connections, without inherited wealth can bring it so far in such a short time . . . what remains unattainable for you gentlemen who, unlike them, have the immeasurable advantages of birth, connections, patronage, an inherited estate—provided that you liberate yourselves from certain prejudices, of course, very honorable prejudices, and seize your chance with energy and relish, as they do." *Sturmflut, op. cit.,* pp. 202 and 219.

16. Quoted in Otto Jöhlinger, *Bismarck und die Juden* (Berlin, 1921), p. 27.

17. On the earlier realism, see one of the few studies on attitudes toward money that has appeared: Hans-Richard Altenhein, *"Geld und Geldeswert. Über die Selbstdarstellung des Bürgertums in der Literatur des 18. Jahrhunderts,"* in *das werck der bucher. Von der Wirksamkeit des Buches in Vergangenheit und Gegenwart,* Festschrift for Horst Kliemann, ed. Fritz Hodeige (Freiburg, 1956), pp. 201–13.

thing is what all the world so greedily presses for: tangible possessions, property, gold . . . I for one stick to the ideal and will never renounce it." Her old suitor, whom she had abandoned for a man of means, saw through the pretense: "She is a dangerous person and the more dangerous because she does not know it herself and sincerely imagines she has a tender heart, and above all a heart 'for the higher things.' But she has a heart only for the tangible, for everything that is substantial and bears interest. . . . They all constantly liberalize and sentimentalize, but that is all farce: when the time comes for showing one's true colors, then the motto is: Gold is trump and nothing else."[18]

Money became scarce after the great crash of 1873. The stock market dropped precipitously, as many of the new businesses ran into trouble or failed altogether. Most of the original promoters had reaped their benefits; the public, its greed aroused, discovered that what had started out as the lure of participatory profiteering quickly turned into the disaster of participatory bankruptcy. Gone was the dream of acquiring instant wealth; gone, too, was the speculative fever. The great boom turned into an unprecedented depression and Germany's laissez-faire phase—of a few years' standing—was virtually at an end.[19] The actual crisis was serious; the effort at explanation and expiation was worse. The nation had suffered a shock that far from inspiring efforts at reform or reappraisal led to bouts of indiscriminate breast-beating, to mendacious and divisive accusations, to still greater obfuscation and suspicion.

The Junkers reacted with predictable peevishness. The crash

18. Theodor Fontane, *Frau Jenny Treibel* (Berlin, 1905), pp. 32 and 96.
19. We now have three important studies that deal with the place of the depression in German development: Helmut Böhme, *Deutschlands Weg zur Grossmacht. Studien zum Verhältnis von Wirtschaft und Staat während der Reichsgründungszeit 1848–1881* (Cologne, 1966); Hans Rosenberg, *Grosse Depression und Bismarckzeit. Wirtschaftsablauf, Gesellschaft und Politik in Mitteleuropa* (Berlin, 1967); Hans-Ulrich Wehler, *Bismarck und der Imperialismus* (Cologne, 1969).

had vindicated their prejudices, though not their actions. They blamed others, Bismarck included, for their misfortunes. Capitalism was evil and un-German. To protect themselves in the face of mounting economic difficulties, the Junkers now turned from private initiative to the ruthless exploitation of their collective political power. With Bismarck's encouragement, the upper classes united to demand material help and satisfaction from the state. By the end of the 1870's, an unacknowledged materialism pervaded the political realm, and the gap between professed ideals and actual practice widened—covered by still greater hypocrisy. By the end of the decade, also, conservatism acquired a cramped, repressive character, as embodied in the Puttkamer regime of the next decade.

Men quickly translated the crash into a political and moral indictment of the whole society. Corruption became the common charge of the day—and one to which Germans were perhaps peculiarly sensitive. Eduard Lasker, Germany's foremost liberal parliamentarian and a Jew, was the first to allege collusion between high public servants—including a protégé of Bismarck's—and the so-called promoters. It was assumed that Lasker had meant to strike a blow against the conservatives, and the latter quickly retaliated with a torrent of abuse. They unmasked what they dubbed the promoters' swindle and laid it at liberal doors: liberalism invited corruption, and liberals indulged in it. For years, the charge of corruption remained a conservative monopoly. Nor did the conservatives hesitate to malign Bismarck—in fact, they rejoiced at having found a popular stick with which to beat the renegade Junker. In some celebrated articles of 1875, the *Kreuzzeitung* blamed Bismarck for the depression, because—according to this allegation—he had surrendered the direction of the German economy to his liberal colleagues and to his Jewish banker, from whom he derived vast gains. Bismarck denounced "those most shameless and most mendacious calumnies," but discovered that his erstwhile Pomeranian neighbors—"the most esteemed and most influential men of the Protestant population"—rushed not to his, but to his traducers' defense.[20]

What the elite began, subterranean literati kept alive. The rottenness of the system, the conspiracy behind the system, the horrendous illicit profits made possible by the system: these were the stock-in-trade of pamphleteers and agitators. The closing words of one of these indictments conveys the flavor of all of them: "As long as Prince Bismarck remains the single, powerful idol, the German nation will be sacrificed to the Reich, the Reich will be sacrificed to the Chancellor, and the Chancellor—belongs to the Jews and the *Gründer*. Hence there is but *one* political order of the day for us: remove the present system and its defender."[21] Just as the promoters had played on people's naïve confidence, so these writers played on their latent paranoia. People had been lured to believe in the feasibility of quick, certain profits and now grasped at conspiratorial theories that explained why they had fallen for promises that never materialized.

But the early 1870's, the *Gründerzeit,* proved to be more than a financial and moral shock. It was a cultural disaster as well. The rise of a plutocracy set standards of dazzling tastelessness that combined maximum expenditure with minimal artistic integrity. In this realm, too, uncertainty prevailed, disguised by garish ostentation. No wonder Nietzsche condemned the absence of all style: elegance consisted in collecting ill-fitting, expensive creations of the past or of aping them in the present. Even the great artists were touched by the confusion of the age. Richard Wagner was a genius—and a superb pro-

20. Siegfried von Kardorff, *Wilhelm von Kardorff. Ein nationaler Parlamentarier im Zeitalter Bismarcks und Wilhelms II., 1828–1907* (Berlin, 1936), p. 100; Dr. H. Ritter von Poschinger, *Fürst Bismarck und die Parlamentarier,* Vol. II, 1847–79 (Breslau, 1895), p. 202.

21. Dr. Rudolph Meyer, *Politische Gründer und die Corruption in Deutschland* (Leipzig, 1877), p. 204.

moter. His Bayreuth shrine of 1876 was a monument to the promotional spirit. Magnificently mercenary, he could create the religious spirituality of a *Parsifal* and utter fashionable laments about the materialism of modernity. He was the German anti-materialist materialist *par excellence.* A popular painter of the day, Hans von Marées, once wrote to a friend, "Do you know what I need? The fist of a Rubens and the speculative spirit of a Strousberg," and the linkage of Rubens and Strousberg said something of the cultural climate of the age.[22]

The *Gründerjahre* held up a distorted mirror to a society that had but a blurred vision of its physiognomy. Self-discovery is rarely an undivided pleasure; self-discovery the day after is bound to be painful and misleading. Endless and exaggerated laments about Germany's moral collapse appeared and paved the way for the creation of a new culprit.

The sudden rise and widespread acceptance of a new, virulent anti-Semitism must be seen as a psychological consequence of the great boom-and-bust experience. Aristocratic consciences had been aroused by the discovery that the lure of wealth had drawn their own class into the world of speculation. They too had contributed to the nation's corruption—and some of them experienced stirrings of unease and guilt. To deviate from one's moral code successfully, without being caught, is a very different experience from violating one's code and ending up in failure and public reprobation. Protestant conservatives, moreover, were uneasy about the *Kulturkampf,* about what they regarded as Bismarck's attack on a Christian religion in what once had been a Christian state—though Bismarck's intentions had been quite different. That transgression also ended in failure, and failure often quickens conscience. Is it an accident that these misgivings and stirrings of guilt coin-

22. Richard Hamann and Jost Hermand, *Gründerzeit "Deutsche Kunst und Kultur von der Gründerzeit bis zum Expressionismus,"* Vol. I (Berlin, 1965), p. 46.

cided with the rise of anti-Semitism? The disaster of 1873 would appear less wounding if it could be charged to the machinations of a foreign agent. The cry went up that the Jew tempted and corrupted, that the Jew lured Germans away from their ancient code of virtue. Anti-Semitism had been waning in mid-century; after 1873, it burgeoned in unprecedented fashion. In 1875, the *Kreuzzeitung* indicted imperial politics as *"Judenpolitik,"* insisting that all policies were being conducted by and for Jews. Two years later, people complained about "Jewish domination [*Judenherrschaft*]."[23] Anti-Semitism now became a doctrine that court chaplains could dispense to the elite as well as to the masses. It constituted an avowal of German Idealism; it became a means to regain a good conscience.

The scapegoat theory of anti-Semitism is never more than a partial and unsatisfactory interpretation, but in this instance it does seem as if the Jew was made to carry dimly perceived Christian guilt, that the upper classes were vulnerable to the rantings of rabble-rousers because anti-Semitism helped to restore their self-esteem. Was this experience an anticipation of later charges that an undefeated, uncorrupted Germany had been stabbed in the back? All of this is hard to document and easy to exaggerate, but the paranoid underworld of politics in an age of affluence and cultural unease cannot be overlooked.

The pillars of German society were not so strong or so solid as had once been assumed. What Bismarck had sought to save at the visible top of the political system, the spread of capitalism undermined at the largely invisible substratum. The adjustment of the upper classes to sudden and profound change was painful—the more so, perhaps, for being largely disguised. Junkers and *Bürgertum* lacked a certain kind of self-assurance: the Junkers because their position required them simultaneously to despise and acquire the fruits of capitalism, the middle

23. *Kreuzzeitung,* June 29, 1875; Dr. Rudolph Meyer, *Politische Gründer,* p. 111.

classes because, challenged from below, they protected these same fruits by accepting the anachronistic and politically emasculating domination of an older caste. Capitalism booming created problems; capitalism in a state of protracted crisis created still worse problems. After 1873, the depression shook the economic self-confidence of many Germans and the specters of corruption and Jew-conspiracy came to trouble anxious people.

The political realm, as we shall see, did not provide the stability, leadership or confidence that the society needed. Quite the contrary. Bismarck sought to handle the political crises of the new nation by making himself the principal arbiter of the country. Here, too, self-reliance and self-governance were gradually corrupted and demeaned—though it is important to remember that this process of political enfeeblement had begun much earlier and had been deeply affected by the outcome of the constitutional struggle of the 1860's. In part, Bismarck became more authoritarian because his opponents were so weak; they grew weaker, as he grew stronger. In the 1860's, he had said that it would be enough to put Germany in the saddle; she would know how to ride. In the 1870's, he thought that it would be best if he stayed in command; Germans turned out to be poor riders, after all. His long and increasingly autocratic rule strengthened existing tendencies to political passivity and submission.

The achievements of 1871 had been extraordinary, and an age that glorified heroes rather than analyzed anonymous social and economic forces attributed them to Bismarck's genius. He had forged institutions that would promote Germany's power by providing for common commercial and foreign policies and that would guarantee Germany's survival by a common military establishment under thinly disguised Prussian hegemony. By creating a national parliament, Bismarck had inserted democratic and popular elements into the structure of the Reich without materially weakening the preceding monarchical-conservative order. By making concessions to modernity, the old order prolonged its life. The new Reich facilitated the immense expansion of material power—though the attendant social transformation undermined Bismarck's political structure. Bismarck was slow to appreciate the danger from that quarter. He was more attuned to foreign dangers. For the great Bismarck was at home abroad, and estranged at home.

He devoted his best efforts to shielding Germany from foreign wars. His greatest accomplishment after 1871 was his assimilation of Germany into the European state system; he persuaded a suspicious Europe that Germany had become a satiated power—and by the time Europe fully believed him, he was dismissed from office, and Germany ceased being satiated.

In the early 1870's, the German Empire was in the historic position of a new nation, even if most Germans, bound by older dynastic loyalties, were unaware of it. It was a time when traditions needed to be founded, patterns set, loyalties formed. A partnership of citizenry and government in the affairs of state needed to be created. In some tangible concerns—the establishment of a national bank or a national railroad system—the Reich did make significant progress, and for a few years Bismarck seemed to have overwhelming popular support behind him. But the dominant note was conflict, not consolidation. In his memoirs, Bismarck acknowledged that fact. He entitled the three chapters dealing with the domestic history of the Second Empire: *"Kulturkampf,"* "Break with the Conservatives," "Intrigues." In retirement, he remembered the antagonisms, not the achievements. In retirement, as in power, he thought himself the victim of malevolent rivals, of indolent and stupid subordinates, of scheming politicians, and of ungrateful monarchs. Bismarck was great in everything—self-pity included.

All societies built on rank and inequalities are riddled with

intrigue and conspiracy—the greater the consciousness of hier-
archy, the stronger the sense of intrigue. Imperial Germany
probably exceeded the contemporary norm. Did the newness
and brittleness of the Empire, its peculiar political structure, its
strident tone and hidden fears, its imbalance between political
and economic power, breed a special combination of insecurity, sycophancy, and intrigue? The diaries and letters of the
period suggest this, and an amateur psychologist might wonder
whether the sexually repressive and largely hypocritical character of the society might not have contributed to its harsh
undertone, which all too often was disguised by an official
veneer of painful sentimentality. Certainly Bismarck contributed to it: his own contemptuous distrust of others and his
often intolerant authoritarianism injected a special kind of
poison into Germany's public life.

It was undoubtedly deleterious for the new nation to have
its politics dominated by one man. Bismarck had defined his
constitutional role in this fashion, and his temperament would
scarcely have tolerated any other role. But he found it difficult
and unrewarding. It was one thing to improvise the startling
victories of the sixties; it was quite another to settle down to
institutionalize these gains in the seventies. "I am bored," he
complained. "The great deeds are done."[24]

His boredom and his health became matters of national
importance, and for most of the 1870's his health was terrible.
His ills made him more prone to anger, and anger aggravated
his ills. As an admirer, Lord Odo Russell, wrote in 1872: "Bismarck, whose nervous system is shattered by overwork and
nocturnal beer and pipe orgies, and who can no longer stand
contradiction without getting into a passion, frets and fumes at
what he calls the ingratitude of a Sovereign who owes him
everything—political power, military glory, and an invincible

24. Poschinger, *Fürst Bismarck und die Parlamentarier,* Vol. I (2nd edn.,
Breslau, 1894), p. 87.

Empire—and whose confidence ought therefore to be bound-less."[25] In his psychosomatic maladies—and perhaps only in them—Bismarck was thoroughly modern. His vicious cycle of complaints was broken intermittently by his ebullient high spirits, his charm, and the resourcefulness of his mind.

Bismarck's capacity for hatred and suspicion is justly renowned and was probably harder on his subordinates than on his foes. He could be incredibly brutal to colleagues as well as unpredictably generous. He said the most devastating things about his fellow ministers, and he vilified some of them with a coarseness that reeked of barnyards. He exaggerated the evil machinations of his putative rivals, and in his celebrated nights of sleeplessness, he endowed these hapless creatures with his own intelligence and toughness. No wonder that the next morning he feared them. But there *were* intrigues against him, even if he vastly exaggerated, for example, the dangers of feminine court conspiracies. Of his favorite target, Queen Augusta, he once said that "her intrigues border on high treason."[26] In the early 1870's, amid various storms and scandals, there was the possibility that Bismarck's rule might not last long, that he might soon be overthrown or resign.[27] In the 1880's, on the other hand, it appeared as if the Bismarck rule would be perpetuated in a Bismarck dynasty, that there would be no end of Bismarcks. Neither prospect lent a sense of security to his subordinates.

Bismarck's entourage was not the happy little band of devoted assistants that has sometimes been depicted. There were

25. *Letters from the Berlin Embassy 1871–1874, 1880–1885*, ed. by Paul Knaplund ("Annual Report of the American Historical Association for the Year 1942," Vol. II, Washington, 1944), p. 58.

26. *Bismarck-Erinnerungen des Staatsministers Freiherrn Lucius von Ball-hausen* (Stuttgart, 1921), p. 110.

27. *Staatssekretär Graf Herbert von Bismarck. Aus seiner politischen Privatkorrespondenz*, ed. by Walter Bussmann ("Deutsche Geschichtsquellen des 19. und 20. Jahrhunderts," Vol. XLIV, Göttingen, 1964), p. 15.

jealousies and animosities, fear and anger, rankling the more for having to be concealed. In his selection and advancement of underlings, Bismarck appeared capricious. He disdained stupidity and rebuffed independence. He wanted intelligent servants without private judgment or ambition, well-wrought tools for his master-hands. The loyal Hatzfeldt once complained that Bismarck's appointments bore no relation to merit and that he preferred nullities.[28] Morale was low around Bismarck.

The personal character of his rule outraged many of his thoughtful contemporaries. The letters and diaries of the 1870's express again and again the fear that it was Bismarck's whim, his caprice, that governed Germany and not the counsels of statesmen or the principles of *raison d'état*. At times, observers may have mistaken inscrutable policy for caprice, but what remains is the impression of considerable unease. There were endless variations on Mommsen's celebrated judgment that Bismarck had broken Germany's moral backbone. Franz von Roggenbach, admittedly a foe, often lamented "the moral degradation" that autocratic rule produced in spineless servants.[29] In 1881, he wrote: "Nobody can deceive himself about the fact that if the elections put him at the head of a slavishly subservient majority and if the dynasty is thereby still further put in check, then the Chancellor will become more extravagant than ever in indulging his passions, his caprices, his hatreds, and his wild ambition."[30]

Bismarck came to sense the precariousness of the new nation. The particularist jealousy of the Reich extended deep into Prussian hearts—and if dominant Prussia resented the new imperial authority, why should Catholic Bavaria feel any special loyalty?

28. Hatzfeldt to Bleichröder, April 15, 1878, Bleichröder Archive.
29. *Im Ring der Gegner Bismarcks. Denkschriften und Politischer Briefwechsel Franz von Roggenbachs mit Kaiserin Augusta und Albrecht von Stosch 1865–1896*, ed. by Julius Heyderhoff ("Deutsche Geschichtsquellen des 19. Jahrhunderts," Vol. XXXV, 2nd printing, Leipzig, 1943), p. 184.
30. *Ibid.,* p. 213.

The major parties constituted latent threats: the National Liberals had not yet consciously surrendered their hopes for a parliamentary regime, hopes that were anathema to Bismarck. The conservatives balked at his seeming closeness to the liberals. Nothing so embittered Bismarck in the 1870's as the sudden enmity of his own class. The Junkers' desertion, which Bismarck largely attributed to their envy of him, left him isolated, without personal friends or dependable political allies. The Junkers, scarred by the financial crash and affronted by Bismarck's liberal and Jewish associates, came to distrust him as a renegade and could not grasp that Bismarck's genius had torn him away from his provincial moorings but that that same genius had devised means to save their political fortunes. The break between the Chancellor and his natural allies illuminates the connections between the social disarray of the early 1870's and the political crisis of the new Reich.[31]

It was one thing for Bismarck to fight Catholic priests, all of whom he suspected—to put it with Ems-like brevity—of maintaining simultaneously illicit relations with both the Pope and Queen Augusta. It was easy for him to persecute socialist leaders whom he suspected of being cousins of the Commune, hirelings of the Internationale. It took no emotional toll to break with the National Liberals in 1879 and to remove, one by one, his liberal associates of earlier years. Only the rupture with the conservatives hurt. As Bismarck put it in his memoirs, "To

31. In November 1873, Lord Russell reported from Berlin: "While shooting in Silesia I met many great and small landed proprietors. They spoke freely of their hatred of Bismarck whose radical German policy and persecution of the Clergy was alienating the Prussian Aristocracy from the Throne. The Prussian Aristocracy had ever shed their best blood in the hour of danger for the House of Hohenzollern, but in the day of prosperity Bismarck used his ambitious influence to mislead their old King into treating them as enemies etc. etc. Most of them said they would not go to Berlin this Winter so as not to mark their disatisfaction [*sic*] with the Court and Government, —but I suspect also, to save money, for Berlin has become simply ruinous." *Letters from the Berlin Embassy*, p. 117.

break existing relations with all or almost all friends and acquaintances is a hard test for the nerves of a man in his mature years."[32] His earlier, intermittent misanthropy now became his steady companion and protection. Gradually Bismarck hardened into an autocrat, convinced not so much of his own greatness or of his ability to impose his will on events, as of the pettiness and utter incompetence of his fellow men.

After the conservatives had broken with him, where were the unshakable pillars of the state—the more needed as new enemies appeared? Or did the putative remark of Count Eulenburg, the Prussian Minister of the Interior, attest a general apprehension? "The old pillars of the government are destroyed. From now on, we have to lean on the Jews."[33]

Bismarck had seen revolution in its liberal and post-liberal guise; he feared it, not so much as the replacement of the monarchical-conservative order, but as the senseless subversion of all order. Hence his genuine fear of democratic socialism, with its revolutionary pretensions. He also manipulated that fear in order to intimidate the electorate. He was no less afraid of the Catholic politicians who would perpetuate a confessional party, under foreign influence, that could mobilize a religious minority and keep it permanently estranged from the state. As Lord Russell once put it: "Thinking himself far more infallible than the Pope he cannot tolerate two infallibles in Europe and fancies he can select and appoint the next Pontiff as he could a Prussian General, who will carry out his orders to the Catholic Clergy in Germany and elsewhere."[34]

Bismarck's response to these threats—which he exaggerated, as he exaggerated all threats—was disastrous. He launched repressive campaigns, dubbed opponents enemies of the Reich,

32. Otto Fürst von Bismarck, *Gedanken und Erinnerungen,* Vol. II (Stuttgart, 1898), p. 156.
33. Dr. Rudolph Meyer, *Politische Gründer,* p. 27.
34. *Letters from the Berlin Embassy,* p. 71.

and almost succeeded in converting them into the creatures he imagined them to be. He knew that he could no longer escape domestic difficulties by foreign adventures; instead he applied the tactics hitherto reserved for dealing with foreign nations to his relations with the different factions of the Reich. Worse, he sought to crush domestic enemies in a way that he would not even try to do with foreign foes. His various stratagems proved harder on liberals and conservatives who always struggled to find reasons to support him than on Catholics and socialists who knew unambiguously that he was their foe. His repressive policies further weakened the principles of the groups that supported the state, even as they strengthened the popular support of the so-called enemies of the state.

The reality of Bismarck's rule, then, was radically different from its appearance. Twenty years of misanthropic autocracy left German politics with a hard, brutal tone and a viciousness that exacerbated the many inherent antagonisms of the new regime. Bismarck's style was as injurious as his policies: need one recall his brutal polemics against political opponents, his systematic denigration of the organs of public life, of parliament and press? The fact that he was superbly skillful in these attacks only sharpened their impact.

Unification was followed by deep divisiveness, much of it caused by social changes beyond the control of any man or government. It is my contention, however, that Bismarck gratuitously added to this divisiveness and made more difficult the resolution of these conflicts. Far from marshaling a consensus behind the new government, far from inspiring trust and tolerance, he poisoned the atmosphere of political life. His critics charged him with promoting the moral degradation and political nonage of the German people. His own diagnosis of the German people was no more complimentary; he would have insisted, however, that he was the victim, not the cause, of these disabilities.

Perhaps we can better assess Bismarck's historic role by looking at it from another perspective. Other new nations had the inestimable fortune that their first leaders also proved to be fathers of their country: one thinks of George Washington and T. G. Masaryk. Bismarck hardly fits that category of leaders, yet his long rule at that particular juncture in his nation's history cast him in the role of a father. He did not play that role, or, at most, he played it occasionally and according to the notoriously different standards of German fatherhood. His talents would inevitably have awed his charges; his autocratic ways confirmed and strengthened their dependence and their fearful adulation of authority. Bismarck, however, should have been aware that precedents were being set, that the success and viability of 1871 depended on the transformation of subjects into citizens, and that subjects, like children, need to learn independence and self-government. Precisely when it was necessary to expand the basis of government, to recruit new talent, to legitimize new institutions, Bismarck, perhaps without realizing it, demeaned the entire political process.

It is ironic to note that Bismarck dead came to symbolize what Bismarck alive could not achieve. The monuments scattered throughout Germany in his honor were intended as mystical representations of national unity: he had become the "Ur-symbol of the nation" he had united. By their massive solidity, these monuments embodied artistic and political protests against the vapid ostentation of Wilhelmine Germany but also sought to express "an insecurity, a secret fear of the dissolution of the national community and of the loss of power because of a hapless *Weltpolitik.*"[35]

William II justified all the fears that wise observers voiced about his reign. But his heritage had not been enviable. Bis-

35. Thomas Nipperdey, "Nationalidee und Nationaldenkmal in Deutschland im 19. Jahrhundert," *Historische Zeitschrift*, Vol. CCVI, No. 3 (June, 1968), p. 582.

marck's legacy had set strict limits to the possibilities of subsequent statesmanship—limits that William II never came even close to testing. William's pathetically unbalanced personality dramatized his political ineptness; Bismark's greatness helped to obscure his failings. The young Bismarck, in particular, had combined an abundance of intelligence, courage, and a certain kind of romantic *Übermut* in so felicitous a fashion that even his critics were understandably awed and captivated by him. The Bismarck of subsequent decades was a curiously changed man, and it had been the Chancellor himself who had set patterns that proved impossible to cast off. It was in the early years of the Empire that a vicious tone crept into German public life, that political institutions were discredited before they had been allowed to develop, that hypocrisy and false self-assessment encouraged suspicion and xenophobic arrogance. Ralf Dahrendorf's suggestive formulation for a later period in German history, that Germany was governed by a "cartel of anxiety," has bearing on this period as well: the roots of that fatal anxiety reach back to the weaknesses of German political culture here discussed.[36]

The people of the new nation suffered from a variety of growing pains, all likely to induce anxiety. Adjustment to capitalism proved hard; the discrepancy between idealized self-image and actual, material behavior was difficult to ignore or explain. Frank acceptance of the values of capitalism would have both undermined the ideological pillars of Junker predominance and lent some legitimacy to the claims of the lower classes for better living conditions and some measure of equality. There was a psychological and moral crampedness in the way most Germans in that first generation of the Empire perceived the realities of the new society. Perhaps there was also something symbolic about Bismarck's hardheaded decision to

36. Ralf Dahrendorf, *Society and Democracy in Germany* (New York, 1967), p. 275.

try to cure Germany's ills by erecting protective walls against foreign competitors; Germans needed to be sheltered from the winds of change and from the outside world. At home, too, Bismarck sought to insulate them from the free, competitive play of political forces and arrogated to himself powers that should have been diffused. Yet, he found it harder and harder to offer leadership or to operate successfully the very regime he had himself devised. The first decades of the Empire, then, saw a political and psychological faltering that affected the growth of the new nation for decades to come.

In 1871, Bismarck had unified the German states, not the Germans. He had helped to give Europe peace, but had left his successors a distrustful, agitated, anxious people who were held together by dynastic traditions, by aggressive nationalist sentiments, and by material prosperity about which they felt intermittently unsure and uneasy. He had done nothing to educate his people in the uses of power; by forging a political culture that bore traces of his own misanthropy and contempt for mankind, he had dulled them to the dangers of unbridled power. All this he bequeathed, but his exquisite skill as diplomat was not hereditary. He had forgotten, as so many statesmen before and after him, that peace, like charity, begins at home, and that power, to be enduring, must have a moral basis.

Gold and Iron

The Collaboration and Friendship of Gerson Bleichröder and Otto von Bismarck

The following was originally delivered as a paper for a
session on "Big Business and German Politics" at the annual meeting of the American Historical Association in
1968. It represents an initial effort to say something about
Gerson Bleichröder. For some years now, I have been
gathering new material from various private and public
archives in Europe in preparation for a full-length study of
Bleichröder's career and influence. That study, I hope, will
be completed in 1972.

In his treatise on big business and politics, George Bernard
Shaw insisted that

the universal regard for money is the one hopeful fact in our civilization, the one sound spot in our social conscience. Money is the most important thing in the world. It represents health, strength, honour, generosity and beauty as conspicuously and undeniably as the want of it represents illness, weakness, disgrace, meanness and ugliness. Not the least of its virtues is that it destroys base people as certainly as it fortifies and dignifies noble people.

Shaw's extravagance in *Major Barbara* was an answer to the hypocritical disdain of money that genteel folk affected and to the scorn of it that mindless revolutionaries scattered about.

Until quite recently Shaw's dictum would have jarred German historians. They were so wedded to the primacy of foreign policy that they ignored or greatly neglected the importance of domestic politics with its inevitable relation to the cruder material interests of life. The treatment of Bismarck's banker, Gerson Bleichröder, is a case in point.[1] In his imaginative, not to say fanciful, memoirs, Bismarck virtually forgot about Bleichröder, and German historians faithfully followed his selective memory. In the important works of Arnold Oskar Meyer and Otto Becker, written during the Nazi period, Bleichröder became an un-person.[2] He simply ceased to exist.

Bleichröder's contemporaries knew better and, if anything, erred by exaggerating the strength of the tie between Bismarck and Bleichröder. They were closer to the mark. For both men it was a central and exceptionally close and persistent relationship. From 1859 to Bleichröder's death in 1893, the two men conferred and collaborated regularly, each deriving profit from the other's help. Despite the obvious inequality of birth and rank, something approaching intimacy ripened. Over the years

1. See also David S. Landes's article, "The Bleichröder Bank: An Interim Report," *Publications of the Leo Baeck Institute, Year V* (London, 1960), pp. 201–21.
2. Arnold Oskar Meyer, *Bismarck der Mensch und der Staatsmann* (Stuttgart, 1949); Otto Becker, *Bismarcks Ringen um Deutschlands Gestaltung* Heidelberg, 1958).

thousands of letters were exchanged, and the two men saw each other hundreds of times. With how many other people, outside his family, did Bismarck cherish such relations? The turnover in his entourage was after all fairly rapid, a fact rarely noted and yet related to the growing loneliness of Bismarck's later years. Chancellor and banker grew old and lonely together. Few people in the 1870's and 1880's still received ten- or twelve-page letters in Bismarck's hand—letters that characteristically enough do not show up in the magisterial edition of Bismarck's correspondence.

There was, to be sure, something incongruous about a relationship between two men so different from each other. What was it that linked the Jew—hedged in by apprehensions and uncertainties, a partial stranger in the land he loved too well, living off his intelligence, his integrity, his inexhaustible industry—and the Junker, with his early, Byronic self-confidence, his half-affected disdain of money, custom, and Jews, his irrepressible courage, and his soaring ambition? What they shared was an appetite for power and an appreciation of intelligence; what brought them together was their usefulness to each other. One of them was, of course, inferior to the other, but Bleichröder had learned the forms of subservience in dealing with that exacting dynasty, the Rothschilds, whose Berlin agent the Bleichröders had been since the 1830's. The Rothschilds lent the House of Bleichröder its initial distinction; the tie with Bismarck gave Bleichröder his unique standing in Germany and the world.

The story of Bismarck and Bleichröder, then, is one of reciprocal need and assistance. Bleichröder's role was in many respects anachronistic. In his service to Bismarck he stood somewhere between a traditional court Jew and a modern trouble shooter like Harry Hopkins. He served Bismarck in a wide variety of roles, in both public and private realms. And what could Bismarck do for Bleichröder? He could use him in these many different roles and, by so doing, give him the imprimatur of national reliability, for a banker who enjoyed the Chancellor's confidence assumed a unique place in the business world of Berlin. By various favors that governments could extend, Bismarck helped to augment—and to legitimize—Bleichröder's fortune. Bleichröder rendered service, and Bismarck conferred status; such a summary does violence to countless other features, but catches something of the essence of their relationship.

Bleichröder's steady usefulness to Bismarck in the political realm constituted one of the highlights of their relationship. Like his model, the Rothschilds, Bleichröder believed in the immense importance of receiving better and faster information than his competitors. He belonged to what must be called the Rothschild intelligence network, and in time he managed to surpass it by adding his own strategically placed informants. His correspondents included some of the leading diplomats and businessmen of Europe; they knew that Bleichröder had easy access to Bismarck, and men like to share confidences with friends who are close to power. Bleichröder may have supplied Bismarck with more information than he needed; in turn the Chancellor used Bleichröder to convey thoughts and inclinations to foreign leaders without having to rely on the more official and possibly less discreet efforts of his ambassadors. No wonder that by the 1860's the Berlin banker Bleichröder considered himself an auxiliary of the Foreign Office and referred to Bismarck as *Der Chef*. Bismarck could rely on Bleichröder's disciplined discretion when it mattered, but Bleichröder's vanity and good business sense combined to let the world know that he was Bismarck's confidant.

In Bismarck's hardest days as Prussian Prime Minister, Bleichröder proved his beneficial loyalty. Dazzled by Bismarck's resourceful diplomacy, historians have lost sight of the fact that the wars of 1864 and 1866 posed major fiscal problems for a government that because of a recalcitrant Diet could raise no extra loans or new taxes. In that crisis Bleichröder pointed the way to an intricate and probably unconstitutional solution. He advocated the conversion of the government's rights to shares of the Cologne-Minden Railway, with which Bleichröder happened to have had long and close connections. The mobilization of that additional capital gave Prussia the necessary fiscal backbone for waging a major war. Both Bismarck and his friend and War Minister, Count Albrecht von Roon, acknowledged the importance of that transaction, and Bismarck treasured Bleichröder's fidelity at a time when, as he put it, he stood as close to the gallows as to the throne.

Actually Bleichröder, like the Berlin business community generally, abhorred the possibility that the Austro-Prussian antagonism could lead to a fratricidal war. Before the outbreak of the war, and almost certainly with Bismarck's knowledge, he urged an old friend and an associate of the Rothschilds in Vienna, Moritz von Goldschmidt, to persuade his government to sell Holstein to Prussia. Bismarck would apparently have accepted a peaceful solution that would have yielded Schleswig-Holstein to Prussia and would at the same time have humiliated Austria by forcing it to trade territory for mere money.

In Bismarck's time of greatest difficulty, Bleichröder also helped him in various subterranean maneuvers. In a world with barely developed intelligence agencies, bankers occasionally had to execute mysterious missions. Bleichröder proved a reliably discreet agent who transmitted 400,000 taler to Hungarian revolutionaries in 1866; four years later, he arranged for the support of Italian agents who even then promised to subvert France by demanding the return of Nice. Also in 1870, the Prussian embassy in London alerted Bleichröder to the possibility of backing Algerian revolutionaries, but the Berlin Foreign Office proved unwilling to foment insurrections in such distant places. Closer to home, however, Bleichröder seems to have played his part in persuading the high-minded King of Bavaria, Louis, that his support of Bismarck's scheme of promoting Prussia's King to be German Emperor would have very precise material advantages for Louis, namely, secret subsidies for his extraordinary artistic and architectural ambitions. All such transactions were made easier by Bleichröder's central involvement with the administration of the *Welfenfond,* that notorious fund that Bismarck had seized from the defeated Hanoverian dynasty.

After 1871 he continued to play a semi-covert role in foreign policy. He was involved in Bismarck's first imperial venture in Samoa. As a friend of Leopold II, Bleichröder was well versed in African politics; he also participated in the German penetration of the Ottoman Empire. He served Bismarck's foreign policy in many different ways; in a few celebrated cases, such as the continued placing of Russian securities on the Berlin market, Bleichröder sought to change Bismarck's policy. In the late 1880's he warned Bismarck that if Germany ceased to supply Russia with capital, other powers would assume that role and reap political advantages from it. Bleichröder's rivals and detractors pounced on these attempts to alter or thwart the Chancellor's purposes, but Bleichröder offered them infrequent ammunition.

In two other fields, Bleichröder managed to serve Bismarck and himself. In the late 1860's Bleichröder played a preeminent role in financing a German equivalent of the Reuters News Agency in London and of Havas in Paris. In negotiating with the government Bleichröder secured important concessions for Wolff's Telegraph Bureau; the government in turn obtained privileges that increased its influence over public opinion and that under some circumstances envisioned controls that would have come close to censorship. More dramatic was Bleichröder's role in saddling the defeated French with a five-billion-franc indemnity. After considerable lobbying behind the scenes in January 1871, Bleichröder obtained Bismarck's summons to Versailles in order to help with the financial aspects of the prospective armistice. For about four weeks Bleichröder stayed at Royal Headquarters, negotiating with the French concerning the payment of their unprecedented burden. At the same time he restored ties with the Paris Rothschilds, hoping that the two partners would collaborate in the immeasurably intricate, but also profitable, business of collecting the French indemnity. Bleichröder's all too visible presence at headquarters, his calls on royalty and military "demigods," as well as his frequent conferences with Bismarck, inflamed the already surprisingly fierce anti-Semitism in those all-Gentile surroundings. Bleichröder seems to have been oblivious to the barnyard humor of which he was the victim: he was too pleased to be at the center of power at the moment of victory to notice, and he willingly accepted the congratulations of his old Viennese friend Goldschmidt about his "great, glorious and, one may indeed say, world-historical trip. . . . I believe you that the stay in Versailles offered things in plenty of the *highest* interest and left you with unforgettable memories for life. Only the elect experience such things."[3] He left Versailles with an Iron Cross, second class, a memento of his share in Prussia's glory. He also helped to collect the indemnity—his share in Prussia's profit.

Before and after the founding of the Empire, Bleichröder helped to salvage the bankrupt fortunes of some of Bismarck's associates and special constituents. In the late 1860's and early 1870's many a Junker found his investments threatened by the collapse of Dr. Bethel Henry Strousberg's railroad schemes in Rumania. These notables, many of whom had the closest links to the Prussian court, had been encouraged by Strousberg's earlier and successful railroad schemes in their own eastern provinces of Prussia. Now, in his more distant Rumanian ventures, they became the victims of their own capitalistic

3. Goldschmidt to Bleichröder, March 9 and 18, 1871, Bleichröder Archive.

appetite. Bleichröder and Adolf Hansemann of the *Disconto-Gesellschaft* provided for their financial rescue. Bleichröder likewise helped to restore Hermann Wagener and Count Paul von Hatzfeldt to solvency, and many a Bismarck aide benefited from Bleichröder's advice and assistance. Bismarck's enemies fared less well: when Count Harry von Arnim, German ambassador in Paris, fell from Bismarck's favor, Bleichröder's excellent connections in Paris contributed to the spiteful surveillance of the hapless Arnim.

In the twenty years of Bismarck's Empire, Bleichröder often counseled the Chancellor on economic policy. He wrote lengthy memorandums on the establishment of the Reichsbank and on bimetallism, urged the adoption of protectionism, and submitted advisory opinions on Bismarck's projected schemes of social insurance. In such matters he spoke with authority. His connections with the German business world, including the *Zentralverband deutscher Industrieller,* were close indeed. Angry contemporaries often exaggerated Bleichröder's influence on Bismarck's economic policies. He was a convenient surrogate for the real villain, Bismarck himself. Even such a well-informed disinterested observer as the French ambassador, the Comte de St. Vallier, reported in July 1879 that Bismarck's appointment of Karl Bitter as Finance Minister indicated that Bismarck would run the ministry himself or let Bleichröder do it, because his race and position as banker made it impossible for him to play an open role.[4]

Bleichröder was probably even more useful to Bismarck in the private than in the public realm. For thirty-four years, he was Bismarck's banker, investment counselor, tax adviser, and helper in all operations connected with Bismarck's cherished landholdings. At times, especially in his youth, Bismarck may have affected disdain for money, for double-entry bookkeeping,

4. Archives du Ministère des affaires étrangères, Correspondance Politique, Allemagne, Vol. XXIX, July 5, 1879.

for sordid material considerations. His banker knew the truth: Bismarck was anything but a Franciscan; he had a most remarkable appetite for augmenting his property, particularly his estates. Even if he had been less passionate in his land hunger, he would have needed Bleichröder's steady help. He lived well, and his salary covered but a third or half of his expenses. The balance had to come as interest from his fortune—a fortune that has remained the subject of continued controversy and mystery.[5] Bleichröder held all threads in his hands, and I hope that my study of Bleichröder will provide a comprehensive account of Bismarck's finances. A few high points must suffice here.

It is well known that Bismarck was one of Germany's largest landowners. Successive gifts from a grateful monarch and nation endowed him with the vast lands of Varzin and Friedrichsruh, to which he gradually annexed neighboring estates. It was fortunate for the peace of Europe that Bismarck's insatiable annexationism had been fixed not on national ambitions but on his private person. Indeed, a cynical observer might infer from various examples, Bismarck included, that the ambition of men of means is generally safer than that of propertyless adventurers. German historians have dwelt lovingly on Bismarck's passion for nature, on his love of trees, on his happy seigneurial relations with his tenant farmers. But Bleichröder saw another side of this idyllic rusticity: Bismarck's relentless determination to make these estates yield a profit. More than six million marks had been invested in the estates and the various industrial enterprises that Bismarck had added to them. Bleichröder was charged with supervising all kinds of details, ranging from handling mortages to checking on the brothers

5. The best, most recent, but still incomplete, account is Alfred Vagts, "Bismarck's Fortune," *Central European History,* Vol. I (Sept., 1968), pp. 203–33. Another recent work, Ulrich Küntzel, *Die Finanzen grosser Männer* (Vienna, 1964), pp. 447–511, is a popular study of Bismarck's fortune, full of errors of fact and interpretation and of allegations offered without proof.

Georg and Moritz Behrend, who for thirty years ran, and through their mismanagement intermittently threatened to ruin, Bismarck's prized paper mills in Varzin. Bismarck, the architect of reinsurance treaties, commissioned Bleichröder to handle his intricate insurance plans.

Bleichröder also had other responsibilities. A substantial part of Bismarck's income came from the sale of his vast timber supply, and he was always concerned to find a lucrative and reliable market. At first much of his timber was sold to England, but Bismarck complained to Bleichröder in 1882 that concerning payment "The English do not want to accept other procedures; they are used to imposing their own conditions in commercial matters."[6] Later on, Hibernia, the huge Ruhr coal mine, became Bismarck's chief buyer through the services of Friedrich Vohwinkel, and the Friedrichsruh forester pleaded annually with Bleichröder to use his good offices so that Hibernia would renew Vohwinkel's contract. Bleichröder had been the principal founder of Hibernia in 1873 and until his death retained his seat on the Board of Directors; he could therefore help to preserve this special tie between Bismarck and big business. By 1886 Vohwinkel had already paid over a million marks to the Prince, who was very grateful for Bleichröder's intervention.[7]

Few of his contemporaries realized the extent of Bleichröder's involvement in the management of Bismarck's estates. Everyone knew—or speculated—about his investment of Bismarck's securities. Bismarck's enemies hinted at all manner of dubious deals and shady profits that the Chancellor allegedly derived from this connection. It was often rumored that Bismarck used his political information to play the market. The truth is at once more prosaic and more interesting. Bismarck had a steadily growing portfolio of securities over which Bleich-

6. Copy of Bismarck to Bleichröder, Feb. 6, 1882, Bleichröder Archive.
7. Peter Lange to Bleichröder, Aug. 21, 1886, *ibid.*

röder had full powers. He rarely needed these powers because he would almost invariably ask for and receive Bismarck's instructions concerning the disposition of funds. Bleichröder bought or sold securities according to Bismarck's oral or written instructions. The portfolio, which I have been able to reconstruct in large part, was essentially conservative, a fitting tribute to the conservatism of both men. There were, however, some notable developments.

Shortly after the American Civil War, Bismarck was a heavy buyer of United States government bonds. By the end of the 1860's, however, his financial interests had shifted eastward: more than half his fortunes went into various Russian securities. In the July crisis of 1870 Bleichröder solicited Bismarck's thoughts on the likelihood of war; on July 10 Johanna von Bismarck answered for her husband

> who is very busy coding and uncoding. . . . He does not indeed believe in war because despite all the frivolity of some people, he thinks it improbable that one would suddenly attack *us* because *Spain* did not vote the way one wanted it to. But he thought that there could still come moments when the belief in war would be stronger than now and since he needs money here anyhow it might be a good idea to sell the railroad preference shares.[8]

The next day the market dropped sharply.

Four years later Bismarck alarmed Bleichröder by suddenly ordering him to liquidate all his Russian holdings. Bismarck's later explanations concerning his sudden selling—that he thought it ominous that Russia's ablest minister, Count Peter Shuvalov, had been moved from the ministry in St. Petersburg to the embassy in London—reflected his poetic hindsight rather than his likely reasons at the time. The portfolio underwent other important and mildly lucrative changes.

The greatest transaction in the history of Bismarck's capital occurred between March 8 and 13, 1890, days before his dis-

8. Johanna von Bismarck to Bleichröder, July 10, 1870, *ibid.*

missal, when he liquidated his vast holdings in German government securities and replaced some of them with Egyptian bonds.[9] Did Bismarck, as has often been alleged, perhaps think of staging a *coup d'état,* which might have depressed the Reich's obligations? Or, more likely, was this Bismarck's final speculation, a speculation against his own downfall? Did he assume, as he had alleged much earlier in Shuvalov's case, that an empire that let its ablest man depart would soon commit political follies? We know that he thought it "very strange that the Emperor names his best general a Chancellor and his best Chancellor a field marshal."[10] This time he was doubly right: the market reacted to his dismissal with a violent, if brief, drop in prices,[11] the Egyptian securities appreciated, and the Reich embarked on its new course of unbridled power and folly.

In the three years between Bismarck's dismissal and Bleichröder's death, relations between the two men grew still more intimate. *Der Bleiche,* as Bismarck's wife had called Bleichröder for decades, was a frequent visitor in Varzin. The two men had known each other in the beginnings of their careers, amidst trials and dangers; they had worked together in the consolidation of their triumphs; and now they watched together

9. There had been a sharp drop on the Berlin market—for financial, not political reasons—for some weeks before Bismarck's dismissal. On March 9 the leading financial weekly, *Der Aktionär* (Vol. XXXVII, p. 157), noted "last week . . . a regular panic dominated [the stock exchange]. . . . The improvement that appeared at the end of the week was . . . to the largest part due to the intervention of others, and in the first place one recognized the House of Bleichröder." It may be relevant to note that on March 5 *Der Aktionär* carried a lead article commenting on the much-improved state of Egyptian finances, in which Bleichröder had long been interested.

10. Herbert von Bismarck to Lord Rosebery, March 30, 1890, in *Staatssekretär Graf Herbert von Bismarck aus seiner politischen Korrespondenz,* ed. by Walter Bussmann (Göttingen, 1964), p. 567.

11. The bearish elements were encouraged by the fact that "the first House of the city, whose connections with the Chancellor are well known, served their purpose by making great sales." *Der Aktionär,* Vol. XXXVII (March 23, 1890), p. 197. Bleichröder had obviously known for some days before Bismarck's dismissal that his position had become precarious.

the passing of their era, defined in some measure by the very possibility of their close association.

How can one finally assess Bleichröder's place in Bismarck's world? Perhaps one measure of his importance was simply the amount of abuse the Chancellor was willing to suffer on account of that relationship. Privately in the 1860's and publicly in the next two decades Bismarck was maligned for giving a Jew so much power, protection, and influence. The anti-Semitic agitators, Franz Perrot and Adolf Stöcker, carried the campaign to the masses, depicting Bleichröder as the evil genius of the *Gründerjahre* and of Bismarck's economic policy. Most aristocrats probably hated the Jew lover more than the Jew; resentful masses and declining classes regarded Bleichröder—an ever more visible target—with revulsion. Despite these animosities, despite the hatred of Bleichröder that Bismarck's favorite son, Herbert, harbored, and despite the fact that Bismarck had often before broken old and amicable ties, the Chancellor stuck by his banker. He was often critical of him, but he rebuffed all suggestions that he should free himself from his "pushy" and nefarious Jew. Sometimes his private, anti-Semitic apologies for retaining Bleichröder showed him to be far closer to his traducers than to his banker. Still he kept Bleichröder. Loyalty, even gratitude, may have played a role, but a modest one at most. He knew that other bankers would have been happy to take over, but Bleichröder survived because Bismarck trusted, respected, and liked him—and because Bismarck profited from the association, not in the crude sense his vilifiers alleged, but in many tangible and intangible ways. His policies, his pocket, and perhaps even his psyche profited and in so felicitous a combination that he apparently was never even tempted to trade his banker for another.

Bleichröder had no reason to think of leaving Bismarck, even though the Chancellor could be exacting, imperious, and unreasonable as well as benevolent and charming. The very fact

that Bismarck could have dropped Bleichröder but not Bleichröder Bismarck exposes the inequality of the relationship. It in
turn deepened Bleichröder's extraordinary subservience, which
at times degenerated into sycophancy.

Bleichröder's embarrassing deference derived from a com-
posite of facts and feelings. Every German would have felt
awed by Bismarck's power, and Jews even more so. Every German banker of Bleichröder's generation would have instinc-
tively understood the primacy of political over material power
—and Bleichröder even more so. The very profit that Bleichröder drew from his association with Bismarck's power heightened his deference and tinged it with fear: he had more to gain
and more to lose than his contemporaries. We have already
seen some of the tangible rewards that Bismarck was able to
bestow on Bleichröder. Bismarck helped to make him richer;
Bleichröder died one of the richest men in Germany. But Bleichröder, like most men, wanted more than wealth. In a society
that was still fiercely inegalitarian, where feudal prejudices
grew stronger after mid-century as a rising bourgeoisie embraced
them, businessmen sought distinction, and Jews did so more
than others. They had to overcome the double stigma of race
and mammon. Outwardly, Bleichröder rose to the pinnacle,
surpassing in his generation all of his coreligionists. In the
1860's he was made a *Geheimer Kommerzienrath,* and in 1872,
at Bismarck's personal behest, William I raised him to the
ranks of the hereditary nobility—the first Prussian Jew who
had been so honored without having previously converted to
Christianity. In the same year the British government appointed
him its consul general in Berlin because, in Lord Odo Russell's
words, he is "not only the Rothschild of Berlin, but also one
of Prince Bismarck's most intimate friends and advisors in
financial and commercial matters. Baron Bleichröder, who
holds an exceptionally good position in Berlin Society, is often
personally consulted by the Emperor and the Crown Prince and

is generally trusted and respected by the governing and commercial classes of Prussia."[22] The great financier of a later time, Carl Fürstenberg, whom Bleichröder gave a start in life, once remarked that in Germany there was no amnesty for titles. Bleichröder would not even have understood such reverse snobbery: he accepted the system and sought to excel in it, not to escape from it. To the coveted "von" he added a host of decorations, German and non-German, and on formal occasions his chest was no longer lamentably bare. Much of this he owed to Bismarck. In 1873 he bought Fieldmarshal Roon's estate near Potsdam. That acquisition, too, was part of Bleichröder's spectacular social rise, which of course further incited his anti-Semitic foes. The higher he rose, the more prominent a target he became.

Amidst all his honors, Bleichröder was never allowed to forget that he was a Jew. To his credit it should be said that he never tried to. Repeatedly he used his influence with Bismarck on behalf of his coreligionists. At the time of the Congress of Berlin, he led an international campaign to convince Bismarck that the Great Powers must compel Rumania to grant civil equality to Jews as a price of recognition. It was a long, tough fight with the wily Rumanians, and many times Bismarck tired of Bleichröder's entreaties. Bleichröder also petitioned Chancellor and King to put an end to the anti-Semitic agitation of the court chaplain, Stöcker. For all his deference, Bleichröder could be extraordinarily persistent—a quality that escaped neither his friends nor his detractors.

Clearly there was something anachronistic in the relationship of these two men. By the time Bleichröder became Bismarck's banker, the age of the court Jew was over; indeed the great

12. Lord Russell to Viscount Enfield, Sept. 28, 1872, Foreign Office, Public Record Office, 64, 749.

age of the private banker was already doomed in the 1850's when the German *Grossbanken* began to dominate the scene. The emancipation of German Jewry and the establishment of a relatively open liberal economy made the role of the court Jew obsolete; against the next great wave of anti-Semitism even powerful individuals would be impotent. Bismarck, too, marked the end of an epoch; no European statesman has since dominated his country for as long and as completely as did Bismarck. The powers of the state became specialized and bureaucratized, and the kind of informal, intimate relationship that existed between Bismarck and Bleichröder became less feasible in the new so-called mass age.

Bleichröder's spectacular rise marked an important stage in the history of German Jewry. His daughter and three sons inherited his fortune but not his talents or disciplined capacity for work. The decline set in rapidly, affecting both progeny and bank. In their rise and fall the Bleichröders describe a kind of Jewish Buddenbrooks. The social and psychological precariousness of their position, always present beneath the glittering surface, became desperately clear after the rise of the Nazis. Bleichröder's descendants appealed to Adolf Eichmann to be exempted from deportation. It was a poignant, futile end to the story of the Bleichröders in Germany. The triumphs and disasters of that family illuminate much of modern German history and offer a new perspective on the titanic figure who dominated so much of that history.

Part Two

Germany and the Great War

Bethmann Hollweg and the War

The Bounds of Responsibility

I wrote this essay in the fall of 1966 for the *Festschrift* for Hajo Holborn, *The Responsibility of Power*, edited by Leonard Krieger and myself. I had long been interested in Bethmann Hollweg. The permission to use the unpublished diary of his assistant and confidant, Kurt Riezler, prompted me to write this essay, which is here reprinted with minor changes and additions.

Bethmann Hollweg, philosopher-bureaucrat, a riddle to his contemporaries, has remained a subject of unending controversy for historians. His responsibility for the outbreak of the First World War and for Germany's conduct of it has been polemically debated for decades. A villain to the Allies, to the German military and their Pan-German allies, he was a weakling and the country's gravedigger. After 1918, German nationalist historians blamed his indecision and defeatism for hobbling Germany's war effort. His few defenders in the 1920's insisted that he had been a "military Chancellor,"[1] only more reticent and circumspect than the Pan-German extremists. The Third Reich interrupted the argument which, a few years ago, Fritz Fischer's massive *Griff nach der Weltmacht* revived. The roles have been reversed: Bethmann Hollweg's detractors now claim that he was an annexationist with philosophical veneer, and his defenders suggest that he was a noble, ill-cast bureaucrat, with occasional annexationist leanings.

Most often, and most ambiguously, he has been called the German Hamlet—as if there were but one Hamlet! Intended was convention's ineffectual Hamlet, torn by self-doubt. If it is to be Hamlet, then a better likeness is that of the prince, who despite doubts and scruples, resorts to various stratagems to dispatch enemies and friends, and leaves the stage littered with corpses.

The controversy is more than an academic exercise about an inscrutable individual. Bethmann Hollweg, Imperial Germany's last effective Chancellor, led Germany into the First World War and left his office only after unrestricted submarine warfare and America's entry into the war had all but sealed Germany's fate. He necessarily is at the focus of all discussions concerning Germany's war guilt in 1914, her war aims during the war, and of the debate but recently started concerning the continuity of German history in the twentieth century. His Chancellorship illuminates as well the mounting internal antagonisms of the Bismarckian Reich. The study of Bethmann, then, has ever been controversial, important, and politically explosive.

For decades he was made to serve as the anchor man in Germany's case for her own essential moderation. After Versailles, German historians were loath to indulge in criticism of

---

1. *Bethmann Hollwegs Kriegsreden*, ed. by Dr. Friedrich Thimme (Stuttgart and Berlin, 1919), p. xxv.

the imperial regime that might bolster Allied charges against Germany. Indeed, they were reluctant to touch at all the "national-liberal" consensus which had virtually dominated German historiography before the November Revolution and which had become both anachronistic and inimical to the spirit of the new Republic. But then the historical guild—isolated exceptions notwithstanding—was more concerned with preserving the untarnished image of the Bismarckian state than with providing a Republic they disdained with an objective account of its origins.

In 1925, at the very beginning of his career, Hajo Holborn called upon historians to turn to the domestic history of the Bismarckian Reich—as against their cherished absorption with the minutiae of Bismarck's *Grosse Politik*.[2] An objective study of Germany's internal development, such as Hajo Holborn demanded, and unprejudiced studies of Germany's wartime and postwar foreign relations, such as his own work in 1932 on war guilt and reparations at Versailles exemplified, would have brought about a revision in this "national-liberal" consensus that kept the German past in the service of essentially conservative interests.[3] The struggle over a new historical consciousness in Germany was renewed after the second war— with greater acrimony because of the enforced delay and the intervening disasters.

This debate has recently centered on the First World War and on Bethmann Hollweg. The legend of German innocence and Bethmann Hollweg's irenic passion has been effectively exploded; in some quarters, there is a tendency to create a legend in reverse by suggesting Germany's sole guilt, and thus to perpetuate the legend in a different form. What Germany

2. Hajo Holborn, "Bismarck und Freiherr Georg von Werthern," *Archiv für Politik und Geschichte*, Vol. V (1925), p. 469.
3. Hajo Holborn, *Kriegsschuld und Reparationen auf der Pariser Friedenskonferenz von 1919* (Leipzig, 1932).

did and Bethmann Hollweg said has now been quite thoroughly investigated—thanks to the impetus given by Fritz Fischer and Egmont Zechlin. The reasons for political decisions, however, are rarely as apparent as the decisions themselves. The present-day controversy over Bethmann Hollweg is marked by a distressing literal-mindedness, every "scrap of paper," every public document, has become sacrosanct and receives its own often exaggerated exegesis. To understand motives and decisions, however, one has to probe not only the conditions of political culture, the tangible pressures and conflicts, but also the less tangible elements of milieu, atmosphere, and private reasoning and character. Bethmann's thoughts and aspirations are difficult to reconstruct because his private papers were destroyed in 1945. The best remaining source is the diary of his longtime political assistant and secretary, Kurt Riezler, which I have been allowed to read and which is the principal source for these reflections.[4] The diary begins in July 1914, but a brief look at Bethmann's early career may be useful for an understanding of his later conduct.[5]

Theobald von Bethmann Hollweg, born in 1856, was a Prussian by birth, not tradition. His ancestors on the paternal side were rich merchants and bankers in Frankfurt; his grandfather became a professor of law in Prussia and in the liberal era under Prince William a Prussian minister. He resigned his post at the beginning of the constitutional conflict in 1862. Bis-

4. I am deeply grateful to Kurt Riezler's daughter, Maria White, and her husband, Professor Howard White, for permission to read the Riezler diary and for an opportunity to discuss it with them.

5. An earlier interpretation of Bethmann on the basis of the Riezler diary, Karl Dietrich Erdmann, "Zur Beurteilung Bethmann Hollwegs," *Geschichte in Wissenschaft und Unterricht,* Vol. XV (1964), pp. 525–40, includes a few references to prewar entries. The copy I saw began with an entry of July 7, 1914.

marck's political adventurism revolted him, and a few hours before the outbreak of the Austro-Prussian war, he wrote the King, imploring him to remove the reckless Bismarck.[6] Time would be when Bismarck would be celebrated as the cautious statesman and Bethmann's grandson censured as the devious aggressor. Theobald's mother was a Swiss, Isabella de Rougemont. He was born on an estate his father had bought in Hohenfinow in the Mark Brandenburg; born in the Mark, but not wholly of it.

He studied jurisprudence, entered the civil service at the age of twenty-five, and in 1905 was named Prussian Minister of the Interior. In 1909 the Emperor appointed him Bülow's successor as Chancellor—and Bethmann had seen enough of politics in Imperial Germany to know the complexities and limitations of that office.

In fact, Imperial Germany could hardly be governed. Time and Bismarck had created a system of checks and imbalances, destined not to work. The political structure was cumbersome at best: a federal system in which Prussia held a central, but not unchallenged, position. The pseudo-constitutional state hid the locus of sovereignty. William, despite his occasional, disastrous outbursts of autocracy, had neither the constitutional prerogative nor the personal capacity to govern Germany. Parliaments, elected according to different systems of suffrage and therefore unequally representative, did not control the executive, though parliamentary approval was needed for the enactment of budgets and laws. The Chancellor's tenure was on the Emperor's sufferance; he was directly responsible to the Crown and indirectly dependent on the Reichstag which reflected the social composition—and cleavages—of an industrialized Germany. In theory, the Chancellor had to translate the Emperor's will—and sometimes whim—into effective political action, and when necessary, obtain parliament's approval.

6. Horst Kohl, ed., *Bismarck-Regesten*, Vol. I (Leipzig, 1891), pp. 286–9.

In practice, the Chancellor was caught between the conservative classes which, economically declining, were desperately clinging to their positions of power, and the liberal and radical groups, representative of a new society, that sought greater recognition of their own steadily increasing popular strength. The political system, already intricate and often unwieldy under Bismarck, had become incompatible with the social realities of the new age.

Bethmann's task was hard and his authority severely restricted. Political power had become much more fragmented after Bismarck's dismissal. The Chancellor had to contend with the military and naval leaders of the Reich who, fortified by their direct access to the Emperor, claimed not only autonomy in their *ressorts* but a strong voice in foreign policy as well. Antiquated court factions and modern pressure groups also sought to wield power or shape policy. In the years before the Great War, Germany faced immense problems at home and abroad. Internally, her industrial power provoked a steadily deepening antagonism between declining authoritarianism and a growing democratic movement. Externally, Germany's might aroused the fears of her neighbors, and her fitful, bullying policy, partly caused by her internal dissension, heightened these fears. Germany's worst problem was that its political system was virtually paralyzed and incapable of coping with these problems.

Bethmann intended to pursue a conciliatory course at home and abroad. He hoped to find a diagonal line, as he often put it, between conservative and liberal-radical pressures. "A clear conservative policy in the Reich was in fact an impossibility— the Right knew that best of all," he wrote after the war.[7] A consistently liberal policy, enhancing the power of the Reichstag, would have been equally impossible—for the Kaiser

7. Th. von Bethmann Hollweg, *Betrachtungen zum Weltkriege*, Vol. I (Berlin, 1919), p. 98.

would not have tolerated it and the Reichstag could not have mustered a workable majority. Bethmann pushed meek measures meekly: he tried, for example, to reform the antiquated electoral system in Prussia which was the parliamentary bulwark of feudal dominance and as such sacrosanct to the conservatives and anathema to the Left. He failed, inevitably, and in the process deeply antagonized both sides, also inevitably. He realized—as did most intelligent contemporaries—that the integration of the proletariat into the nation was the principal requirement of the age, but he saw no way of achieving it. In the years before the war, the antagonisms instead waxed stronger, and the opposing groups pushed each other into more radical and recalcitrant positions, as they did again during the war. The Socialists scored a great electoral triumph in 1912; a year later, the military flaunted their contempt for the *Rechtsstaat* in the Zabern affair, and enjoyed the Chancellor's full backing.[8]

Germany's external position was also precarious. The dangers were far more real than those Bismarck invoked to rally nation and Reichstag for military expenditures, and Bethmann always managed to obtain increasing army and navy appropriations. Foreign danger was sometimes a domestic convenience. It was always a source of the deepest worry to Bethmann, who, unlike his predecessors, had had no military or diplomatic experience. The danger of war had mounted steadily since 1905, especially since the Bosnian crisis of 1908. Bethmann realized that Germany's exposed position between France and Russia had been rendered still more dangerous by its *Weltpolitik* and by its naval ambitions which had prompted England to seek closer ties with France and Russia. He found no comfort in Tirpitz's promises that his navy would frighten England

8. See Hans-Ulrich Wehler, "Der Fall Zabern. Rückblick auf eine Verfassungskrise des wilhelminischen Kaiserreichs," *Die Welt als Geschichte,* Vol. XXIII (1963), pp. 27–46.

into neutrality or negotiations, and in either case remove it as a threat to Germany in case of war. Instead he found England supporting France in the second Moroccan crisis and he heard with dismay of the Anglo-French naval conversations of 1912. His fear of German encirclement was genuine. He saw Germany, with decrepit Austria its only ally, surrounded by a ring of enemies, ready to block its continued growth. Bethmann certainly shared the nation's claustrophobia. He, too, had abandoned Bismarck's premise that Germany was a satiated power, and had embraced that curious blend of contradictory beliefs—social Darwinism, misunderstood Romanticism, and cultural pessimism—all pointing to German expansion as the only alternative to stagnation. In January 1912, for example, he spoke privately of a great colonial empire in Africa, which Germany would be able to organize out of the Belgian Congo and the Dutch and Portuguese colonies.[9] Later that year, during the Balkan wars that clearly involved and damaged Austrian interests, he declared before the Reichstag: "If our allies while asserting their interests should against all expectations be attacked by a third party, then we would have to come resolutely to their aid. And then we would fight for the maintenance of our own position in Europe and in defense of our future and security."[10] Germany's future in Bethmann's eyes, to say nothing of his colleagues', had to be open and dynamic, commensurate with its steadily growing economic power. Bethmann rejected the idea of a preventive war, but was determined to safeguard this expansionist future by all means, including war.

Germany's diplomatic position deteriorated during his tenure. At the time of the Haldane mission, he was already afraid of an Anglo-Russian naval convention, which would tighten

---

9. *Der Kaiser . . . Aufzeichnungen des Chefs des Marinekabinetts Admiral Georg Alexander v. Müller über die Ära Wilhelms II,* ed. by Walter Görlitz (Göttingen, 1965), p. 107.

10. *Bethmann Hollwegs Kriegsreden, op. cit.,* p. xxiii.

the ring around Germany still more. He was ready to slow down German naval construction in return for a political agreement virtually involving an English withdrawal from Europe, giving Germany a free hand. Despite the failure of the Haldane mission, Anglo-German relations improved during the Balkan crisis. Austria's position, on the other hand, grew still more precarious and her reliability as an ally declined accordingly. The specter of an isolated Germany, gradually overshadowed by an ambitious, rapidly industrializing Russia, with its appalling multitudes, allied to France and probably England, haunted Bethmann and all German leaders.

Bethmann knew that in many quarters he was held responsible for Germany's mounting difficulties. In an age of national bombast and impetuosity, his plodding caution and conciliatoriness won grudging acceptance at best.

Berlin wits already called him *Bethmann soll Weg* (Bethmann should go), and there were always rumors of his impending ouster. The Crown Prince detested him, and the Kaiser, though respectful of him at most times and aware that he needed him, often railed against his *Schlappheit*, his brooding, and his philosophical airs. William's contempt for diplomats and civil servants was universally known, even if particularly crude outbursts against "stupid and anxiety-ridden diplomats, indeed [against] stupid civilians generally"[11] did not always make the rounds. The Kaiser preferred the often brainless virility, the *Schneidigkeit,* of soldiers. In this, too, he epitomized his age. Though tiresomely repeated, it is nevertheless true—and important to an understanding of Bethmann—that Germany was a thoroughly militaristic country in the years before the war. Gerhard Ritter cites one revealing instance: "It became good form even for higher state officials to wear military uniform at every conceivable fitting occasion. Thus Bethmann Hollweg in his first appearance as Chancellor in the

11. *Der Kaiser, op. cit.,* p. 68.

Reichstag appeared in a major's uniform—an exercise for which Bismarck with his endless masquerading as *Kürassiergeneral* certainly was not blameless. Only the person who could wear the uniform with the silver epaulettes counted as a real man [*ganzer Kerl*]."[12]

Outwardly Bethmann accepted the values of this system of creeping militarism, though he probably realized the attendant danger of eroding civilian control and political reason. At the same time, it seems probable that this exaltation of things military must have grated on his sensitive civilian soul.

It is generally agreed that Bethmann's abiding sense of responsibility and his brooding over every decision were his outstandingly attractive traits. What a contrast there was between the unevenly ebullient Kaiser, ever boastful of German prowess, so representative of his age, and Bethmann, the enigmatic, taciturn worrier! The slippery, smiling Bülow had certainly been more attuned to William's age and personality than his successor. As Riezler noted: "The Chancellor [is] a child of the first half of the nineteenth century and of a better education [*Bildung*]. Strange that he with his old humanistic convictions, his seriousness, and his incapacity for all sham should have gained power in the new German milieu and should have been able to hold his own against parliamentarians and jobbers."[13]

The stark contrast in style and character between Bethmann and almost all the other leaders of Imperial Germany had encouraged the belief that there was a fundamental divergence of political aims as well. For this, however, the general consensus about Germany's national destiny was too broad and the Kaiser's tolerance for dissent too narrow: Bethmann Hollweg, as we will see, was perspicacious in his worries about Ger-

---

12. Gerhard Ritter, *Staatskunst und Kriegshandwerk*, Vol. II (2nd edn., Munich, 1965), p. 129.
13. Riezler Diary, entry of July 7, 1914; hereafter referred to as R.D.

many's course, but he had no alternative to propose and would have been powerless to implement one.

Bethmann resisted all efforts at the diminution of his office, and particularly all efforts to enhance the power of state secretaries. He had difficulties with his own appointee, Kiderlen-Wächter, who liked to conduct his foreign negotiations without informing him. Bethmann successfully resisted even the Kaiser's encroachments: in March 1912, at the time of the Anglo-German talks, William, impatient with what he thought Bethmann's dilatoriness, gave important orders directly to the ambassador in London and to the war minister in Berlin. Bethmann replied by submitting his resignation, warning the Emperor against a precipitous policy that in the end might force Germany into an attack on France in which the victim, but not the aggressor, would have the support of its allies. Bethmann argued that he could not take the responsibility for such a policy "and certainly not if Your Majesty informs an ambassador directly on such decisive measures as possible mobilization without listening to me first. By virtue of the office with which Your Majesty has entrusted me, I bear responsibility for the policies Your Majesty orders before God and country, before history and my own conscience. Even Your Majesty cannot relieve me of this responsibility."[14]

It was a manly avowal, and the Kaiser immediately retreated. Bethmann's letter points to a revealing distinction: he could reconcile himself more readily to a dangerous policy than to the imperial flouting of his authority. He would resign rather than accept both simultaneously. Bethmann's implicit distinction may help us to understand his complicated sense of the responsibility of power.

I have already suggested that he had a highly—in Imperial Germany, perhaps uniquely—developed sense of responsibility.

14. *Kiderlen-Wächter, Der Staatsmann und Mensch,* ed. by E. Jäckh, Vol. II (Stuttgart, 1924), pp. 159–61.

He knew that future generations would hold him accountable for German policy, and his intelligence and realism made him recognize the potential dangers of that policy. He was cautious and circumspect and pondered the likely consequences of decisions. Often he appeared racked by doubts. Still, his sense of responsibility and his constant brooding did not paralyze him, as has sometimes been suggested. They may have given him the psychological reassurance for action. He stared before he leapt, but he leapt nevertheless.

Bethmann's sense of responsibility was attenuated by his political ideas and experiences and by certain personal beliefs. He sensed intuitively what Max Weber posited in his celebrated "Politics as Vocation" immediately after the war, that a politician "allows himself to come into contact with diabolical powers lurking in every form of violence."[15] Bethmann probably would have agreed with a wartime observation by Riezler that "politics is really the art of doing evil and attaining the good.—To be wise enough to know how everything is interlocked [and] through malice to lead the ill-intentioned [*die bösen Willen*] to something good."[16] He appreciated the ambiguity of power, and the distinction between private and public morality.

He had, moreover, suffered from the fragmentation of power in Imperial Germany, and he understood the limits on its exercise. Hence the responsibility of power was parceled out as well. Bethmann bent to the decisions of others in authority, often assuaging his conscience by the correct assumption that if he were to resign, his opponents would follow a still more reckless course, aided by a Chancellor less conscientious than him-

---

15. Max Weber, *Gesammelte Politische Schriften* (Munich, 1921), p. 447. Weber's lecture, delivered in 1919, recalls in so many ways the predicament of Bethmann, surrounded as he was by vain *Machtpolitiker,* that one wonders whether, unconsciously, he may not have been thinking of Bethmann as a tragic model of the politician without vocation.

16. R.D., March 4, 1915.

self. He defended, as I have suggested, his office more stoutly than his policy. A sign of diffidence, perhaps, but of something deeper also. Max Weber's distinction between the civil servant and politician is relevant: the politician's "conduct is subject to quite a different, indeed, exactly the opposite, principle of responsibility from that of the civil servant. The honor of the civil servant is vested in his ability to execute conscientiously the order of superior authorities, exactly as if the order agreed with his own conviction. This holds even if the order appears wrong to him and if, despite the civil servant's remonstrances, the authority insists on the order. Without this moral discipline and self-denial, in the highest sense, the whole apparatus would fall to pieces. The honor of the political leader, of the leading statesman, however, lies precisely in an exclusive *personal* responsibility for what he does, a responsibility he cannot and must not reject or transfer."[17] Bethmann's sense of responsibility, I think, was an uncertain mixture of these two types.

A further point must be considered: Bethmann was by temperament and perhaps conviction a pessimist. As the Great War drew closer, he seems to have become a fatalist as well. This foreknowledge of disaster probably eased his sense of responsibility and reinforced the feeling of resigned duty that he had to stick to his job, however heavy the burden of decision, because a successor would be so much worse. In July 1914, his sense of responsibility, modified by these considerations, allowed him to take extreme risks and seek crafty subterfuges. For as the devoted but not uncritical Riezler wrote on July 7 and repeated later: "His cunning appears to be as great as his clumsiness. [*Seine Gerissenheit wohl ebenso gross wie sein Ungeschick.*]"[18]

The bulk of the Riezler diary pertains to the war itself, but the

17. Max Weber, *op. cit.*, p. 415.
18. R.D., July 7, 1914, and Oct. 30, 1914.

entries from July 7 to 23 offer unique insights into Bethmann's thoughts and conduct during the crisis weeks. They also record Riezler's gradual understanding of Bethmann's daring and complicated policy, designed to end what he thought was Germany's plight.[19]

On July 6, the two men traveled to Hohenfinow together, and Riezler was struck by Bethmann's melancholy, attributing it to his wife's death a few weeks before. That night, Riezler learned of the appalling dimensions of the crisis that had begun that morning with Germany's issuance of the "blank check" and her insistence that Austria honor it quickly and with aplomb. Bethmann told the unsuspecting Riezler "the secret news . . . which gives a shocking picture" of Germany's situation. Bethmann began with the Anglo-Russian negotiations for a naval convention and the prospect of a landing in Pomerania, "the last link in the chain."[20] Russia was growing steadily stronger, Austria steadily weaker and incapable of ever fighting "as an ally in a German cause. The Entente knows that we are therefore entirely paralyzed."

The sequence of Bethmann's account makes it clear that his response to the murder of Sarajevo was determined by what he had long thought was Germany's precarious condition, not by the immediate effects of the assassination itself. Sarajevo unrequited would worsen Germany's situation; Sarajevo properly

19. Ever since the Riezler diary was first introduced as an historical source by Karl Dietrich Erdmann, *op. cit.*, the present-day critics of Bethmann Hollweg have tended to damage Riezler's reputation as well by giving compressed and one-sided interpretations of his two prewar books. A balanced study of this sensitive scholar who for a decade was close to the center of German power would be desirable. The diary offers a rich source, of course, and incidentally contains some poignant hints about how it felt to belong to Germany's governing elite, with its undercurrents of anti-Semitism, and to marry during the war the daughter of the German Jewish painter, Max Liebermann.

20. On the importance Bethmann attached to these Anglo-Russian naval negotiations, see Egmont Zechlin, "Deutschland zwischen Kabinettskrieg und Wirtschaftskrieg. Politik und Kriegführung in den ersten Monaten des Weltkrieges 1914," *Historische Zeitschrift*, Vol. CIC (1964), pp. 347–52.

exploited might lead to a dramatic escape from that situation.

On July 6, Bethmann spoke of "grave decisions." Official Serbia was implicated in the assassination, Austria sought to rouse herself, and Francis Joseph had asked the Emperor whether Germany considered the crisis as a *"casus foederis."* Bethmann added: "Our old dilemma with every Austrian action in the Balkans. If we encourage them, they say we pushed them into it; if we discourage them, they say we left them in the lurch. Then come the Western powers with open arms and we lose the last powerful ally." This remark seems in odd, but not atypical, contradiction to the fear that Austria was practically worthless as a German ally anyhow.

Bethmann warned that "an action against Serbia can lead to world war. The Chancellor expects that a war, whatever its outcome, will result in the uprooting of everything that exists. The existing [world] very antiquated, without ideas." He thought it was a symptom of the general blindness that conservatives hoped that a war would strengthen the monarchical order in Germany. "Thick fog over the people. The same in all of Europe. The future belongs to Russia. . . . The Chancellor very pessimistic about the intellectual condition of Germany."[21]

What a strange mixture of motives and forebodings, of realism and pessimism! Yet this mixture constituted the background to Bethmann's decision to run the risk of war in July 1914.[22]

On July 8, Bethmann added that if the war "comes from the east" and Germany goes to Austria's help and not the other way around, "then we shall have prospects for winning it. If the war does not come, if the Czar does not want it, or France, thoroughly bewildered, counsels peace, then we still have pros-

21. R.D., July 7, 1914.

22. For an important and ingenious effort to relate Riezler's prewar writings to Bethmann's July policy, see Andreas Hillgruber, "Riezlers Theorie des kalkulierten Risikos und Bethmann Hollwegs politische Konzeption in der Julikrise 1914," *Historische Zeitschrift*, Vol. CCII (1966), pp. 333–51.

pects of breaking up the Entente through this action." The Riezler diary sustains the view that Bethmann in early July had resolved on a forward course; by means of forceful diplomacy and a local Austrian war against Serbia he intended to detach England or Russia from the Entente or—if that failed—to risk a general war over an opportune issue at a still opportune moment.

But Bethmann realized the dangers of a military showdown. Already on July 14, he correctly assessed the likely line-up of nations. "If in case of war, England starts at once, then Italy will under no circumstances come in." No wonder Riezler wrote on the same day: "Our situation is terrible."

On July 23, the Chancellor pointed out that if war came, it would come through precipitous Russian mobilization, before any negotiations. After mobilization, it would be too late for talks because the Germans would have to attack at once in order to have any chance of victory. "But then the whole people will feel the danger and will rise up." Bethmann envisioned the sequence of events that would lead up to a "defensive" war, provoked by Russia, which alone could unite the nation and perhaps even deceive other nations. Hence Bethmann was furious at the Crown Prince, who had sent bellicose messages to Pan-German groups. Such royal saber-rattling would obviously impair the credibility of this defensive war! In the same conversation he discussed the treatment of the socialists; in order to make sure of their support he would negotiate with them at once and in case of war forestall army action against them. Three days later, he was appalled at the recurrent idea of some generals to arrest all socialist leaders on the first day of war.[23] The principal components of Bethmann's tactics for the outbreak and conduct of war appear here for the first time with remarkable clarity: the war must be defensive, the utterances

23. The Riezler diary reinforces the conclusions by Egmont Zechlin, "Bethmann Hollweg, Kriegsrisiko und SPD 1914," *Der Monat,* Vol. XVIII (Jan., 1966), pp. 17–32.

of the Pan-German chauvinists subdued, and the socialists wooed. During the war, he discovered that these tactics proved his only possible strategy.

In a sense, the most damaging evidence that the Riezler diary provides for the July crisis lies in what it does *not* say: it contains no hint or thought of any move by Bethmann to arrest the crisis, to save the peace. Why, we must then ask, did Bethmann opt for and persist in this forward course that he recognized from the beginning was fraught with danger? Riezler confirms what we would suppose: he chose this course regretfully, broodingly. On July 14, he said that a war would destroy the familiar world and that it represented for him "a leap in the dark and [his] hardest duty." Time and again, during the war, he worried over his responsibility for leading Germany into it. The "defensive" character of the war offered little solace to him.

Did it have to come to this? he asked on July 20. Should he have stuck to his resignation in 1912? But his successor—perhaps Tirpitz himself—would have been worse. Why was Germany in this predicament? "The earlier errors: simultaneously Turkish policy against Russia, Morocco against France, the navy against England—challenge everybody, put yourself in everybody's path, and actually weaken no one in this fashion. Reason: Aimlessness, the need for little prestige successes and solicitude for every current of public opinion. The 'national' parties which with their racket [*Radau*] about foreign policy want to preserve and strengthen their party position." A better analysis—or clearer indictment—of the fatality of Germany's prewar foreign policy could hardly have been made. It bears out completely a general observation that Riezler made in a prewar book: "The threat of war in our time lies . . . in the internal politics of those countries in which a weak government is confronted by a strong nationalist movement."[24] Bethmann's judgment corresponds to Admiral von Müller's later view as to

24. Quoted in Hillgruber, *op. cit.*, p. 339.

why the German government in July 1914 did not pursue a conciliatory policy: "The government, already weakened by domestic disunity, found itself inevitably under pressure from a great part of the German people which had been whipped into a high-grade chauvinism by Navalists [*Flottenvereinler*] and Pan-Germans."[25]

Bethmann overcame or suspended his doubts. In fact, once he had resolved on this forward course, he shook off his habitual hesitancy. Already on July 20, Riezler noted that the mood was serious, "the Chancellor resolute and silent." A week later, he recorded that Bethmann "sees doom [*Fatum*] greater than human power hanging over Europe and our own people," but added on the same day, "he is entirely changed, has no time to brood, and is therefore fresh, active, and lively, without any disquiet." The juxtaposition of fatalism and energy is not odd or unusual: Calvinists, too, believe in predestination and act decisively.

Obviously fatalism was a psychological condition, not a rational ground, for Bethmann's decision to run the risk of a world war. His fatalism went beyond the not uncommon assumption of the times that such a war was inevitable; he also believed that the world such a war would destroy was hopelessly superannuated, destined to be swept away. This, too, eased his sense of responsibility.

It has recently been suggested that Bethmann cherished expansionist aims, which he hoped to realize through war. Perhaps, but compelling evidence is lacking, and the Riezler diary offers no corroboration. Rather it suggests that his principal motive was fear for Germany's future. Bethmann's aims for the future were vague, his fears concrete, and the discrepancy allowed for the psychologically comforting half-truth that a war would be a defensive struggle. The diary does attest Bethmann's real terror at Russia's "growing demands and colossal

25. *Der Kaiser, op. cit.*, p. 140.

explosive power." In a few years she would be supreme—and Germany her first, lonely victim.[26]

In his dread of the future he seems never to have reckoned with the fluidity of the European political system or the likely workings of the balance of power. He feared the day when a thoroughly prepared Russia, supported by England, would crush Germany. But would England ever have supported the attack of a stronger Russia on a weaker Germany, thus establishing Russian hegemony in Europe? Or again: if Austria had in fact defected to the West, would not a return to a Russo-German alliance have offered a more than adequate counterweight? Bethmann barely considered these alternatives; in any case, he would not have persuaded the other rulers of Germany of their plausibility. Instead he remembered in those July days that Kiderlen-Wächter had always assumed the inevitability of war, and the implication was that Bethmann now at last accepted the dead man's judgment. Not that there was a dearth of living colleagues who urged him on.

Bethmann's anxiety about Germany's eventual isolation seems so exaggerated—as compared with even his own earlier estimates—that it may be legitimate to ask whether its intensity may in some small measure represent a kind of projection of his own melancholy stemming from his recent bereavement. His decision to risk war and his reluctance to do anything to save the peace was probably related to still another condition that combined personal and historical elements. For years he had been decried as a weakling. The military—but others too—frequently warned against another "Fashoda," which popular wisdom in those days, much like the indiscriminate warning against "Munich" today, adduced in order to preach a hard line against any compromise.[27] Is it not likely that Bethmann's resolution in July 1914 was strengthened by a feeling that his

26. R.D., July 20, 1914.
27. *Der Kaiser, op. cit.,* pp. 74 and 140.

policy of so-called conciliatoriness had yielded nothing, strengthened by the weariness of the civilian who had for so long been attacked by his tougher colleagues? It is a curious fact that in his postwar memoirs he defended his July course by arguing that the opposite course—accommodation of Russia—would have amounted to "self-castration" (*Selbstentmannung*)—an unconscious allusion perhaps to the frequent charges of civilian effeminacy?[28] It is significant that two other principal actors of the July drama, Leopold Berchtold and Serge Sazonov, also smarted under their countrymen's allegations of earlier weakness.[29] It is difficult to assess the importance, if any, of such often unconscious factors, but it seems arbitrary to ignore them altogether.

It is incontrovertible that Bethmann consciously risked a world war, but there is no evidence that he did so in order to establish German hegemony. It is naïve and excessively rationalistic to suppose that aggression must spring from lust of conquest. Fear, too, impels aggressive action, and if the action succeeds, then, as Bethmann remarked in August 1914 about Moltke's war aims, "*l'appétit vient en mangeant.*"[30]

Kurt Riezler's notes from the war years offer a magnificent *mélange* of events, impressions, and reflections, attesting his own searching mind and his continuous proximity to power. During the war he served as Bethmann's principal aide on domestic issues and their relations became closer still. By training a classicist, by cast of mind a philosopher and moralist, Riezler was an unlikely partner for Germany's war-time Chancellor. Yet Bethmann clearly found him congenial. He unbur-

28. Th. von Bethmann Hollweg, *Betrachtungen, op. cit.*, pp. 142-3.
29. Luigi Albertini, *The Origins of the War of 1914*, Vol. II (Oxford, 1953), pp. 124 and 181.
30. R.D., Aug. 20, 1914.

dened himself to Riezler as he could to no one else, and he indulged his pessimism with seeming relish. We see a somber side of Bethmann then. The heart of the diary remains their conversations, though Riezler's own political education is mirrored in these pages as well. At the beginning of the war, he found himself still "dreamily uninterested" in political matters, but his political sophistication and passion grew steadily.[31] The diary consists of hastily composed, stylistically compressed, often aphoristic entries, recording his thoughts, not his daily duties or encounters. It has the double advantage of political immediacy and philosophical detachment; it deserves to be published.

Riezler's diary reflects a remarkable continuity of mood and problems. Neither he nor the Chancellor experienced the great exaltation that led Falkenhayn to say to Bethmann on August 4: "even if we end in ruin, it was beautiful."[32] Despite moments of high hopes and a steady appreciation of the quiet heroism of the common people, Bethmann and Riezler persisted in their pessimism about Germany's future. They lamented the world without culture—the putative mass age *à l'américaine*—that would emerge from the war. For Germany, victory would bring spiritual corruption, defeat, political revolution. Still Bethmann saw no alternative but to continue the war and to attain for Germany the illusory goal of permanent security. With mounting anger and exasperation, they noted the ever-worsening internal problems: the encroachment of the military, the disintegration of unity, and the re-emergence of political divisions rendered worse by the demands of war.

The diary reveals neither the heady atmosphere of victory nor the certainty of some master plan of conquest; rather it suggests gloom, confusion, uninspired improvisation in planning, and endless wrangling in execution. Bethmann appears

31. R.D., Sept. 25, 1914.
32. R.D., Nov. 22, 1914.

once again as racked by uncertainties and occasional self-recriminations. In his daily struggles, however, this "strange man," as Riezler habitually called him, acted with tenacity, discretion, and considerable finesse.

The question of Germany's war aims arose early and retained a central place in the preoccupations of Bethmann's entourage, as did the larger and vaguer question of the shape of the post-war world.[33] The first recorded discussions took place on August 21 at General Headquarters in Koblenz: "In the evening, long conversation about Poland and the possibility of a loose incorporation [*Angliederung*] of other states with the Reich—a Central European system of preferential tariffs. Greater Germany with Belgium, Holland, Poland as close, Austria as more distant satellite states [*Schutzstaaten*]." This clearly adumbrates the famous September program, published by Fritz Fischer, and its full discussion on August 21 and subsequent days rather explodes the ingenious idea of some of Fischer's critics that the September program was suddenly slapped together, as one would a list for Santa Claus.[34] Nor does it support the recent argument that German leadership embraced *Mitteleuropa* only after it realized that English resoluteness was turning a limited conflict into a world war.[35] On the other hand, Riezler never mentioned the September memo-

33. In this essay I cannot deal with the present controversy about German war aims. The Riezler diary illuminates the atmosphere of the wartime debate, but contains no new hard facts that would resolve the question. If one had read the Riezler diary ten years ago, it would have come as a shock. After Fritz Fischer's book and the rash of recent works on the subject, it tends merely to amplify and confirm what we now know. The best analysis of the controversy is James Joll, "The 1914 Debate Continues," *Past and Present*, No. 34 (July, 1966), pp. 100–13. Cf. also the articles by Klaus Epstein, Imanuel Geiss, and Wolfgang J. Mommsen in the issue on 1914 of *The Journal of Contemporary History*, Vol. I, No. 3 (July, 1966).

34. Fritz Fischer, *Griff nach der Weltmacht. Die Kriegszielpolitik des kaiserlichen Deutschland 1914–18* (3rd edn., Düsseldorf, 1964), pp. 116–18.

35. See Egmont Zechlin, "Deutschland zwischen Kabinettskrieg und Wirtschaftskrieg," *op. cit., passim*.

randum, which he presumably thought a provisional statement without any binding force.

In fact, the chief goal throughout the war remained *Mitteleuropa* as an economic union girded by political institutions guaranteeing German supremacy, even if details were refined, revised, and endlessly debated. Riezler believed that such a new order in Europe promised far greater permanency than the outright annexation of foreign territory. Others, he noted, wanted grandiose annexations; he preferred vassal nations to festering truncated states. Belgium and Poland should be turned into willing vassals, exposed to a gradual process of Germanization, as he often but ambiguously called it. Riezler and Bethmann knew what this "Middle-European Empire of the German Nation" really meant: "It was the European disguise of our will to power. [*Die europäische Verbrämung unserers Machtwillens.*]"[36]

Riezler thought that the "petty" nationalisms of Central Europe could be supplanted by a kind of super-loyalty to this new Reich which would be dominated by *Grossdeutschland* as Imperial Germany had been by Prussia. He even spoke of the extinction of Prussia and *Kleindeutschland* and the return to the traditions of the Frankfurt Parliament of 1848.[37] Bethmann seems to have been more reticent in these matters, less given to grandiose schemes, but apparently never restrained, let alone rebuked, his more candid assistant. They often agreed concerning tactics; both, for example, feared that the military would insist on a formal assertion of German dominance: "hegemony itself can be enforced. The caudinian yoke of its formal recognition never."[38] The Riezler diary contradicts Gerhard Ritter's recent assertion that Bethmann's policy toward war aims reached "a decisive turning point" in November 1914, after

36. R.D., April 18, 1915.
37. R.D., Nov. 22, 1916.
38. R.D., Dec. 2, 1916.

Falkenhayn's report that a clear-cut military victory over all of Germany's enemies was no longer possible.[39] As late as January 1917 Riezler wrote: "It is clear, after all, that the insulated life of a small Germany in the middle of Europe is tenable only for decades, that it remains exposed to the greatest dangers and that it cannot have a very big future."[40] A few days before the First Russian Revolution he noted: "The policy of the Chancellor: to lead the German Reich which by the methods of the Prussian territorial state . . . cannot become a world power . . . to an imperialism of European form [*Gebärde*], to organize the Continent from the center outward (Austria, Poland, Belgium) around our undemonstrative [*stillen*] leadership . . ."[41] The major obstacles Riezler saw in March 1917 were internal, that is, upper-class opposition to the domestic complement of Bethmann's policy, democratic reform, and military opposition to any policy that was not openly based on German power.

The dream of a German *Mitteleuropa* died hard, if at all. When the war went badly for Germany, the means shifted, not the end. It persisted because it seemed to endow the war with some meaning. On September 4, 1914, Riezler lamented that "people today do not have a single idea that corresponds to the greatness of the age. But it would be the ruin of Europe if on this occasion it should not find a possible form of permanence and community." The civilian's *Mitteleuropa* was the alternative to the military's wild annexationism that would leave partitioned nations thirsting for revenge. It was also the only means for safeguarding Germany's future. When Falkenhayn in November 1914 counseled immediate peace with Russia, and

---

39. Gerhard Ritter, "Bethmann Hollweg und die Machtträume deutscher Patrioten im ersten Jahr des Weltkrieges," *Festschrift Percy Ernst Schramm zu seinem siebzigsten Geburtstag von Schülern und Freunden zugeeignet* (Wiesbaden, 1964), p. 210.
40. R.D., Jan. 6, 1917.
41. R.D., March 11, 1917.

Bethmann demurred, Riezler noted: "If we make peace now, we will have to wage war in ten years' time, alone and under entirely unfavorable conditions."[42] The goal was to fight until Germany could create a new European order that would render her inviolable from attack, and would establish and, if possible, disguise German hegemony.

Would England—the most hated and envied country even in Bethmann's entourage—ever have accepted a Europe dominated by Germany? Riezler sensed the answer and dimly realized that the goal of permanent security could be attained only through a long war ending in England's defeat. In this way the limited goal of *Mitteleuropa* implied the unlimited, unwelcome goal of world dominance. This dizzy prospect was repeatedly invoked—casually, as an inevitable, indeed regrettable, consequence of the constellation Germany was fighting. Bethmann and Riezler discussed Germany's capacity for world dominance a month after the battle of the Marne.[43] Later they thought: "Perhaps the heroic attempt of this war to secure us an impregnable position of world power of the first order is half impossible and therefore the people's eagerness so moving and so tragic."[44] In August 1916, in a long disquisition about the war, Riezler noted that for Germany it had a "triple significance . . . defense against the France of today, preventive war against the Russia of tomorrow (as such too late), struggle with England over world dominance [*Weltherrschaft*]." German policy before 1914, he added, mistakenly pursued all three goals simultaneously.[45]

Riezler's cryptic sentences should not be overinterpreted: he did not believe that Germany had entered the war to attain these goals, merely that they had been intermittent and contra-

42. R.D., Nov. 26, 1914.
43. R.D., Oct. 11, 1914.
44. R.D., Nov. 22, 1914.
45. R.D., Aug. 1, 1916.

dictory motives during the prewar era. The war itself joined them together, and Riezler as well as Bethmann was appalled by the magnitude of the stakes. They feared that "England's tragic error might consist of compelling us to rally all our strength, to exploit all our possibilities, to drive us into world-wide problems, to force upon us—against our wills—a desire for world dominance."[46] Some might dismiss this as self-exonerating bombast. They would, I think, be wrong. Bethmann and Riezler genuinely believed that fate or a concatenation of deep forces in world history was thrusting world dominance upon Germany. Bethmann found the prospect uncongenial; as Riezler once remarked, the Pan-Germans were right in sensing that world dominance was repugnant to the Chancellor.[47] I doubt if Bethmann and Riezler regarded such dominance as intrinsically evil or undesirable; they merely feared that Germany would perish in the effort. Already in August 1914, Riezler noted: "The difficulty for the German to accustom himself to the mien of world dominance which he *must* wear after a victory."[48] In December 1914, he wrote of "the tragedy in the development of modern Germany: if it is victorious, all its energies will be absorbed in tasks for which Germans have no talent—world dominance, which is contrary to its spirit and greatness."[49] Finally, in April 1918, he still thought: "Never was a people more capable of conquering the world, and less capable of ruling it."[50]

Bethmann hid from himself the fact that Germany could gain permanent security, which he wanted, only by defeating England and by establishing world dominance which he neither wanted nor thought feasible. Once again, he failed to reckon with the unwanted consequences of Germany's ambitions, as

46. R.D. Oct. 4, 1915.
47. R.D., July 16, 1915.
48. R.D., Aug. 21, 1914.
49. R.D., Dec. 13, 1914.
50. R.D., April 15, 1918.

he had in July 1914. It is perhaps a common convenience for statesmen to believe quite genuinely that goals not wanted in the mind cannot be goals implicit in their actions and decisions. For Bethmann it was enough that he and Riezler knew, and said to each other countless times, that Germany was totally incapable of ruling the world, of ruling Europe—or herself.

Their despair over Germany's political incompetence may have been tinged by their *Weltuntergangstimmung,* but it was gallingly confirmed in Bethmann's daily struggles. The bureaucratic Chancellor and his idealistic assistant were at one in their horror at the daily face of German politics: intrigues, party jockeying, false and reckless promises. They expected, especially in wartime, order, rationality, and public rectitude—and they encountered virtual chaos and mounting unreason. They feared that Germany would perish because of the political *Unbildung* of its people.

The foremost cause of discord was the continuous struggle between Bethmann and the military, though the latter fought among themselves as well.[51] The prewar fragmentation of power had turned into the bitter competition for power during the war, with the final arbiter, William, gradually relinquishing his leadership altogether. A brilliant French officer, who was himself to become something of an expert on the question of political authority in his own country, wrote in 1924 about a particular instance of William's fickleness: "Extraordinary

51. The literature on Bethmann has of course grown substantially since I wrote this essay. On the question of civil-military relations, see Karl-Heinz Janssen, *Der Kanzler und der General. Die Führungskrise um Bethmann Hollweg und Falkenhayn (1914–1916)* (Göttingen, 1967). The reader will find *Erster Weltkrieg, Ursachen, Entstehung und Kriegsziele,* ed. by Wolfgang Schieder (*"Neue wissenschaftliche Bibliothek,"* Geschichte, Bd. 32; Cologne and Berlin, 1969), a valuable collection of recent articles. At once a summary of the existing Bethmann literature and a critical analysis of historians' judgments on Bethmann can be found in Klaus Hildebrand, *Bethmann Hollweg—der Kanzler ohne Eigenschaften? Urteile der Geschichtsschreibung. Eine kritische Bibliographie* (Düsseldorf, 1970).

The Failure of Illiberalism · 104

retreat of the supreme power, indisputable proof of that crisis of authority which was despite certain appearances the true spiritual cause of the defeat of the Empire."[52] The military continually expanded their sphere of control and as early as September 1914 Riezler lamented, "the concept of the purely military concern is having a field day here."[53] The soldiers lacked, however, all political intelligence, and Riezler's diary is the record of mounting exasperation and anger at these powerful incompetents in uniform and their blind, brutish faith in force. By harassing the natives, they wrecked Germany's chances in Belgium and Poland. By their alliance with conservatives, industrialists, and Pan-Germans, they poisoned Germany's internal politics. They understood neither friend nor foe, and they meddled in realms where even their technical knowledge was inadequate. "It is a real wonder that this dilettantism, in which the German people has unshakable faith because it wears a uniform, does not ruin it."[54]

There were individual culprits, too. Tirpitz was the archvillain, dubbed "the liar," "the father of the lie," or the "Jesuit." He and his uncompromising policy against England were responsbile for the war. Bethmann knew that Tirpitz was a charter member of the *fronde* against him and that the Admiral was intermittently plotting for his removal. Most generals were political infants, and the party leaders a disaster.

Bethmann and Riezler saw beyond personalities. They were appalled by the political immaturity of all Germans, by the antagonisms within Germany, by the hopelessness of governing the country under such conditions. Time and again they complained of "insane political unreason, of the dominance of blind passion."[55] The ruling classes were the worst. Bethmann

52. Charles de Gaulle, *La discorde chez l'ennemi* (2nd edn., Paris, 1944), p. 51.
53. R.D., Sept. 20, 1914.
54. R.D., Jan. 9, 1917.
55. R.D., April 28, 1915.

despaired of any future with the Thyssens, the *Krautjunker,* and the Hohenzollerns in whom "the intellectual decline of the day finds its most rapid expression. . . . He does not know how the new Germany of power and finance supremacy could find its harmony with Goethe."[56]

The somewhat lofty, even snobbish, tone should not disguise the very practical import of Bethmann's thoughts. He feared that the war—and most especially a victory—would brutalize the ruling elites still further, making them still more uncultured, selfish, and blind, and still less able to govern the country. Bethmann was genuinely impressed by "the idealistic strength of the common people," by the idealism of the trade unionists.[57] But he feared that the loyal Left would be goaded into revolution by the selfish, chauvinistic Right, and he spoke of "the incubus of the postwar Revolution which oppressed him."[58]

Bethmann had to contend with the political stupidity and power-drunk arrogance of Germany's ruling classes throughout the war. The worst struggle occurred over the use of the submarine—a struggle that began in 1915 and ended with the fatal announcement of unrestricted submarine warfare in February 1917.[59] From 1915 on, Tirpitz and his colleagues at the Admiralty boasted that their "miracle weapon," if fully unleashed, not hedged in by restrictions about who could be torpedoed and how, would bring England to the negotiating table—or to her knees—in a matter of months. Bethmann, supported at first by Falkenhayn and Admiral von Müller, the Kaiser's chief of naval cabinet, opposed indiscriminate sea warfare because he

56. R.D., July 28, 1915.
57. R.D., July 28, 1915, and March 4, 1915.
58. R.D., June 14, 1916.
59. For a comprehensive survey of this struggle, see Gerhard Ritter, *Staatskunst und Kriegshandwerk,* Vol. III (Munich, 1964), Chs. 5 and 8, and Karl E. Birnbaum, *Peace Moves and U-Boat Warfare: A Study of Imperial Germany's Policy Towards the United States April 18, 1916–January 9, 1917* (Stockholm, 1958).

rightly thought that Germany had too few submarines to wage an effective campaign, and he feared that the only certain result would be the enmity of the remaining neutrals. Bethmann persuaded the Kaiser to stave off unrestricted submarine warfare. Thwarted by the Chancellor, the naval clique launched a great and mendacious propaganda campaign promising a *Siegfrieden* through submarines. The bourgeois public, incited by renowned academics and by most of the non-socialist deputies, proved thoroughly receptive, and Bethmann found himself in a crossfire between the putative experts of the Admiralty and an aroused, greedy public. Riezler records the stages of the conflict and provides a chorus for the unfolding of the tragedy.

In February 1916, the Chancellor weighed once again the arguments for and against the full use of submarines. He hesitated a long time, realizing that without them, England could not be decisively beaten, and hence would refuse concessions. Riezler feared he would yield: "My suspicion that the main argument—unconsciously—is his fear of rejecting the weapon that all the Emperor's military advisers contend they cannot do without, while not being able to present anything which will end the war in 1916."[60] The vilification of Bethmann mounted: in six weeks' time, his opponents claimed, England could be finished, "but the requisite courage is lacking"—in Bethmann.[61] Riezler hoped Bethmann would resign rather than accept a defeat on this issue. "His style is caution and intelligent reflection. . . . If he lets himself be forced into something which is against his conviction and style, he is lost. . . . For some, the unrestricted submarine warfare is like an orgy of ruthless force which intoxicates them. Their clamor almost confirms what the English always say: the Germans have become mad."[62] In February 1916, Bethmann once more prevailed. As an aftermath of this exhausting struggle, Tirpitz resigned, his hatred for

60. R.D., Feb. 4, 1916.
61. R.D., Feb. 11, 1916.
62. R.D., Feb. 22, 1916.

Bethmann hardly diminished, and the agitation gathered new strength in his wretched *Vaterlandspartei.*

The submarine issue hung fire all through 1916. Germany's chances for a victory on land seemed nil; even her chances to hold out in a defensive position were rapidly diminishing. As more submarines became available, their unrestricted use made more sense. The question was: could total warfare knock out Britain or would her losses be offset by America's entry into the war? Would the submarines then merely clinch Britain's resolution to destroy German power and give her the American means to do so? The dilemma was real, and the Chancellor sighed that the U-boats would follow him to the grave: "It will always remain the great enigma what would have happened if they had been unleashed without restrictions."[63]

The public howl for their full use never ceased, and Bethmann gradually weakened. Did he share Riezler's view that the Pan-German madness could never be overcome "save it be permitted once to run wild so that the damage could be seen"?[64] Would unrestricted warfare bring total victory over all enemies —or necessary catharsis for the Germans themselves? In the event, it brought neither.

Bethmann had urged the Kaiser to replace Falkenhayn with the immensely popular Hindenburg and Ludendorff, hoping that perhaps Hindenburg would make a reasonable peace respectable. Instead the new military leaders became champions of the U-boats, and Bethmann was caught between folk heroes promising victory and politicians branding caution treason and cowardice. Bethmann weakened in his opposition, partly because the promises of the military had begun to impress him, too. On January 9, 1917, he surrendered to the military. Their victory marked the virtual end of the Bismarckian Empire, for power had slipped from civilian into military hands. The next day Riezler wrote: "Despite all vows of the navy, a leap in the

63. R.D., Aug. 10, 1916.
64. R.D., March 22, 1916.

dark. We all have the feeling that this question hangs over us like a doom [*Fatum*]. If history follows the laws of tragedy, then Germany should be destroyed by this fatal mistake which embodies all her earlier tragic mistakes." A few days later, in a slightly different vein: "We have signed a piece of paper without knowing whether it contains our own death sentence or the acceptance of a legacy of millions, William the Very Great or William the Last."[65]

Bethmann had now agreed to play what a year earlier he had called "a game of *va banque*, the stakes being our existence as a great power and our entire national future."[66] If he had stuck to his refusal but a few months longer, Germany's chances for a favorable peace would have been excellent. Seven years after the disastrous decision, de Gaulle wrote: "If it had not been for American intervention and the hope it inspired in the Entente, the Reich—considering the Russian Revolution and the Russian peace a few months later, the failure of the French spring offensive with the moral crisis that ensued as a consequence, and the efforts in London of the Lansdownes and Ramsay Macdonalds—would have found itself in a very favorable position for negotiating peace, with the help of mediation that President Wilson had just offered."[67]

The decision, however, had become ineluctable—given the internal politics of Germany—and Bethmann hoped that the desperate gamble might pay off. But could it—without sanctifying militarism and perpetuating its rule? Riezler probably spoke for both men when the U-boat agitation made him cry out: "Germany is like a person reeling [*Taumelnder*], staggering along the abyss, wishing for nothing more fervently than to throw himself into it."[68]

65. R.D., Jan. 31, 1917.
66. Quoted in Karl E. Birnbaum, *op. cit.*, p. 59.
67. Charles de Gaulle, *op. cit.*, pp. 26–27.
68. R.D., April 24, 1916.

The submarine crisis deepened Bethmann's disillusionment with Germany's ruling classes and parties. Only the Social Democrats, he had thought, retained any idealism, and this almost aesthetic appreciation turned practical when he realized that sensible policies could be made only with the Left, never with the Right.[69] The Social Democrats, he said, could teach all other parties the meaning of *Staatsraison,* and he was grateful for their restraint and rationality. He needed their support and they deserved his solicitude—and yet what a necessary gulf remained between them. In private, Bethmann could bewail the selfish idiocy of Germany's elites; in public, he was their representative and protector. In private, he could say to Riezler that "to change East Elbia is an impossibility; [it] must be broken . . . disappear."[70] But he worried lest the socialists should publicly expose the chauvinism and selfishness of the upper classes. In his relations with the socialists, Bethmann had something of the *grand seigneur* who liked his servants better than his equals, treated them accordingly in private, and was much pleased by his own largesse. Some of the socialists were impressed and flattered, too.

But Bethmann knew that more tangible rewards for socialist loyalty were needed. As early as 1914 he realized the inevitability of postwar reform at home, and he told Riezler he would resign after the war rather than abandon the reform of the Prussian suffrage. The sacrifices of the lower classes and their mounting suspicion of the war aims and postwar plans of the ruling classes made it increasingly difficult to postpone reforms until later. Even the promise of reform, however, was anathema to the Right. It was Bethmann's task to keep the two extremes from open warfare: he could not govern in defiance of the Right nor could Germany carry on the war without support of the Left. Bethmann's sympathies in the short run were with the

69. R.D., Nov. 3, 1916.
70. R.D., June 14, 1916.

socialists; in the long run, he feared both sides for he had little faith in a parliamentary-democratic future.

Bethmann's surrender on the submarine question threatened his tie to the socialists. He strove hard to keep them in line. Predictably, the U-boat decision merely emboldened his foes: "The whole *Kanzler-fronde* apparently full of fear that the war might be coming to a successful end before they succeed in overthrowing the Chancellor."[71] The socialists were accommodating at first: "Touching—the modesty of the socialists and touching their patriotism."[72]

Still the lines were drawn clearly: on the Right, Pan-German war aims, unrestricted submarine warfare, and die-hard resistance to domestic reform; on the Left, demands for a compromise peace, democratic reform, and skepticism or opposition concerning submarine warfare. The surface calm was shattered by reactionary moves in the *Herrenhaus,* which Bethmann countered on March 14 with the forthright promise of internal reforms after the war. The next day came the news of the Russian Revolution, and Riezler noted that Bethmann's speech had come at the last possible moment: after the Revolution, his promises would have been attacked as a sign of weakness. The Russian Revolution acted as a sudden gale fanning Germany's discord: the conservatives and industrialists saw the Revolution as the harbinger of things to come in Germany, especially if Bethmann were allowed to continue his conciliatory policy. The socialists demanded immediate reforms—and needed them, if they were to keep even their moderate supporters in line. Bethmann promised them, but was defeated by his ministers who feared that the promulgation of a democratic franchise in Prussia would mean "that one would not be able to work any more with the bourgeois parties, great agitation of the League of Farmers against the cities—dire consequences for the food

71. R.D., Feb. 18, 1917.
72. R.D., Feb. 25, 1917.

supply."[73] Once more Bethmann had to retreat and the socialists had to be disappointed because the King's ministers, themselves opposed to reform, conjured up the specter of upper-class
sabotage! No wonder Riezler sighed: "Only a few sense how
closely we brush catastrophe all the time."[74]

The mood remained grim throughout the spring: Riezler
thought it would be a miracle if Germany survived the madness
of its ruling classes. "The Chancellor's heroic struggle against
the soldiers—but the great policies we could be carrying out
are ruined by it."[75] The Chancellor's position was rapidly weakening even before the final crisis in July: "If the people identify the Supreme Army Command with the Pan-Germans, if it
leaks out that the Chancellor has lost all his political freedom
of movement in internal and external affairs because of the
army leaders, then will come the rebellion against the rule of
militarism and the beginning of the collapse."[76] But before the
Chancellor's captivity was realized, rebellion and intrigue
finally felled him.

A newly constructed Reichstag majority grew impatient of
Bethmann's temporizing and sought to develop its own initiative in the form of the peace resolution. Ludendorff exploited
the disaffection of the moderates in order at last to get rid of
Bethmann. Despite everything, the Kaiser probably regretted
having to part with his Chancellor. De Gaulle's portrait of their
relationship was amazingly apt: "Bethmann, moderate without
weakness, hardworking without ostentation, respectful without
servility, was the very model of a good servant, and this character pleased William whose superficial authoritarianism and
prickly prestige he did not vex."[77] In taking leave of the Kaiser
at the end, Bethmann did not mention "the true reason [for his

73. R.D., April 6, 1917.
74. R.D., April 10, 1917.
75. R.D., May 8, 1917.
76. R.D., June 9, 1917.
77. Charles de Gaulle, *op. cit.*, p. 155.

resignation], Ludendorff's blackmail, in order to spare the Emperor, already *de facto* abdicated." He merely complained that his telephone had been tapped and that when he hears the click he shouts into it, "What *Schweinehund* is listening in?"[78] Shaken when Bethmann yielded on submarine warfare, Bismarck's Empire ended when Ludendorff and Hindenburg, banking on their glory and backed by their nationalist allies, imposed their will and finally their dictatorship on Emperor and populace.

Riezler's notes on the July crisis apparently were lost, but his predictions during the final eighteen months of the war attested his clairvoyant pessimism. In April 1917, he thought the Allies might soon announce their willingness to negotiate with the German people, not the Hohenzollerns.[79] He foresaw the internal consequences of defeat: "If we collapse because of hunger and the agitation of Haase and comrades—or if it looks that way—then the bad peace will be blamed on the workers, everything will be misconstrued in favor of the Right, and Germany, mortally wounded physically, will have her soul completely confounded as well."[80] After Bethmann's departure, he sensed the beginning of a reactionary plot to "goad and provoke the socialists by all possible means—the war demagogy [*Kriegshetze*], etc. serves this purpose principally, the socialists should be forced to turn their hatred of the *Vaterlandspartei* against the state . . . and in this way should be pushed from the state."[81] Bethmann's feeble successor could hardly maintain his laborious efforts to coax and bully the socialists into the state. Agrarians and industrialists, parliamentarians of the Right and rabid annexationists, always urged on by Ludendorff, preferred to keep the nation cleanly divided: either our

78. R.D., Aug. 4, 1917.
79. R.D., April 13, 1917.
80. R.D., April 19, 1917.
81. R.D., Feb. 11, 1918.

state or theirs. In victory, the upper classes were resolved to hold on to their own, and make no concessions; in defeat, they were determined to accuse the Left of treason, spreading spiritual poison, which would corrupt all public order.

On October 1, 1918, Riezler grasped the totality of Germany's defeat and dreaded its implications: "The defeat in its worst form—if no miracle intervenes, or if the enemy coalition does not become disorganized, we will practically have to accept *das Diktat*. Slavery for a hundred years. The dream about the world [*Welttraum*] finished forever. The end of all hubris. The dispersion of Germans around the world. Fate of the Jews."

Riezler was a perspicacious judge of people and situations. His impressions of Bethmann, however, may have been occasionally distorted by loyalty and admiration, for he was devoted to his chief, as young advisers to men of power often are. Riezler's Bethmann may have been wiser, more detached, than he appeared to most others. Sometimes Riezler was critical and impatient, but he was always puzzled by "this strange man." To some extent, we still are.

Before the July 1914 crisis, Riezler thought of Bethmann as a highly intelligent and cultivated civil servant. The July crisis made him disavow that judgment: "He is great—as a man and because of the breadth and independence of his mind. He is entirely free of all prejudice and pettiness and entirely independent of public opinion and suggestion. His judgment is autonomous. . . . If only he did not have the dreadful habit of pretending doubts even when he has firmly formulated his own opinion, of saying things that he himself does not believe only to hear the contradictions of others."[82] At the beginning of the war, Bethmann's *Gejammer*, his stubborn anxiety, his reluc-

82. R.D., July 20, 1914.

tance "to think big," exasperated Riezler, who longed for something more dynamic, more inspiring—who longed in fact for the charismatic leader that Weber depicted after the war. He wished the Chancellor would cease playing *advocatus diaboli*, would fortify his will to power, would gain some of that passion and magnetism that would inflame the people. He praised his defensive energy, his toughness and tenacity, his caution and perspicacity, but hoped he would occasionally seize the initiative. Toward the end of the Chancellorship, Riezler's admiration rose and silenced all criticism. He saw Bethmann, lonely, ever unbefriended, heroic, martyrlike. The Chancellor had always been at his best when things were at their worst; when optimists collapsed, he was calm and confident. Perhaps a critical situation confirmed his private view of the world, and he could adapt to it more readily. His defeat left his dignity unimpaired and indeed something like nobility clung to him as he departed. Riezler once wrote and always believed: "He is superior to others in human as well as intellectual qualities. [*Seine menschliche Überlegenheit über die anderen tritt zu der geistigen.*]"[83]

With this judgment there can be no quarrel, though the competition for greatness in wartime Germany was obviously not keen. Riezler's impressions of Bethmann are invaluable, though the historian's perspective and questions are necessarily different. We are not principally concerned with Bethmann's person, but with the statesman and his relations to society.

Perhaps the most extraordinary quality that emerges from Riezler's portrait is the realism and reasoned pessimism of Bethmann's views about Germany. He understood the divisions and antagonisms of German society, and he feared that the struggle between blind ruling classes and aspiring lower classes would lead to revolution, particularly under the stress of war. He saw in wartime Germany the same danger of violent

83. R.D., March 7, 1916.

upheaval that he had seen in prewar Europe. His commitment in the struggle with foreign nations, however, had been unambiguously national whereas his sympathies in a divided nation were not so easily identified. He admired the socialists as they were during the war, but feared a social-democratic future as jeopardizing authority and culture. He detested the wartime politics of agrarians and national bourgeoisie, doubted that they would ever reacquire the qualities of leadership, and yet by background and tradition belonged to them. At his best, Bethmann had no political home in Germany.

He clung to the only course he could find: conciliation, the policy of the diagonal, which in the end, fleetingly, united the two opposites against himself. Perhaps there was no other way, save revolution, which was anathema to the monarchical, bureaucratic Bethmann. Slightly lugubrious by temperament, he was hardly buoyed up by his vision of the future. "To fear the worst often cures the worst" did not apply to Bethmann.

He was a Puritan gambler: he worried about plunging his country into war, but he took the leap nevertheless; he feared Pan-Germanism in its effects at home and abroad, and he consented to the submarine gamble anyway. His personal weakness has been blamed for his failure to defend his cautious course— and to some small extent, with justice. There were weightier reasons for his repeated, if disguised capitulations: it must be remembered that to a large extent, he accepted the values of the very system he criticized. Much as he railed against individual generals, he probably shared his countryman's excessive faith in the authority of the uniform. Much as he inveighed—in private—against the *Unbildung und Verblendung* of his colleagues and compatriots, he too had a fatal blind spot when it came to appraising Germany's place in the world or the likely effect on others of her "defensive" ambitions. The chief reason, of course, for his failure to achieve his goals at home was the political system itself. The upper strata of German society had enough power and resolution to block their own political en-feeblement. The system kept Bethmann confined to a very narrow area of maneuverability, and the fact that he himself hesitated to move beyond that area was secondary. Personal hesitancy was functional: the system enjoined it.

The remarkable thing about Bethmann was not his failure to achieve pacification at home, for no man could have done that. Rather it was the fact that this seeming moderate, so clearly hounded by his sense of responsibility, could cover with his own authority such fateful decisions as the forward course of July 1914 and the submarine war of 1917. As Chancellor he presided over the subversion of political authority by the military. On several occasions, he thought of resigning—the traditional means of disavowing responsibility for the political acts of others. In the end, he always shrank back—and certainly not for love of power.[84] His devotion to the monarch—whatever his thoughts about William or the affronts he suffered at court —made him hesitate to leave his post in wartime. His patriotism and his pessimism combined to keep him in his office: he knew that his successor would abandon his conciliatory, moderate course altogether. He was psychologically prepared for unpalatable decisions because he expected the worst anyhow. His pessimism, too, had its functional aspects.

84. Amidst his own dismissal crisis in 1932, Heinrich Brüning insinuated that Bethmann Hollweg had clung to power for unworthy reasons. After Hindenburg had ousted Brüning, he asked him in a three-minute interview to retain his post as foreign minister. Brüning declined and added sanctimoniously: "Mr. President, you must not forget that I am no Bethmann Hollweg. When I have reached the conclusion that a policy is wrong then I depart without rancor . . ." Brüning at least was right in saying he was not Bethmann. Bethmann had tried to reform a monarchical system in order to strengthen its popular basis—and failed; Brüning had tried to restore a monarchical system in order to find an authoritative balance against Weimar's popular forces—and also failed. In any case, it is revealing that in the hardest moment of his career, Brüning thought of but one man, Bethmann. A study of how German chancellors fell—from Bismarck to Brüning—would shed much light on the style of German politics. Heinrich Brüning, *Memoiren, 1918–1934* (Stuttgart, 1970), p. 602.

Thus it came about that this moral man became the uniquely useful agent of reckless, selfish leaders. Unwittingly, probably unconsciously, he slid into the position of being a front for the very forces he detested. Riezler saw this tragic irony: "There persists the strange paradox: that we can follow such a foolhardy policy in the domestic and foreign realm is made possible exclusively [by the fact that we have] the most cautious and circumspect man at the helm who alone can make it credible. This paradox from the beginning of the war."[85] And again, "All his bad qualities have one advantage. The people outside politics have confidence that if this man demands something it is really necessary. . . . This was already an important asset at the outbreak of the war."[86] Or again, "strange irony of fate, that this great hard man, earnest and prudent, with the warmest heart must conduct and cover the most foolhardy policy—that the only accomplishment of him who had the best interests of Germany at heart is to keep the mass of the people—the only thing that is great and worthy of respect in today's Germany— in line with the policy of Ludendorff, Tirpitz, etc."[87] Bethmann meant to be a brake on political irresponsibility, but at critical moments he served as the mask of conscience and character for the very devils he detested—and without which they would have been far less effective.

Worse still, Bethmann could have rendered a signal service to the pacification of Germany after the war and revolution if he had rendered an honest account of his years as Chancellor. As early as 1916, Riezler hoped that Bethmann's struggles against the military would be described precisely, "after the war, as an example for the Germans to learn from."[88] Later he cried out: "Will the history of this U-boat war, this profoundest [*imgeheimsten*] lie, ever be written? If yes, then it must

85. R.D., Feb. 14, 1917.
86. R.D., April 28, 1915.
87. R.D., Jan. 31, 1917.
88. R.D., Dec. 2, 1916.

unmask the *Unbildung,* stupidity of militarism, and the rottenness of the whole chauvinist upper strata."[89]

Bethmann's memoirs went but halfway. He gently criticized
Tirpitz and Ludendorff, who had already vilified him. But he
could not bring himself to write a full, objective, and hence
scathing account of how German leadership was corrupted during the war and why. His motives were undoubtedly mixed and
honorable. A full account would have substantiated Allied
charges of German militarism and imperialism. He shrank from
denouncing Germany's erstwhile leaders for fear of deepening
the divisions within Germany. But he knew better than most
men the quality of those who were already poisoning the life of
Germany by their infamous stab-in-the-back legend and their
cries of treason. Perhaps Bethmann's most culpable act was to
have seen and understood so much and to have said so little.
His semi-silence, though understandable, facilitated the second
and worse triumph of the very passions he deplored.

Despite his personal integrity, his biting sense of responsibility, and his own exceptional intelligence, his historic role
abetted the disastrous course of Germany's history in this century. To say that he was more a victim than a villain is an obvious tribute that puts him in a class with most well-intentioned,
unsuccessful statesmen of modern Germany.

89. R.D., April 13, 1917.

The First World War

An Evocation

This essay was originally written in 1966 for *The Columbia History of the World*. It is intended as an evocation of what the Great War meant to Europe rather than as an analysis or a narrative account. Its form may not strike the reader as orthodox scholarship, but its substance reflects years of interest and study. Footnotes could have been added, but even mammoth footnotes would have given the reader little guidance to the prolific literature on the war. To recall the dimensions of the war may in itself be useful, particularly at this time. When I first wrote the article five years ago, I was struck by the pertinence of many of the themes to our own tragedy in Vietnam. The military delusions, the escalation of propaganda, the impact of the war at home, in short the dynamics of that war seemed to have echoes in the present.

I have made minor changes in this version.

Historic Europe did not survive the Great War. When the fire finally burned itself out in November 1918, the old Europe with its hard-won pre-eminence in the world, with its liberal beliefs and practices, with its power and prosperity, and its admittedly precarious unity, was gone. The war, straining the social fabric beyond endurance, turned into revolution; the specter that had been haunting Europe since the Commune had become ominous reality in Russia. Peace in 1919 signified the continuation of war by different means. The Great War ushered in a period of unprecedented violence. A second Thirty Years' War had in fact begun.

With what innocence, with what enthusiasm, did the Europeans of 1914 respond to the tocsin! No one foresaw even the contours of the disaster ahead, and most people thrilled to the war as a great patriotic adventure. After a decade of worsening crises and a spiraling arms race, they had come to expect a final showdown; after decades of peace, they had forgotten what war was like and only the fewest had an inkling that a modern war would multiply the terrors of earlier conflicts. Europeans marched off to battle with something close to exultation, proud in their patriotism and certain of their cause, confident of a victorious end in a short time. It was the last time in our civilization that war could be greeted in this fashion.

The enthusiasm for war did not bespeak a great bloodthirstiness. For some, it signified a yearning to escape insufferable boredom, to get rid of bourgeois sham and oppressiveness. To Thomas Mann the war promised an end to that "horrible world, which now no longer is, or no longer will be, after the great storm passed by. Did it not crawl with spiritual vermin as with worms?" The dream of finding cultural salvation in political upheavals was shattered soon enough—only to reappear periodically in different guises.

Patriotic exultation had been preceded by the solicitous efforts of all governments to save the appearances of peacefulness, to make it seem as if the enemy was also the unprovoked aggressor. None had pursued this policy of deception with more cunning or under greater difficulties than the German government, and nowhere was the appearance of fighting a defensive war more important than in Germany, where the Socialist Party, with its avowed pacifism, represented a third of the electorate. Indeed, international socialism, pledged to oppose all imperialist wars, became the first victim of the war. Its most attractive leader, Jean Jaurès, was assassinated at the end of July, and socialists everywhere felt their national allegiance far more strongly than their commitment to international class solidarity. Socialist backing of the war made possible that instantaneous closing of national ranks—epitomized by the formation in France of the *union sacré*—that promised the adjournment of political conflicts for the duration of the war. In the passion of the moment, all parties and all classes pledged their full support to the nation, in what everybody expected would be a short, decisive test.

At the beginning of the war, the sides were rather evenly balanced. In a short war, the Central Powers, with the German army as the backbone of their strength, would enjoy certain advantages. They were superbly poised for action, and their interior lines of communication allowed for the quick transport of troops and equipment. The Allies held potential advantages in a long war: the vast manpower of Russia and the great naval superiority of England that guaranteed free access to foreign, especially American, supplies. In such intangible matters as leadership and morale, the great contestants—Germany, France, and England—were evenly matched, at least at the beginning.

German strategists had long hatched meticulous plans for a lightning war and for nothing else. In August, they set them in motion. By attacking France through Belgium, they expected to capture Paris from the west and to break French resistance in a matter of weeks. Germany's Eastern front, meanwhile, was to remain virtually undefended until, after France's defeat, the bulk of the German army could be used to crush the Czarist armies. For four weeks, the German advance proceeded like clockwork, as Belgian defenses crumbled and French armies retreated.

In early September, German troops were within sight of Paris; the High Command, however, had changed its mind about Russia and had weakened its Western offensive by sending troops eastward. The French, at the same time, rallied for the defense of their capital. With magnificent, if costly, gallantry, they counter-attacked, and the miracle of the Marne, as it came to be called, threw German troops back and ended the threat to Paris. Fighting then shifted to the northwest, with each side aiming to outflank the other; the Germans also hoped in the process to capture the channel ports, thus depriving the British army of its vital supply routes. The British bore the brunt of this savage "race to the sea," and denied the Germans this strategic prize as well.

Even after the Marne, the German people could comfort themselves with their gigantic victories in the East, which they wrongly credited to the genius of Hindenburg, and which had weakened, but not destroyed, the Russian army. Everywhere German troops stood triumphant on enemy soil. They had scored impressive victories, but the decisive victory had eluded them. Forever. Six weeks after the outbreak of the war, most German leaders realized that their chances for winning a clearcut victory had virtually vanished. The Allies, injured, but intact and resolute, faced a Germany that had won enough in those early weeks to reject a peace that did not bring it large gains but had not won enough to impose its own terms on a world of enemies. The tragedy was that neither side could win.

The losses in those early weeks of fighting had been monstrous, especially to the British and French, whose losses then and for the rest of the war consistently outran those of the

Germans. The young elite of each army had been decimated, and the great bloodbath which was to prove so infinitely destructive of Europe's genius had begun in earnest. The cost of a long war should have been clear to all, but war enhances man's immense capacity for self-delusion.

By the end of 1914, the Western front had become stabilized, and the vast armies stretching from the Channel to the Alps dug themselves in, built trenches behind barbed wire, with a narrow gap between lines, known as no man's land. In trenches that were wet and crawling with rats, millions of soldiers huddled together, battling alternately monotony or death. Never before had so many soldiers faced each other in such futility, terrorized by the all-powerful machine gun which made every offensive action, every patrol, a death trap. And still military wisdom decreed that the decision had to come where the bulk of the armies lay, i.e., in the West—even after it became obvious that neither side could achieve a breakthrough.

Were there no alternatives, no way of escaping this bloody stalemate? The answer proved to be no, but not for lack of ingenious ideas and clever projects. The Germans, for example, sought to attack their enemies from behind, by fomenting revolution in the Near East or India or even Ireland. They were successful only in Russia—and with questionable results for themselves. The British, meanwhile, perfected their weapon, the blockade, which was aimed at weakening the resistance of the enemy's civilian population. New weapons were invented; the Germans introduced zeppelins for bombing purposes, and poison gas for land attacks, forgetting that prevailing westerly winds would vitiate all but initial successes. Lloyd George, the British Minister of Munitions, championed armored vehicles, later known as tanks, and pushed their construction despite Kitchener's sneer: "A pretty mechanical toy; the war will never be won by such machines." How was it to be won?

Two traditional means remained to be tried: the winning of

new allies and the opening of new fronts. Diplomats on both sides worked on the remaining neutrals. In September 1914, not unexpectedly, Turkey joined Germany and Austria, thus blocking Allied access to Russian ports in the Black Sea. A few months later, the Allies persuaded—or bribed—Italy to enter on their side, in violation of her treaty obligations but in pursuit of her *sacro egoismo,* her immense annexationist appetite. The greatest neutral, the United States, admonished by its President to remain neutral in thought as well as deed, became an ever more important supplier of food, weapons, and credit to France and Britain, who controlled the sea. Germany's efforts to use her few submarines to cut off English supplies proved risky because, as the sinking of the *Lusitania* in 1915 showed, effective submarine action entailed the loss of neutral lives and evoked the threat of American retaliation. The English blockade of Germany also violated the rights of neutrals—and humanitarian scruples—but spared American lives and hence aroused less opposition. Still, the submarine proved an enticing new weapon to the Germans, and her military leaders ceaselessly urged its unrestricted use.

There were some leaders in England, notably Winston Churchill, who agitated for the opening of a new front that would break the Western stalemate. After months of wrangling, an expedition for the capture of the Dardanelles Straits was launched; if it had been successful, it would have separated Turkey from its allies and provided much-needed help for Russia. But staggering incompetence ruined the enterprise—and very nearly eclipsed Churchill's fortunes. Years later, he still viewed it as the decisive turn to disaster: "Thereafter events passed very largely outside the scope of conscious choice. Governments and individuals conformed to the rhythm of the tragedy, and swayed and staggered forward in helpless violence, slaughtering and squandering on ever-increasing scales, till injuries were wrought to the structure of human society which a century will not efface, and which may conceivably prove fatal to the present civilization."

The main reason for the failure of Gallipoli had been the unwillingness of Anglo-French military leaders to do anything that might weaken the Western front. They—and their German counterparts—were mesmerized by that front, certain that the next time around, "with one more push," they could achieve a breakthrough and regain mobility. To that hope were sacrificed millions of men. Even on ordinary days, when all was quiet on the Western front, men would be killed on useless reconnaissance missions, while for the rest, the monotonous and debilitating routine remained unbroken. Both sides launched gigantic offensives as well, which at best gained a few useless square miles, bought with the lives of tens of thousands per day. The French launched such futile attacks in 1915, and the next year both sides resorted to a strategy of attrition, hoping to wear down the enemy. In February 1916, the German High Command opened an attack on Verdun, a stronghold of strategic and symbolic value, which it assumed the French would defend at all costs; French armies would be bled white, while German losses would be lower. For four months the battle raged; the French held Verdun, at immense cost to themselves —and to the Germans. In the West, men were sacrificed to a military Moloch without reason, without intelligence, and without compassion. War had lost what glory it once possessed, and terrified men were killed by machinery that human reason had devised but could no longer control.

In the East, the war bore a more traditional mask. Armies moved over large tracts of land, hoping to trap or encircle enemy formations—and sometimes succeeding in doing so. In 1915, the Central Powers were everywhere successful, and Russia was deprived of her Polish possessions, leaving Germany and Austria quarreling over the spoils. In 1916, the Russian Commander, Brusilov, launched a counter-offensive which attested and strained Russian resiliency and by its failure hastened the final collapse of Czardom. The Eastern front never acquired the horrid glamour of the Western front; the territory was unfamiliar and the fighting less gruesomely novel. But it determined the shape of things to come for over half a century; successive Russian Revolutions would have been unthinkable without the prior breakdown of Russian life due to the war.

In fact, the war imposed a tremendous burden on all belligerent societies, and the universal response to this new burden was a degree of social regimentation undreamt of in earlier decades and centuries. The anticipated short war had become protracted and total—the first war in history that deserved the epithet. As there was no precedent, there was no master plan of regimentation. There was only step-by-step innovation and improvisation in order to mobilize, clothe, feed, and equip millions of combatants, to maintain production when manpower was short and raw materials became scant, to feed the civilian population and keep up their morale. The problems were legion and bedeviling in their intricacy and unexpected interrelatedness. In the early months of the war, the British carried on under the motto "Business as usual," while the German High Command was stunned when a great industrialist, Walther Rathenau, asked what provisions had been made for the stockpiling of raw material. War as usual, war as it had been taught at Sandhurst or St.-Cyr, was dead. The Great War, to paraphrase Georges Clemenceau, France's fiery Premier, was too complicated to be left to the soldiers.

Under the duress of war, the modern Leviathan was born. The state—so exquisitely circumscribed by decades of liberal theory and practice—suddenly assumed new powers over realms hitherto deemed immune from its control. The state as night watchman, as the English myth had it, now became the mobilizer of men and property, the commander of economic life, the censor of men's expressions, and the manipulator of men's minds. All this took place while traditional politics were adjourned, while dissent was often denounced as unpatriotic, so that governments could assume these new powers with a minimum of struggle or opposition. Indeed, as governments began not only to conscript their male citizenry—this was novel only in England, where it was adopted in 1916—but also to impose rationing, to control prices, and to allocate labor and resources, their own powers vis-à-vis parliament greatly increased. Laissez-faire was another wartime casualty. It was discredited in theory and curtailed in practice. By 1918, for example, the British government was the direct buyer of 90 per cent of all imports. War socialism, as the Germans called the new statist regimentation, went hand-in-hand with war dictatorships, and even in the democratic countries like England and France, parliaments lost much power. Lloyd George entered office in December 1916, and Clemenceau in November 1917; in July 1917, the seemingly moderate German Chancellor, Bethmann Hollweg, had to surrender power to a thinly disguised military dictatorship under Ludendorff and Hindenburg. In Russia, on the other hand, where autocracy had been the rule of centuries, the government's gross inefficiency stimulated demands for some measure of parliamentary control. In all countries, however, the freedom of individuals contracted—temporarily, it was assumed. But would governments relinquish or forget all the new devices of control that they had discovered during the war? The prewar balance between individual liberty and public authority would never be restored.

Civilians everywhere sacrificed comforts and suffered deprivations; soldiers suffered incomparably more, but at least the common terror at the front bred a kind of camaraderie, of fraternal companionship, that sustained their spirits. Soldiers and civilians alike lived under the shadow of sudden death, lived with the fear that their lives or the lives of those close to them might suddenly be snuffed out in one of the futile battles in what gradually appeared to be an endless, futile war. By winter 1916, the enthusiasm of August 1914 had long since turned into a grim, sullen mood, relieved by bursts of mordant cynicism.

Governments did their best to whip up ever fresh enthusiasm for the killing, and in the process received ample help from the established classes. The chauvinistic cant that poured from press and pulpit was meant to rouse flagging spirits to new sacrifices. The techniques of propaganda, borrowed from pre-war modes of advertising, became so important in the hands of governments, that one English wit spoke of "propagandocracy" as the new type of rule. Wartime propaganda became ever cruder and uglier: it started with the theme "love your country and defend it" and gradually turned to "hate your enemy and kill him."

Allied minds were poisoned by atrocity stories about the Huns mutilating bodies of Belgian children and German minds by horror tales about English greed and hypocrisy that were responsible for the war and the starving of innocent women and children. Truth was devalued along with life, and hardly a voice was raised in protest. The guardians of God's word led the martial chorus. Total war came to mean total hatred— though least, perhaps, among soldiers, because they knew that the enemy across the trenches were fellow-pawns, equally mortal and equally desirous to live.

The systematic poisoning of men's minds by paroxysms of nationalism—which at the time Corporal Adolf Hitler found most impressive and worthy of emulation—further obstructed the search for peace. As the war dragged on, as the vilifications of the enemy mounted, appetites increased and war aims became more grandiose in order to justify past and future sacrifices. "They shall not have died in vain" became the monstrous slogan by which the meaning of the war was escalated, and the still living were led to ever greater slaughter—to justify the already dead. Could those who had died, thinking they were defending their country, be justified by others dying for some new annexation? Thus the war fed on itself, and governments became prisoners of their own propaganda.

The definition of war aims proved divisive among and within nations. The French demands were deceptively reasonable: they wanted the restoration of Alsace-Lorraine—which only a defeated Germany would yield; the British sought to destroy Prussian militarism and terminate the German threat to the European balance of power. Colonial gains would be incidental rewards. Germany harbored the most ambitious war aims, which would in fact have established her as the hegemonial power in Europe, and hence a world power in England's place. The heart of Germany's programs—different groups embraced different varieties of avarice—was the establishment of a Central European Confederation, dominated by a victorious *Reich*. Many Germans thought of this new order as establishing in the twentieth century a *Pax Germanica* to replace the *Pax Britannica*. Whether flamboyant or seemingly reasonable, the war aims of the belligerents ruled out a compromise peace such as the Pope or President Wilson hoped to mediate. The appetite grew with the eating—or, this time, with the dying.

The escalation of war aims had political origins and consequences. By and large, the traditional Right in Europe propounded harsh war aims, hoping that visible, national gains would redound to the prestige and profit of the upper classes. German industrialists were vehement exemplars of this combined greed and fear. The European Left was far more diffident concerning war aims, and a steadily growing minority of socialist militants demanded a peace without annexation or indemnity that would put an end to "the imperialist war." The suspicion that the war was being continued to serve class ends began to spread among radicals and working-class groups, particularly in Russia and Germany—in the very countries where the lower classes had to bear the brunt of mounting hardships, such as inflation, with wages lagging far behind the rise in prices, malnutrition, and the worst form of class warfare: the fight for bread. This suspicion and the daily experience of inequality fostered a new socialist militancy, which in Germany, for example, led to a schism in socialism and the founding of the Independent Socialists, a radical antiwar party. On the international plane, in neutral Switzerland, Russian exiles, led by Lenin, and radical socialists from other countries, vowed to turn the imperialist war into a revolutionary struggle, to end the war by first ending capitalist oppression, as they called it. Socialists who disagreed—whether prompted by patriotism or by a sense of practicality—were quickly vilified as "social chauvinists." By 1916, the passion for national unity that had swept across Europe in August 1914 was shaken; in 1917, that unity collapsed in one country and was severely tried in all others.

In retrospect, 1917 looms as one of the decisive years in the history of European civilization. For in that year, the old system collapsed, as America's entry into the war signaled the end of the more or less autonomous European states-system, and the Bolshevik Revolution signaled the beginning of a new revolutionary challenge to Europe's social order. In 1917, Wilson and Lenin appeared simultaneously on the scene and faced each other across a prostrate Europe. In a sense both had been called forth by the challenge of German power; neither would disappear with its destruction. The implications of America's entry into the war and Russia's revolutionary secession from it were not evident at first; they became clear gradually, as for half a century of disaster Europe fitfully suffered from the constellation that dominated 1917: German power, Bolshevism, and the intermittent need for an America that was by unpredictable turns too remote and too close.

These three elements were strangely intertwined from the

beginning. Without the direct challenge of German power, embodied in Germany's declaration of unrestricted submarine warfare, the United States would not have entered the war. Gratuitously, Germany's ruling classes, made arrogant by their victories and frantic by the elusiveness of victory, provoked their own nemesis: the Allies would never have been able to defeat Germany without American help. German power also paved the way for Bolshevism: indirectly, by precipitating the collapse of Czardom and of its immediate, liberal successors, and directly by transporting Lenin from Switzerland to the Finland Station, and by supplying Bolshevism with subsidies. Ludendorff's hope to use Lenin, and Lenin's to use Ludendorff, were but early examples of that collaboration between Right and Left extremists that was to prove so debilitating to political stability in the ensuing half century. Revolutionaries and counter-revolutionaries either lived off each other—or died because of each other. In 1917, Germany drew short-term advantages both from unrestricted submarine warfare and from her support of Bolshevism. The long-term advantages accrued to her enemies. The Germans, however, were not the only ones to stumble onto tactics that would defeat the very ends they were to serve: the politics of Europe had become so obscure, so filled with blinding hatreds and uncertainties, that clarity in political thought and action was virtually unattainable. The very pace of events suddenly outstripped the power of comprehension.

By the beginning of 1917, all the belligerents suffered a further intensification of hardships. Food shortages in England, Germany, and Russia worsened perceptibly and people were alarmed lest chronic malnutrition turn into famine. In Russia, the workers first struck because of the breakdown of supplies; once out on the street, they demanded the end of Czarism itself, and no group, not even the army, thought that Nicholas was salvable. A provisional bourgeois government was organized and vowed to fight on, but radical pressure forced it, against its will, to promise to seek a "peace without annexations and indemnities." War weariness spread insidiously in the East as well as in the West, where the stalemate continued bloody and unbroken. The much-heralded spring offensive of the French ended in failure—and widespread mutinies. For the first time in the war, the military's principal virtues, discipline and obedience, were flouted by weary, disillusioned men who, having lost their faith in their officers, refused to return to the trenches. Their new commander, Pétain, went on the defensive: "I will wait for the Americans and for tanks." In Germany, wildcat strikes erupted and mutinies racked naval bases. War weariness —and the suspicion that the war was continued only for reasons of national greed—inspired an upsurge of Left-wing militancy.

Workers and soldiers everywhere had had enough. French soldiers boggled at the murderous idiocy of trench warfare. German workers suspected that their masters demanded proletarian sacrifices in order to pursue their capitalist profit and their imperialist ambition. Radical propaganda gained credence at a time when, as the British writer C. E. Montague noted, "the air stank of bad work in high places. . . . Wherever the contrary had not been proved to their [the soldiers'] own senses, the slacking, self-seeking and shirking that had muddled and spoilt their own training for war until they were put, half-trained, in the hottest of the fire must be assumed to be in authority everywhere." Even so conservative a leader as Winston Churchill echoed the sentiments of desperately war-weary soldiers: "As in the shades of a November evening, I for the first time led a platoon of Grenadiers across the sopping fields which gave access to our trenches . . . the conviction came into my mind with absolute assurance that the simple soldiers and their regimental officers, armed with their cause, would by their virtues in the end retrieve the mistakes and ignorances of

Staffs and Cabinets, of Admirals, Generals and politicians—including, no doubt, many of my own." Consistent failure at the top could only stimulate discontent at the bottom.

The greatest socialist victory came in Russia, when the provisional government's offensive ended in total disarray. Lenin's Bolsheviks seized power and demanded an immediate peace. France and England, close to collapse themselves, realized that the Bolsheviks intended to desert them militarily and subvert them politically. The Bolshevik victory greatly stimulated the socialist agitation everywhere for an immediate revolutionary peace; it was only Wilson's promise of a liberal peace, based on national self-determination, that enabled the moderate Left in the other belligerent countries to continue supporting the war.

From the fall of 1917 to the following spring, the Germans had it all their own way, and they imparted some of their own new energy to their lagging ally, Austria. In October, the Austro-German armies inflicted a monumental defeat on the Italians at Caporetto—a defeat that years later Mussolini's aggressive antics still sought to exorcise. At Brest-Litovsk, the Germans dictated a Carthaginian peace to the stunned Bolsheviks who had expected succor from their German comrades and instead saw the German military tear most of industrial Russia from their hands. By March 1918, Ludendorff, having shifted all but a million men from the East, threw the German armies into a series of offensives in the West that repeatedly broke through Allied lines. So precarious was their outlook that the Allies, who for three years had fought under separate and often poorly coordinated commands, finally appointed a French general, Ferdinand Foch, as supreme commander. By July, the Germans were once again across the Marne and within thirty-five miles of Paris. But this time, they quickly succumbed to Allied, including American, counterattacks. Weary, without reserves of men or supplies, they began a retreat which—if the

Allies had had more strength or self-confidence—could easily have turned into a rout.

Defeat threatened Germany's allies as well. Anglo-French offensives in the Near East and the Balkans—offensives that were not unrelated to imperialist aims—brought the Ottoman Empire and Bulgaria close to disaster. The tremors were felt further north, and as Allied troops advanced in Southeast Europe, the Austro-Hungarian monarchy, long plagued by internal strife, finally disintegrated into its national components. The Czechs and Slovaks, the Poles, the Hungarians and the Yugoslavs proclaimed their independence. The venerable empire which, as Trotsky put it maliciously, "had long before hung out a sign for an undertaker, not demanding any high qualifications of him," ceased to exist. The Central Powers were crumbling at last—faster indeed than the Allies thought credible.

In late September, Ludendorff precipitously demanded the creation of a democratic government that should immediately appeal to President Wilson for an armistice. The choice of Wilson was deliberate and cunning. His moral ascendancy in Europe was such that the Germans could hope that he would break Allied vindictiveness and insist on a "soft peace." For the moment, American power was the arbiter of Europe; Wilson told the Germans that they must first rid themselves of the imperial dynasty and told the Allies that they must grant Germany an armistice on the basis of his Fourteen Points. Weeks passed, until Foch finally presented the Germans with the terms of a harsh armistice. They had no choice but to accept, and on November 11, 1918, at eleven in the morning, the fighting stopped. Europe experienced its last day of universal rejoicing. The agony was over.

But life could never be the same. The very fact that the peace conference in Paris was dominated by a non-European, by Woodrow Wilson, who had won the hearts of Europeans as no leader ever had before, symbolized the tremendous changes that the war had wrought in Europe. The physiognomy of Europe had been decisively altered, and historians have been debating ever since whether the war created or merely accelerated these changes. It certainly created the conditions for change, as witness the Bolshevik Revolution: Bolshevism, long nurtured in prewar thoughts and antagonisms, could never have triumphed without the war. Nor would America's power have grown so rapidly if it had not been for the war—and for the new challenge from the East.

The war had brought immense changes, and it took an incalculable toll of European life. It is relatively easy to measure the material cost: the homes and factories destroyed, national economies exhausted, existing assets wasted, currencies ruined by inflation, and national debts acquired that a few years before would have been unimaginable. The total cost of the war has been estimated at 350 billion dollars—the dollar reckoned at 1918 value. Europe's place in the world economy was impaired beyond recovery; two new giants, America and Japan, had been making colossal strides while Europe bled itself.

The human cost is harder to assess. Over ten million Europeans had died in battle—as well as 115,000 Americans. At least twice that number had been wounded; many of them were left to live out their lives as cripples, millions of mutilated men, walking the streets of Europe as reminders of the ravages of war. France lost half its men between the ages of twenty and thirty-two—and other countries suffered almost as much. But numbers fail to tell the full story. Among the dead was the promise and flower of Europe's youth. The potential leaders of the 1920's and 1930's had been decimated, as thousands of men of recognized talent died alongside others whose talents and genius would remain undiscovered forever. In those futile charges across no man's land, junior officers and young volunteers were mowed down first: nearly 20 per cent of all Oxford University men who served in the war were killed. Of 346 students of the *École Normale Supérieure* mobilized, 143 never returned. Even Europe, with its historic abundance of talent, could not suffer such losses without greatly impoverishing its future.

Nor had the talent of the next generation been better protected. In all the belligerent countries, the young had been undernourished and undereducated. Millions of young people experienced privations, both physical and psychic. In England, 600,000 children had to leave school prematurely, because their mothers needed their financial support. It was the same story elsewhere. Those fortunate enough to stay in school were taught by fewer and fewer teachers, by rapidly trained women or by men too sick or too old to fight. The young suffered grievously if less dramatically than their elders. The reckoning of the costs came later.

And what of the millions that finally returned from the trenches—to families that had been living in dread of their not returning? Had their collective outlook, their moral expectations, not changed radically? The war, as one veteran turned historian put it, had scorched the minds and character of a generation. To many the war had been a discovery of violence, a lust for violence even in their own selves, that nothing in the genteel, repressed world of before 1914 had prepared them for. "Most men, I suppose, have a paleolithic savage somewhere in them. . . . I have, anyway. . . . That's the beastliest thing in war, the damnable frivolity. One's like a merry, mischievous ape tearing up the image of god," wrote a gentle English scholar about his experience in the trenches. In other ways, too, that earlier world had been thoroughly discredited. It had been discredited by the bloody bungling of incompetence, by the failure of leadership, by the greed of war aims, and by the hollow claims of church and state. The rough "deference" for church, fatherland, and social superiors that still existed in

1914 was hopelessly compromised four years later. Superiors had been proven inferior, and the old notion that there was a rough equivalent between performance and reward, that there was a social order that made sense, this too had broken down. What was to take its place? What faith would claim the disillusioned? The immediate reaction of many was a hunger above all for peace and "normalcy," though not a few, particularly among the defeated peoples, thirsted for the renewed glories of military companionship. The war left a legacy of cynicism and skepticism as the dominant mood—and a spiritual thirst for action among others. The fascist spirit and the *squadristi* tactics were a legacy of war and revolution as well.

It is an ill wind that blows no good, and even Europe's worst catastrophe brought hope and betterment to some. The war hastened the development of egalitarian democracy and brought new benefits to long-suffering minorities. By the end of the war, nationalities long oppressed attained their independence. Independence, however, brought new problems in its train. Statehood for old minorities involved the creation of new minorities. Eastern Europe could not be neatly sorted out into different nation states, but probably there were fewer minorities with fewer grievances in 1919 than had existed in 1914. During the war, as nations became more and more dependent upon women's capabilities, women's rights were more generally acknowledged as well. Religious minorities were further assimilated into national societies, and cherished prejudices were suspended, at least for the duration. In Central Europe, for example, Jews, needed in wartime, were rewarded with greater privileges. The full integration of trade unions into national life greatly advanced the rights and expectations of labor. "A country fit for heroes" was Lloyd George's promise to the English, and the drabness of the postwar performance contrasted ill with the new deal that had everywhere been expected.

Europe had suffered too much to honor its pledges, to

satisfy the aroused expectations of millions of its citizens. By 1918, most parts of Europe were ready for some form of democratic socialism. The war had been a great leveler, and the Soviet Revolution had quickened hopes everywhere for greater equality. But the Bolsheviks had also split the European labor movement and had frightened the upper classes into still greater intransigence. Victor and vanquished alike were too enfeebled to build material conditions that would protect and promote the precarious stirrings of a new democracy. The war had not only immeasurably weakened the old order; it weakened the forces that could have built a new order as well.

After 1918, Europe succumbed to a new kind of international civil war. Victorious nations and ruling classes felt threatened and insecure while defeated or aggrieved peoples seethed with additional resentments. In that kind of climate, the rationality of imperfect democracy appealed less than the wild irrationality of fascism. Despite the resiliency of man, despite brave beginnings, Europe proved incapable of dealing with this tangled legacy of war and revolution, without first succumbing to another war that in its violence and terror surpassed even the tragedy of the Great War.

A Liberal Historian
and the War

Élie Halévy's
"The World Crisis of 1914–1918"

I first read Élie Halévy's "The World Crisis of 1914–1918"
as a student and have admired it ever since. It offers a new
perspective on the Great War and it suggests the absurdity
of studying diplomatic history in isolation from domestic
politics. In the early 1960's, I urged R. K. Webb to translate *L'ère des tyrannies*, of which "The World Crisis" is a
part. To his edition of *The Era of Tyrannies*, published in
New York in 1965, I was asked to contribute a note, here
reprinted with minor changes.

Élie Halévy was forty-four years old when the Great War broke
out. He was too old to fight, too austere a patriot and a philosopher to stay at home. He volunteered for the ambulance corps,
preferring the companionship of common soldiers to that of
Paris intellectuals who led the chorus of chauvinists. "In war-

time, if pacifistic eloquence sounds false, martial eloquence sounds falser still. At the present time, only one writer satisfies me and that is Joffre. The rest is, or should be, silence."[1]

Halévy had sensed the coming of the war and he quickly sensed its revolutionary character. His wartime letters to friends—moving testimony to an abiding patriotism tempered by wisdom—reveal his constant efforts to apprehend the meaning of the war. Gigantic issues had brought on the war, he thought, and these must be solved before the war could or should end. Anything less would signify only an armistice, and the slaughter would have to be resumed after a brief pause. In his published correspondence he did not identify these issues, and it may well be that they remained obscure in his own mind. All he knew was that the war marked a terrible *caesura* in the life of Europe, that that life would never be the same, that a new era was being born amidst the collective exertions and sufferings of the war. In March 1916, before any revolutionary movement had become visible anywhere, he wrote: "I always come back to my thesis. The day when Jaurès was assassinated and when the conflagration of Europe was lit, a new era opened in the history of the world. It is foolish to believe that in six months this could be extinguished, and that the same parties, the same groups, the same individuals could resume the same rhythm of their combinations as if nothing had happened in the interval. Don't make me say, in the fashionable style of the day, that Europe is going to emerge regenerated, purified by this baptism of fire. I say she will emerge changed; and I say that she is not at all near emerging from all this."[2]

Over a decade later, when for a fleeting moment Western Europe thought itself secure, as it had not since 1914 and as it has not since, Halévy, invited to deliver the Rhodes Lectures in

---

1. Halévy to Xavier Léon, Dec. 15, 1914, in Alain (Émile Chartier), *Correspondance avec Élie et Florence Halévy* (Paris, 1958), p. 343.
2. Halévy to Xavier Léon, March 24, 1916, in *ibid.*, p. 358.

Oxford, returned to the task of interpreting the war. In three deceptively simple lectures entitled "Towards War," "Towards Revolution," and "Towards War and Revolution," and published under the title *The World Crisis of 1914–1918: An Interpretation,* he presented a model of explanation which in its profundity and suggestiveness has never been rivaled. The lectures exemplified perfectly his historical method. By bold hypothesis and intelligent and honest marshaling of facts, he presented a new interpretation of an intractable subject.

The subject had become the most controversial of the post-war decade. The Treaty of Versailles had injected into European politics the issue of responsibility for the outbreak of the war; the war-guilt question intrigued historians and incited peoples. The search for alibis and culprits had become an all-consuming passion, especially among the defeated nations. What side had started the war, what nation, what statesmen? How to distribute the proper measure of responsibility? In this search, no one asked whether one was looking in the right places or asking the right questions. The race was on, and each man ran roughly over the same course.

As a consequence of this fascination with immediate origins, people lost sight of questions about the deeper forces that plunged Europe into war and determined the course and meaning of that war. They explained the causes of the war in categories that were either excessively concrete or excessively abstract. Historians fastened on the principal statesmen of the crisis of July 1914 and scrutinized their every move and telegram as if reality could be recovered by the more or less objective compilation of those minute facts. Marxists, on the other hand, insisted that the war was the necessary result of capitalistic contradictions and imperialist rivalries, while nationalists in every country blamed the war on the inherent rapacity of the opposing side. Historians were captivated by the ever swelling supply of available minutiae, as every major government published some of its prewar records. Other writers fell back on generalities of doctrine or expressions of resentment that would readily appeal to the already converted. The great tomes of historians and the impassioned outpourings of publicists provided little enlightenment to a generation that wanted to know what had happened to Europe during those catastrophic years.

Halévy offered an entirely different perspective. He abandoned the search for immediate causes because that search would never be able to uncover the nature of the war or its historic meaning. "The object of my study is the earthquake itself. I shall attempt to define the collective forces, the collective feelings and movements of public opinion, which, in the early years of the twentieth century, made for strife."[3] His hypothesis was that the strife of the prewar years exploded into the great war, and that once the war had started it consumed many of the remaining barriers to violent changes. In seeking to identify the forces making for strife, Halévy, true to his habitual style of analysis, pursued the social career of great ideas. Socialism in its many forms constituted the principal force making for revolution, and nationalism and the nationalist grievances in East-Central Europe the principal force making for war. The two forces, he argued, were closely related, and both were responsible for the outbreak of the war. The Austrian Empire was threatened by revolutionary nationalist agitation, and the European diplomats could neither banish the threat to Austria nor preserve the peace of Europe while a great power was in danger of disintegration. In the early stages of the war, the revolutionary forces within nations were contained; as the war dragged on, these forces became ever stronger, because they now added the urgent plea for peace to their older revolutionary aims.

3. Élie Halévy, *The Era of Tyrannies,* trans. by R. K. Webb with a note by Fritz Stern (Garden City, N.Y., 1965), pp. 210–11.

For Halévy there was no merit, then, in the prevailing, nostalgic view that a peaceful, stable Europe had been overwhelmed by the outbreak of the war which then raged senselessly until the energies of nations had been burned out. From his vantage point, the "good old days of before 1914" appeared as a foolish myth and an obstruction to right understanding.

He had wanted to study "the earthquake itself," and his metaphor helps us to understand the extraordinary scope of his interpretation. He had pointed to the deep stresses and strains that finally led to a series of eruptions called the world crisis. In this way, he illuminated the continuities between prewar and wartime society, but he also was one of the first to understand the discontinuity that the war had brought about. The very image of an earthquake suggests that while the tremors had built up for a long time, the final eruptions did create something new, even if the rubble did not at first allow a clear view of the new landscape.

His wartime letters and his later essay, "The Era of Tyrannies," clearly express what is only hinted at in "The World Crisis": the new order in Europe, which was characterized by an accommodation of socialism and nationalism, was built more on force than freedom. The war had left a terrible legacy of constraint, and the ever precarious balance between liberty and authority had tipped in favor of the latter. No wonder that he had singled out Jaurès's assassination as signaling the opening of a new era: in the world after 1914, the humane socialism of Jaurès was all but extinguished by the ruthless Soviet socialism and the equally ruthless national corporatism of Italy or national socialism of Germany.

His three lectures were beguilingly neat and modest. He did not celebrate his own originality by denigrating his predecessors. He had sketched a new interpretation which offered a unified explanation for the various phases of the war. In this new view the traditional distinction between diplomatic and political history, between a nation's external relations and internal order, lost relevance. The relationship between domestic and foreign politics has always been closer than historians have grasped; in Halévy's view the two are so closely intertwined that to separate them is to understand neither. In these lectures, he did not fully work out the many connections between the forces making for revolution and those making for war. Only in one case did he say that "it is legitimate for historians to ask, whether one of the reasons—we are far from saying the main reason—why the German military aristocracy decided, in July 1914, to run the risks of a great European war was not a growing sense of discomfort under the increasing pressure of Social Democracy, and a surmise that a bold attempt to give a set-back to socialism, by asserting themselves once more as the party of war and victory, might prove the wisest course."[4] It is likely indeed that this conscious or unconscious fear of revolution played a considerable role in the prewar conduct of foreign policy everywhere in Europe, and it seems incredible that questions of this sort have rarely even been asked by historians since Halévy.

Halévy's achievement has yet another dimension. Somewhat like Tocqueville in his work on the French Revolution, Halévy —who in his conservative defense of liberty, his austere moral outlook, and his astounding historical perspicacity resembles Tocqueville—discovered the underlying continuities between an *ancien régime* and a revolutionary upheaval. He lifted a recent historical process, which people were still treating politically and in isolation, to the level of past history. He connected the war with the great recognized stream of past events.

Today's reader may not at once recognize the novelty of Halévy's approach and insight. His interpretations of many details have finally filtered down to us and have become common coinage. It is worth recalling, however, that his interpre-

4. *Ibid.*, pp. 215–16.

tation of prewar socialism in Germany and of the impact on
Europe of the Russian Revolution of 1905, his comprehension
of the overshadowing importance of the year 1917 and his
sense of a kind of ideological rivalry between America and
Russia in 1917, were startlingly new when he delivered these
lectures.

We may be surprised, on the other hand, that Halévy said
relatively little about Germany's role in prewar Europe. Before
and during the war, he acknowledged the fact that her striving
for hegemony posed a threat to the established balance of
power, just as the France of Louis XIV had done two centuries
earlier. Germany's foolish and intermittently aggressive policy
before the war merely exacerbated the fears of her neighbors,
which were initially aroused by her mere strength and exist-
tence. Indicative of a more serious misreading, perhaps, is
Halévy's erroneous assertion that the world crisis came to an
end in August 1920, "when the last of the postwar treaties
was signed at Sèvres, when the Bolshevik army was defeated
in Poland, when an attempt at a Communist revolution in Italy
proved abortive, and the rise of Fascism began."[5] Halévy's
exceptional perspicacity failed him when he was first confronted with the phenomenon of Fascism. He saw in it at first
only a new form of *étatisme* and a new ideological mixture of
socialism and nationalism. Only later did he see that it embodied a power of unreason and hatred, more violent and dangerous than he had imagined possible. But his judgment in
1929 about the end of the world crisis reflected the happy glow
of the Locarno spirit. That spirit evaporated a year later, and
the world crisis reappeared in still uglier form. By 1936, he
warned that Fascist Italy and Nazi Germany "are narrowly
nationalist. They can offer us nothing but war."[6] The forces of
revolution and war were once more on the march.

The greatness of Halévy's lectures cannot be measured by

5. *Ibid.*, p. 245.
6. *Ibid.*, p. 277.

the accuracy or inaccuracy of details. The enduring value of these lectures lies in the totality of his vision, in the fact that every thought could have inspired a separate study, while the conception as a whole could lead to a better understanding of the world since 1900. Few historians have followed the path he laid out, preferring instead to tread familiar tracks or ruts. One of the reasons for this failure may have been the fact that, paradoxically, Halévy had gained more distance from the Great War, from violence and revolution, than any historian since. In the nearly forty years since he wrote these lectures, historians have lived with war and revolution and in their political engagement may not have found his detached and supra-national analysis to their taste or within their grasp. Perhaps we have now regained the necessary distance, and Halévy's lectures together with his other writings on contemporary history may help us to go back to the tasks which he long ago perceived.

Halévy had meant to be more than an historian's historian. In these lectures—as in much else he wrote—he had a moral purpose as well. "In looking for the 'causes' or 'responsibilities' of the War, not in the acts of individual statesmen, but in collective anonymous forces, against which individual statesmen were powerless," Halévy had meant to show that "the wisdom or folly of our statesmen is merely the reflection of our own wisdom or folly."[7] Hence every citizen shares political responsibility, and Halévy hoped to fortify that sense of civic virtue. In this, too, he was right. For the wars and revolutions of our time have been made possible not so much by a few leaders or sects as by the multitude of passive citizens who smugly thought that politics was the responsibility of statesmen.

7. *Ibid.,* p. 245.

German Historians and the War

Fischer and His Critics

Fritz Fischer's book on Germany's bid for world power during the First World War provoked instant controversy among German historians. The substance of that debate was important, as was the style. Most of the German participants fought their battles with great ferocity. Intrigue and innuendo quickly outpaced argument, and the scene allowed a close look at the practices of illiberalism.

The climax of the controversy came at the Berlin meeting of the German Historical Association in 1964. I was invited to speak to that session at which the Fischer affair was to be adjudicated. Four years later, I published my speech in *International Affairs*, adding a few paragraphs about the debate itself. I am here reprinting that version, with some minor changes. My speech was a *pièce d'occasion*, and I have not tried to convert it into a survey of the field of German imperialism and the First World War.

When Fritz Fischer's study of German war aims during the First World War appeared in 1961, it caused an immediate uproar and shattered the surface calm of the German historical guild. Fischer had dared to reopen the most explosive of all issues and had in fact launched a frontal attack on the long-cherished defense of Germany's essential moderation during that conflict. Backed by a massive array of new—and to the German cause, damaging—evidence, he presented a picture of aggressive imperialism, as it inspired both civilian and military leadership, both moderates and annexationists. Moreover, he hinted at the proposition that there was a continuity of German expansionist aims before, during, and indeed after the First World War until well into the Second World War. Implicitly this was a challenge to the comforting notion that the Third Reich was an historical aberration.

The reaction was violent. The older historians, many of whom had fought in the Great War, were appalled by the book's *Tendenz;* Gerhard Ritter, indefatigable master of the guild, led the attack on Fischer's method and conclusions. Some of the younger generation, though critical of details, rallied to its defense. By the spring of 1964, the attacks on Fischer had become shockingly personal. He was arraigned for faulty scholarship, but the impetus for the polemic came from injured patriotism. Fischer "was fouling his own nest," some charged, and his patriotism was impugned. A lecture trip to the United States, sponsored by an agency of the German government, was cancelled, and there was ample reason to suspect that his own colleagues had prompted the bureaucratic decision. American historians, myself included, then took over the sponsorship of the trip and came to the aid of Fischer, who had become a kind of Ralph Nader among German historians. In Germany, the polemics, vigorously pursued by both sides, continued.

In October 1964, the German Historical Association, at its triennial convention in Berlin, placed the controversy concerning German war aims on its agenda. The session, chaired by the wise and impartial Hans Herzfeld, took place in the Auditorium Maximum of the Free University before an impassioned audience of over one thousand listeners, whose boos and catcalls lent drama to the occasion. In fact, the atmosphere was as different from the conventional mode of scholarly debate as Fischer's book had been different from the traditional version of patriotic history. In some sense, both the book and the conduct of the audience bespoke a break with old mores and beliefs. Fischer's critics, notably Gerhard Ritter, Egmont Zechlin, and Erwin Hölzle, scored important points regarding particulars, while Fischer's side was defended only by himself and his two assistants. The last two speakers at the three-hour session were foreign historians, especially invited for the occasion: Professor Jacques Droz of the Sorbonne and myself. What follows is a compressed text of my remarks on that occasion, remarks that were given wide publicity by *Der Spiegel's* decision to publish them—without troubling to ask my permission. The meeting was widely reported in the press, and it was generally contended that the intervention of the two foreign historians on Fischer's behalf helped to dispel the polemical atmosphere that for so long had embittered the debate.

Politics and the writing of history have ever been closely connected, and this book by Professor Fischer seems to touch the most tender points of German political and historical consciousness. It is not easy for an outsider to take a position in such a profound controversy that touches the historical self-consciousness of a nation. I believe, however, that the present debate is one of the most decisive and most important moments in German historiography in the postwar period, and hence it would be wrong if I held back for reasons of tact.

In America, Professor Fischer's book did not at first cause

any controversy. American historians admired his comprehensive work in the archives and a few new documents took us by surprise, a few formulations appeared a bit strained, but the fundamental thesis of his book came as no particular surprise. American historiography had long before abandoned the revisionism of Harry Elmer Barnes or at least modified it through the perspectives offered by Bernadotte Schmitt, Luigi Albertini, Ludwig Dehio, and Hans Gatzke, and by sources such as the diaries of Admiral von Müller. American historians do not believe in the sole guilt of Germany for the outbreak of the First World War, and it occurred to no one in America that Professor Fischer wanted to advance that thesis. There had never been any doubt among us, however, that German war aims had been very far-reaching indeed. Only when the attacks on Fritz Fischer and his book mounted, when his lecture trip to America was canceled, suddenly and under dubious circumstances, when the *Frankfurter Allgemeine Zeitung* printed an attack against him, only then did we understand the explosive effect that his book had had. Only then did we realize with what different assumptions American and German historians viewed the period 1890 to 1933, although our historical understanding of the periods before 1890 and after 1933 coincided in most aspects. Only then did we realize that in Germany the main accent was being put on the weaknesses of Fischer's book, whereas we, recognizing these weaknesses, valued the achievement more.

The book touches on the most complicated and delicate questions of the German past. From now on this book will have to be reckoned with in any discussion of the character of the Wilhelmine Empire or of German imperialism, of the origins of the First World War or of German war aims. Professor Fischer raised—in part only hinted at—the question concerning the continuity of recent German history. Are the connections among *Weltpolitik* before 1914, the outbreak of the war, the direction of war aims, and the postwar period so clearly establishable that one dares speak of continuity? I would like to touch briefly on a few of these themes, particularly those that bear on the *Problematik* of historiography.

"Continuity" is the most problematical question put forward by Professor Fischer. But can this continuity be established by documents and quotations, as Professor Fischer attempts, or must not every utterance and every decision be considered in light of a given situation and the conduct of others? Professor Fischer's portrait of prewar Germany is perhaps somewhat one-sided, though on the basis of my own work I can only support his picture of pervasive imperialistic sentiments as well as his insistence upon the extraordinarily close ties between the economic and political realms. In my opinion, however, he underestimates the opposition to imperialism in Wilhelmine Germany: before 1914 the largest party in Germany, the Social Democratic Party, was still totally free of imperialist appetites, and among the bourgeois groups as well there were some who viewed Germany's yearning for a place in the sun with the greatest concern.

I would, in fact, suggest that it is this internal opposition that decisively influenced the style of German imperialism. If instead of speaking of the continuity of expansionist war aims, we were to speak of a continuity of mood, a continuity of the form and manner in which these aims were defended, propagated, and occasionally translated into political action, then we would probably recognize a continuity much more easily. In one of his important essays on this subject Professor Erwin Hölzle[1] has written about the style of imperialism; this style should be the subject of serious historical research. I believe that the German style would distinguish itself from that of the

---

1. Erwin Hölzle, "Das Experiment des Friedens im Ersten Weltkrieg 1914–1917," *Geschichte in Wissenschaft und Unterricht,* Vol. XIII, No. 8 (Aug., 1962), p. 520.

older imperialist powers, in part precisely because German leadership was afraid of the domestic foe. The style of German imperialism shows a rare combination of *Angst,* arrogance, and —in assessing the non-German world—political ignorance and insecurity. The dread of which I speak is not only the exaggerated dread of a great power in the heart of Europe surrounded by other, and perhaps, hostile powers, but it is also the dread of sections of one's own people. German imperialism confronted two enemies simultaneously: the enemy at home and the enemy abroad. This is perhaps most clearly reflected in the so-called Fatherland Party at the end of the war. If in July 1914 one already had to be very careful about internal opposition, if already during the war the fear of democratization and internal reform was by no means restricted to the Pan-Germans, then one can hardly wonder at the instantaneous appearance in 1918 of the stab-in-the-back legend and of charges of high treason. Perhaps the style of political thought and action represents the continuity that is only hinted at in the documents. What we need are studies on how important groups and leading men conceived of Germany's future, how they conceived of *imperium,* what they thought of other nations and the relations among them. What were their often unspoken premises about human behavior? Did the Germans have confidence in their political abilities, did they see in their midst empire-builders like Lyautey or Cromer? Or did they think of Empire in rather vague generalities, with a more or less conscious reliance on force not as the last but the only recourse? It is not my aim even to sketch the main aspects of this style: to do justice to that kind of theme one would need more time as well as the empathy of a Huizinga and the political perspicaciousness of a Dehio.

Still, there are those who deny that Germany ever bid for world power and who contend that Fischer's formulation and defense of this thesis exaggerate Germany's planning and conscious striving for world power. It has often been asserted that German policy before and during the war was of a defensive character. This may indeed have been the opinion of German leaders at the time. But dread can be an even more dangerous motive of expansion than cold-blooded calculation of conquest. Out of dread before enemies that were getting ever stronger, Bethmann Hollweg may have led the German people into the war; out of the same dread he may have striven for the war aims of 1914 and a German position of hegemony in Europe.[2] *Angst* leads not to circumspect action but to a blurred perspective, to irrational and impulsive action, to what might be called self-fulfilling prophecies of disaster.

A case in point was the widespread belief in Germany that the country was being encircled at a time when the Triple Entente was in no way firmly constituted. Professor Ritter referred to "a [German] miscalculation which borders on blindness," in connection with July 1914; this term might more generally be applied to the consistent miscalculations of Germany's prewar policy. This chronic blindness, this false estimation of oneself and others, demands an historical explanation. The terrible decline from Bismarck's realistic statecraft cannot be explained simply by the absence of genius. This blindness, I believe, is connected with the whole structure of German society, with its internal conflicts, and with the style of its governing classes. This same blindness was responsible for the utopian idea that so many leading Germans embraced during the war, i.e., that this must be the last war—as if Germany could have won a victory so decisive that the other world powers would have been forced to accept its domination. The notion of "a last war" sounds defensive, even pacifistic; actually it was bellicose and represented a total misunderstanding of the conditions of the European state system.

Let me briefly turn to the controversial "war guilt question."

2. See Chapter 4.

I have already said that American historians do not believe in Germany's sole responsibility, and that we did not interpret this book as making such an allegation. We have assumed for years, however, that in July 1914 the German government had resolved to use the murder at Sarajevo not only to strengthen Austria's deteriorating position, but to improve Germany's own position and to destroy the Entente. In this connection, one thinks of Bethmann's remark of July 8: "If the war does not come, if the Czar does not want it, or France, thoroughly bewildered, counsels peace, then we still have prospects of breaking up the Entente through this action."[3] In July 1914, German policy embarked on a forward course and was ready to accept a great risk; in this connection, too, one should study not only the documents of the other nations involved, but also consider the patterns of thought and the style of the leading groups in Germany. Before 1914 all nations accepted war as an *ultima ratio,* but Riezler was quite right when he spoke of the "authentically German, idealistic belief that the German people needed a war."[4] According to Riezler, Bethmann shared this belief. The idea of war as salvation and as liberation from social and cultural abuses had currency among various writers of other countries as well, but hardly among the leaders of other nations at the time. This idea played a great role in the exultation of August 1914, but that the German Chancellor should have had it even before the war is indeed remarkable. Such nonpolitical factors must also be considered—and they are perhaps not adequately emphasized in Professor Fischer's book. In most cases they would sustain his theses.

I know that one cannot prove the correctness of a view by the absurdity of its antithesis. Still, I would like to refer to a

3. Karl Dietrich Erdmann, "Zur Beurteilung Bethmann Hollwegs," *Geschichte in Wissenschaft und Unterricht,* Vol. XV, No. 9 (Sept., 1964), p. 536.

4. *Ibid.,* p. 534.

recently published account of the origins of the war. The argument runs thus: the murder at Sarajevo occurred at a time when Europe suffered from other tensions that were due to three factors, i.e., Serbian aspirations to establish a great Serbian state, Pan-Slavism in Russia, and *revanchisme* in France. Germany, so this argument continues, had no need to strive for a position of world power: "it already was a world power." It had no territorial ambitions and nobody in Vienna or Berlin thought of war. This view is tantamount to the declaration of Germany's sole innocence. This picture may seem a caricature that I invented, but I am in fact recapitulating an argument advanced in July 1964 by one of the leading historians of the Federal Republic[5] in the *Deutsche Korrespondenz,* destined for foreign distribution.

Let me say one more word concerning the fundamental question of continuity. Perhaps Professor Fischer has construed this continuity too narrowly in *Germany's Aims in the First World War.* Some aspects of foreign policy, however—Germany's *Ostpolitik,* for example, from before 1914 until 1945—strongly suggest the notion of continuity. Can one really doubt that Germany's ambitious war aims and her revolutionary war measures to attain them intended to give Germany a position in Europe that would make it a world power equal to other world powers? Can one deny that the inflamed nationalism, the hatred of former enemies that dominated Germany between the two wars, derived from the people's disappointment that instead of scoring utopian successes they had been forced to accept the Peace of Versailles which, to boot, was usually depicted as more draconian than it really was? Indeed, one *must* reckon with the continuity of mood and hopes, for otherwise one cannot understand the sad history of Weimar. Perhaps Professor Fischer has strained the continuity thesis, but the counter-thesis which posits that all the miscalculations and derailments of

5. Walther Hubatsch.

German policy in the twentieth century were but accidents (*Betriebsunfälle*) is still less satisfactory. Is it in fact possible to have a series of accidents without coming to the surmise that there may be something wrong in the whole enterprise? (*Gibt es überhaupt so etwas wie eine Folge von Betriebsunfällen, ohne dass man auf den Gedanken kommt, dass in dem Betrieb etwas nicht stimmt?*) Is the continuity of intentions and hopes, of style and aims, not altogether amazing?

The great English historian Sir Lewis Namier once said that "the crowning attainment of historical study is a historical sense—an intuitive understanding of how things do not happen. . . ." If one applies this wise standard to the question concerning the outbreak of the war, then one will realize that Fischer's exposition is possible and its opposite entirely impossible. If we apply this standard to all of Fischer's theses, we would not be driven to conclude that history could not have happened in this way.

Of course it would have been better if Professor Fischer had taken account of the war aims of Germany's enemies. But material concerning Allied war aims was insufficiently available and, furthermore, German war aims depended more on German prewar conceptions and on a given military situation than on the goals of the Entente. The dialogue among the belligerent nations had ceased.

In conclusion, let me briefly say something about the relation of this book to the discipline of history. True originality in our field is usually achieved either through the discovery of new sources or through a systematic reinterpretation of known sources. It is rare for an historian to do both at the same time. I think Fischer did combine these two ways. Theodor Mommsen once spoke of the historian's "stroke which forges a thousand links." Was Fischer's book such a stroke perhaps?

Some have attacked the book for making wrong connections —perhaps with justification. But is not every new historiographical thesis formulated too sharply and too one-sidedly when first advanced? The French historian Mathiez, the English historian Namier, and the Americans Beard and Hofstadter all formulated their fundamentally new theses too sharply—content to introduce modifications and clarifications at a later time or through their successors. All disciplines need shocking stimuli occasionally.

We can, indeed we must, criticize, clarify, and differentiate some of Professor Fischer's theses. But should we not first of all express our grateful recognition to Professor Fischer for his new perspective? How fruitful and stimulating his perspective is seems demonstrated by the discussion that his book engendered. Perhaps one should also acknowledge that it took greater courage to present new perspectives on this subject than on a less sensitive subject.

Clearly this book would not have produced such a public storm had it not touched the tragic complex of events of the recent past. In the debate on Fritz Fischer's work there is more at stake than the clash of historical opinions. Professor Ritter's words concerning this book are moving: "Thus I cannot lay down this book without deep sorrow: sorrow and concern in view of the coming generation." Can one relieve or absolve the coming generation of this problematical past? Must not that generation learn to understand historically the truth of Dehio's warning: " . . . the prerequisite for any really creative German response after the period of the two World Wars is the unconditional recognition of the terrible role that we have played in this period. We were the last, and the most daemonic, power to exercise hegemony over the declining old continent of Europe." It is precisely the duty of the historian to help youth attain this creative reaction. The young should at least have the consolation and the satisfaction of knowing that the tragic history of the last fifty years was grasped by German historiography, and that modern historiography, which has always been closely connected with German thought, was adequate to deal even with this infinitely difficult task.

Since 1964, the debate concerning war aims has spread more widely but has lost most of its political intensity. German historians have gradually assimilated Fischer's views, and some have added valuable refinements to his original thesis. Fischer himself has sharpened rather than modified his views, and in some instances has moved to the very positions that his critics originally and at that time wrongly attacked him for propounding. His book is now available in many languages, including Japanese, and, as James Joll rightly says in his introduction to the English edition, it should stimulate further investigation of the war-aims questions in all belligerent countries. The total impact of Fischer's book has been to realign German and non-German historical thought concerning the era of the Great War, and in this way Fritz Fischer has helped to overcome an unfortunate rift, the origins of which he sketched in his pioneering work.

Part Three

From Weimar to Bonn

Adenauer in Weimar

The Man and the System

In 1957, I reviewed Paul Weymar's authorized biography of Adenauer which contained Adenauer's own notes about his attempt to form a government in 1926. Adenauer's account, at once intriguing and inadequate, aroused my curiosity and led me to consult the unpublished Stresemann *Nachlass,* which had just then become available. This, in turn, led me to other unpublished sources, and the result was this article, published in 1958, and here reprinted, essentially unchanged, except for expanded footnotes. In the latter I call attention to the abundant literature that has appeared in the intervening years. The new evidence, while not contradicting my findings, offers much more detail than I could furnish. I would write the article differently today, but include it here as a study in the political milieu of Weimar.

Born in defeat, humiliated by Versailles, mocked and violated by its irreconcilable enemies at home, the Weimar Republic never gained the popular acceptance which alone could have given its parliamentary system permanence, even in crisis. The upper classes, unreconciled to the passing of the old Wilhelmine order, regarded the Republic as an unworthy and potentially dangerous successor to the monarchy. The aristocracy resented the loss of its predominant position and the bourgeoisie lamented what they now remembered as their secure, comfortable, untroubled existence of before the war. Both groups might have accepted a conservative republic if it had not also been democratic, even socialistic; they might have accepted a democratic regime if the monarchy had remained to restrain it. As it was, they felt alien in the new Republic, the more so for the fact that the hitherto alienated, the lower classes, having attained political equality, were now aspiring to the privileges of culture and leisure that had traditionally been the monopoly of the few.

Throughout Weimar the legitimacy of the Republic was a subject of debate and division; the virtue of the Republic was proclaimed by some, vilified by others, taken for granted by none. If German democracy had been a daily plebiscite, the result would have been a daily manifestation of the most profound and embittered division.

The past, in other words, dominated and divided the present, and the absence of a common historical consciousness of the recent past—of the defeat and the revolution—intensified all the hatreds and resentments that afflicted a defeated and impoverished Germany. Just as the mounting conflicts of material interests sharpened existing class antagonisms, so the postwar mood of defiance and disillusionment, the cynical debunking of all the old proprieties, hardened the intellectual and sentimental differences separating the several classes of Germany. Because of a deep, though not disinterested, nostalgia for an idealized past, because of a traditional disdain for politics and social egalitarianism, the upper classes, as well as a high proportion of ministers, teachers, and bureaucrats, remained aloof from the Republic, and mistook their unfriendly attitude for a noble kind of nonpolitical idealism.

Still, Weimar had the inestimable advantage of existing—and that gave it a presumption of survival. Between 1924 and 1929, the Republic even enjoyed an apparent period of prosperity and stability. The wave of terrorist assassinations and *Putsches* seemed spent, the Allied forces were gradually withdrawn from the Ruhr and the Rhineland, and American capital flowed into the country. But even in its halcyon days, the deep divisions, the hatreds, and the ensuing political instability persisted.

How feeble and divided Weimar really was, how the basic issue of republicanism would inject itself and poison every parliamentary crisis, how the past and the future cast their shadows over Weimar's middle years and prevented the forming of any kind of political consensus—all this appears in microcosmic form in the sudden, unexpected, and thoroughly gratuitous cabinet crisis of May 1926. Outwardly not much happened: one more cabinet had been toppled and another, just like it, was formed. But in the brief interval between governments all the perplexing difficulties of Weimar, all the obstacles to an enduring parliamentary system came to the fore, and suggested that underneath the often frivolous factiousness lay deeper fissures which ultimately could bring about the destruction of the Republic. The course of that crisis, which is the subject of this article, strengthens one's sense of doom about Weimar, and yet in its unfolding it offered a fleeting prospect of reversibility—a tantalizing reminder that even Weimar had its lost opportunities. One of the minor human "ifs" of Weimar must surely be the pros-

pect that Adenauer, this conservative democrat, this statesman of exceptional stature and courage, might have become
Chancellor in 1926.[1]

It was characteristic of Weimar that a seeming triviality—the
government's attempt to alter the disposition of the national
colors—should lead at once to an eruption of the struggle
between republicans and anti-republicans and to the government's overthrow. It was equally characteristic that Weimar's
official flag was a symbol of national discord, not of national
unity.

The flag dispute was one of the legacies of the November
Revolution and the National Assembly of Weimar. With their
habitual mixture of doctrinaire zeal and political timidity, the
Left republicans of the Assembly decided to abandon the
national flag that Bismarck had invented for Imperial Germany
—the black-white-and-red—and to put in its place the liberal
tricolor of the *Vormärz* and of 1848—the black-red-and-gold.
At the same time, they agreed that the old imperial colors, with
the republican colors added in a small inset, should become the
official merchant flag, because, so the argument ran, the gold
could not be easily distinguished at sea. Accordingly Article III
of the Weimar Constitution prescribed two flags for Germany—a reflection of past division and a provocation to new
antagonism.

In April 1921, President Ebert issued an administrative
decree, providing for no less than ten variations of these two

1. Weimar had more than its share of human contingency. It has often
been remarked that the German Republic lost many of its responsible leaders
by their accidental or early deaths: Ebert, Erzberger, Rathenau, Stresemann,
even Helfferich. It may be ungracious to add that the unnatural longevity of
others—Hindenburg, Ludendorff, and Tirpitz, for example—did quite as
much to weaken German democracy. Under Weimar, death itself was anti-
republican.

basic colors, including a special flag for the postal service. The basic conflict continued to be between imperial and republican flags, and throughout Weimar these two flags remained in competition with each other.[2] The extreme Right wing carried on its terrorist work under the defiant sign of the old flag. Even moderate republicans had a sentimental longing for the symbol of the old order, and certainly a man like Hindenburg, despite his grudging display of the constitutional flag, was genuinely attached only to the old. The same was true of the millions of Germans abroad who had always associated German power and protection with the old flag, and who habitually hoisted it, even when the local consular authorities used the new, republican flag. The republicans, on the other hand, timid and uncertain, were afraid of any tampering with their flag. It was the government's inept attempt to resolve this conflict and conciliate some of the discontented groups that brought about yet another crisis in the unstable parliamentary order.

By virtue of the multi-party system, not only the doctrinal conflict over the existence of the Republic, but also all the antagonisms of German society—confessional, material, regional—were reproduced in parliament, and obstructed, even paralyzed, its proper functioning. During most of the Republic the two largest parties found themselves in opposition, encouraged in this by their extreme opponents who rejoiced at their self-imposed isolation: the Socialists left the Stresemann government in 1923, and the Nationalists [*Deutschnationale Volkspartei*], unable to swallow Locarno, walked out of the first Luther government in 1925. Thereafter it was possible to govern only through the temporary minority governments of

2. Echoes of this conflict could be heard even under the Bonn regime, which recognized only the republican flag. Before a decision allowing German soldiers to wear their Second World War medals, without the swastika, there was a vigorous debate in parliament whether the ribbons should carry the imperial or the republican colors. Over the opposition of the Socialists, the old won out. For the revealing debate, see *Das Parlament*, July 3, 1957.

the middle parties—the Democrats, Center, and People's Party. The spectacle of a weak and uncertain political authority, ever on the brink of crisis, confirmed and emboldened the contemptuous anti-republicans of the Right.

The second Luther Cabinet was organized in January 1926, after two months of protracted efforts to restore a great coalition government—from Socialists to People's Party—had been frustrated by the uncompromising Socialist demand for a return to the eight-hour day. In the end, Hindenburg called on the former Chancellor Luther, a remarkably uninspiring and uninspired conservative bureaucrat, who was without party affiliation or even a seat in the Reichstag, to form another minority government.[3]

The survival of the Luther Cabinet depended on the alternating support of the Socialists and the Nationalists.[4] In most instances, the Socialists obliged, and on Socialist sufferance the Luther government staggered along, despite the sharp increase in unemployment and despite Stresemann's reversals in Geneva, where for petty and humiliating reasons Germany's admission to the League had been postponed. The government survived even the Socialist and Communist agitation in favor of the expropriation of former dynastic property, which in early May

---

3. From 1918 to 1922, Luther had been Lord Mayor of Essen. Many of the prominent politicians of Weimar—Luther, Adenauer, Jarres, Koch-Weser, Gessler—came to national politics from careers in local or provincial administration, a tribute to the one persistently successful political tradition in Germany. At the time of the Adenauer candidacy, the *Berliner Tageblatt* remarked: "All our politicians are born mayors, and all our mayors are born politicians." (May 15, 1926.)

4. Out of a total of 493 Reichstag deputies, the government could count on no more than 171 supporters (the Center had 69 deputies, the Bavarian People's Party 19, the People's Party 51, and the Democrats 32). The Socialists had 131 deputies, the Communists 45, the Nationalists 103, and the Nazis 14. The rest belonged to splinter parties. For an excellent analysis of the political structure of Weimar's middle years, see Michael Stürmer, *Koalition und Opposition in der Weimarer Republik 1924–1928* (Düsseldorf, 1967). This particular episode is discussed on pp. 146–51.

1926, these two parties, in unaccustomed unison, were getting ready to submit to a popular referendum. Its fall was brought about from within, by Luther and Hindenburg, who, with Stresemann's sanction, drafted a new flag decree and thus reopened at a most inopportune time a troublesome and intractable issue.

On April 20, Chancellor Luther wrote to Stresemann suggesting that Hindenburg, on the occasion of his much-heralded visit to Hamburg on May 4, should issue a presidential decree ordering all German diplomatic missions abroad to fly not only the official republican flag, but the merchant flag as well. After legal experts had assured him of the constitutionality of the decree, Stresemann concurred, although he anticipated "political difficulties." Moreover, he "entirely agreed with the suggestion that the President should on this occasion express the wish that Germans overseas should henceforth fly the German merchant flag on their houses as well."[5] On May 1, after considerable debate, the cabinet unanimously agreed to the projected decree.[6]

Still, sometime between the first and the fifth of May, the government seems to have taken fright at its own boldness. Hindenburg made his great tour of Hamburg, but the decree was not issued. Outsiders may have cautioned the government.[7]

5. Gustav Stresemann, *Vermächtnis: Der Nachlass in drei Bänden,* ed. by Henry Bernhard, with the collaboration of W. Goetz and P. Wiegler, Vol. II (Berlin, 1932–3), p. 389. Stresemann, though scrupulously loyal to the new flag, was at heart a partisan of the old. More than a year after the flag debate, he noted with regret that there were so few "people who would vote for the restoration of the black-white-and-red flag—like myself." *Ibid.,* Vol. III, p. 278.

6. Cabinet Protocols, Alte Reichskanzlei, German Foreign Ministry documents, in the National Archives, Vol. 65, Container 1838, Frames D 768612-3.

7. Among them was Ulrich Rauscher, German ambassador in Warsaw, who had been told of the projected decree a few days before by Stresemann. In a "strictly confidential" letter to Stresemann, on May 3, Rauscher warned "that the choice of time . . . appears unfortunate." Abroad, where admittedly foreigners were accustomed to the old flag, "it is not difficult to interpret the re-introduction of the old flag for the German missions as a deliberate and

At a ministers' conference on May 5, Dr. Külz, the Democratic Minister of the Interior, reported that Centrists and Democrats were developing "strong resistance to the projected decree." The Chancellor recommended a return to an earlier compromise, whereby the new decree would apply only to non-European areas and to those European cities outside Germany that were accessible to merchant ships. Otto Meissner, Hindenburg's *Staatssekretär,* "emphasized that the President would be unlikely to approve of such a distinction and that he would not give in." Luther declared he would talk to the President, who apparently did give in.[8] Still, the opposition's charge that the flag decree was another instance of unwarranted presidential interference had far more justification than contemporaries knew.

On May 6, the morning papers announced that Hindenburg had signed the flag decree the night before; henceforth all German diplomatic and consular missions outside Europe, and those in European cities that were accessible to merchant ships, were to hoist the merchant flag as well as the official Reich flag.

---

bragging sign of Germany's regained status as a great power, and as an emphatic end to the 'Versailles episode,' i.e., of a condition that unfortunately but understandably has not yet been attained." Rauscher urged instead a genuine compromise, including "respect for the home flag inside the home boundaries." He predicted that the extreme Right would oppose the decree— as a surrender of the hallowed flag to the Republic. Stresemann Papers, microfilm at Columbia University, Vol. 37, Reel 3145, Frames H 161431-7.

8. Cabinet Protocols, *Alte Reichskanzlei,* Vol. 65, Container 1839, Frames D 768743–4. In his memoirs, significantly entitled *Politiker ohne Partei,* Luther claims that the flag decree had been his initiative, not Hindenburg's. He had been prompted to make the change by pressure from abroad—and even in retrospect he had no regrets about introducing the measure at that time or in that form. The psychological finesse he lacked in 1926 he seems not to have acquired in old age. Hans Luther, *Politiker ohne Partei* (Stuttgart, 1960), pp. 412, 417–18. Andreas Dorpalen, *Hindenburg and the Weimar Republic* (Princeton, 1964), pp. 104–6, stresses Hindenburg's passivity during the May crisis, while Michael Stürmer, *op. cit.,* pp. 149–51, confirms my impression that Hindenburg and Meissner put great pressure on the recalcitrant ministers and coalition parties.

The republicans responded swiftly and violently.[9] The decree was unconstitutional, they charged, because it altered the Constitution without observing the prescribed constitutional procedure, and it was anti-republican because it infringed on the republican symbol. So strong was their outcry that it seemed unlikely that the Chancellor, who had had to countersign the decree, would be able to survive.

That same afternoon, the Socialist veteran, Scheidemann, speaking to the Reichstag on the question of expropriating dynastic property, denounced the government's action as an obvious "anti-republican demonstration." With great gusto he vilified the old imperial dynasty and ridiculed his parliamentary opponents.[10] The decree, he said, would be the subject of a full-scale Socialist interpellation: "We cannot tolerate a Chancellor who dares to play in this fashion with what is sacred to the German Republic."[11]

During the next few days, news and rumors about the onrushing crisis dominated the papers and pushed aside the other important news—the British general strike and the final crisis of Polish democracy. In the country at large the republicans organized mass protests; in Berlin alone, twenty thousand mem-

9. Theodor Wolff, the editor of the influential *Berliner Tageblatt,* summed up exasperated republican feeling: "With us Germans, if no great stupidity is committed for ten days we can be sure that on the eleventh a formidable one will see the light of day." (May 6, 1926.) The official Socialist paper *Vorwärts* carried the news already on May 5 and commented: "The flag decree is incompatible with the spirit of the Constitution."

10. His attacks were no less resented for the kernel of truth they contained. His apt remark, for example, "Oh God, on the 9th of November, 1918, they all preferred to be live republicans instead of dying monarchists," must have wounded greatly. *Verhandlungen des Reichstags,* 195th session, Vol. 390 (Berlin, 1926), p. 7034.

11. *Ibid.* The Chancellor, of course, had not thought he was playing with anything that was sacred. The unpolitical Luther thought—or pretended to think—that the whole matter was a bagatelle, an administrative and not a political matter. As the Center's *Germania* wrote on May 6: "We would like to see the decree which the politically color-blind Mr. Luther would consider politically important." Quoted in *Berliner Tageblatt,* May 7, 1926.

bers of the republican guard, the *Reichsbanner Schwarz-rot-gold,* were mobilized and belligerently proclaimed republican solidarity. The leaders of the *Reichstag Fraktionen,*[12] who would decide the future of the government, moved a good deal more cautiously. This suggests once again that Weimar may have had far greater support among the people than among the leaders, most of whom had inherited and were still bound by the forms and fears of the deferential *ancien régime.* What angered the Reichstag leaders even more than the substance of the decree was the fact that none of them, not even the leaders of the government parties, had been consulted before its promulgation—another instance of the frequent tension between government members and parliamentary leaders of the same party.[13] Despite these hesitations, it became increasingly clear that the government would not be able to ride out the storm.

In order to shore up the regime, Hindenburg, on May 9, sent Luther an open letter, intended to be conciliatory.[14] Germany's comeback in the world economy, he wrote, "demands a more vigorous participation of all Germans abroad and their enthusi-

12. *Fraktion:* all the Reichstag deputies of one particular party.

13. Nor had the government consulted the *Reichsrat,* and on May 10, the Socialist Prime Minister of Prussia, Otto Braun, formally protested to Hindenburg that in the matter of the flag decree the constitutional prerogatives of the *Reichsrat* had been ignored. The Reich government maintained that the decree had been a purely administrative matter and that hence it had not exceeded its competence. Otto Braun, *Von Weimar zu Hitler* (2nd edn., New York, 1940), pp. 188–91. Stürmer, *op. cit.,* p. 148, stresses the previous suspicions that Luther had stirred up: " . . . the [government] parties did not regard the flag decree so much as a unique instance but rather as the culmination of an authoritarian and downright anti-parliamentary attitude on the part of the Chancellor."

14. Stresemann and Meissner seem to have drafted the letter. *Cf.* the memorandum of Henry Bernhard, Stresemann's private secretary, of May 8, regarding a phone call from Meissner who reported that the President had agreed to write the Chancellor in the sense agreed upon by Meissner and Stresemann. As motto Meissner cited: "Ebert gave the German people the *Deutschlandlied,* Hindenburg wants to take steps to give Germany a uniform flag." Stresemann Papers, Vol. 281, Reel 3100, Frame H 149643.

astic expression of loyalty to Germany at all public affairs."[15] This, the President feared, was being frustrated by the "unhappy flag dispute," which the decree sought to resolve. "Nothing is further from my mind, as I have repeatedly told you, than to remove the constitutionally established national colors." But "this recurrent flag conflict, fraught with danger and disaster," must be ended through a conciliatory compromise, achieved by constitutional means. "That this compromise will fit the contemporary Germany and its goals and at the same time do justice to the origin and history of the Reich is my most devout wish." The Chancellor was instructed to consult with the legislative bodies and other representative groups in order to attain these ends: "May the time not be far distant when the German people will again harmoniously rally around one and the same symbol of its political existence."[16] Far from assuaging the republicans, the President's letter strengthened their suspicion that the flag decree was the first installment in a presidential plot to effect a final, anti-republican solution of the flag problem.

On May 10, the cabinet met again and Luther reported that the Democrats would not oppose the Socialist motion of censure. Stresemann, obviously afraid of a crisis, sought to impress on the recalcitrant Democrats that a fall of the cabinet or a failure of the flag decree might lead to a presidential crisis, "even if he [Hindenburg] should hold out at his post," which, Stresemann added, he considered unlikely.[17] He warned the

15. The solicitude of the conservative Germans, and of Stresemann in particular, for these overseas Germans was extraordinary and suggests that this was a more or less peaceful afterglow of prewar imperialist fervor.

16. *Deutscher Geschichtskalender,* ed. by F. Purlitz and S. H. Steinberg, 42nd Year, Vol. I, Part A, January–June 1926 (Leipzig, n.d.), p. 17.

17. Hindenburg, of course, was an old hand at this game of threatening to resign in order to buttress his personal power. The Hindenburg-Ludendorff wartime dictatorship used precisely that weapon in order to browbeat and silence all opposition. The *Vorwärts* of May 9 reported rumors of a possible resignation by the President and correctly noted that this threat, used in this instance to intimidate the republicans, had been heard too often and hence had lost its sting.

Democrats that if they should bring about the fall of the Luther government, his party would find it difficult to join them in another cabinet of the middle parties.[18]

On the next day the Reichstag debate began, and the republican Left attacked the decree which it thought a blow against the Republic, a reactionary reconnoitering by the soldier-president whose loyalties had always been suspect. Rudolf Breitscheid, representing the Socialists, introduced a motion of no confidence and declared: "We have the impression that in the recent past it has become governmental practice to push parliament more and more into the background and to treat it with an intentional or unintentional condescension."[19] In rebuttal the Chancellor sought to squelch all fear of further Right-wing moves and hinted that the need for the simultaneous introduction of the new flag everywhere might delay the execution of the decree. This did not appease the Left, but rather incited Count Westarp, the leader of the German Nationalists, to ridicule the government's timidity and to demand immediate implementation.[20] The Center—that chameleon of Weimar politics—pushed forward one of its most stalwart republicans, a former worker, Johann Giesberts. Bravely straddling the fence, Giesberts pronounced his party's loyalty to the past— "we want to cherish the [imperial] tradition"—as well as to the Republic: "I want it understood that we who are loyal to the Constitution are loyal to the colors that the Constitution

18. Cabinet Protocols, Alte Reichskanzlei, Vol. 65, Container 1839, Frames D 768784–90.

19. But surely this kind of usurpation was facilitated, indeed invited, by the Socialists' pathetic vacillation between cooperation and opposition, between being a party of parliamentary compromise and a party of proletarian purity.

20. Characteristic of Weimar parliamentary manners were the catcalls during the debate. When Count Westarp said there was no particular need for the simultaneous introduction of the new flag everywhere, the Left shouted, "Honolulu! Liberia!" and the Nazis retorted, "Don't forget Palestine!" This was thought very funny by the entire house. *Verhandlungen des Reichstags,* 199th session, p. 7168.

prescribed and we shall fight resolutely against any attempt to obscure or ignore the national colors." Although critical of the government's action, the Center would nevertheless refrain from overthrowing the government.

Stresemann's party was squarely behind the government: "The overwhelming majority of the Germans abroad is for the black-white-and-red," and among these were counted the 35 million Germans who had accepted foreign citizenship.[21] Like Luther, the People's Party thought that German profits and prestige would be enhanced by the return of the old flag. The day's debate ended with the Chancellor's promise that the decree would be implemented by the end of July—a delay that infuriated the Nationalists without conciliating the Socialists. The fate of the cabinet now depended on the Democrats, and it was generally assumed that they should oppose and thus overthrow the government.

During the night the government, or at least the Foreign Minister, thought that the Reich was being threatened from quite a different quarter. In his Reichstag speech Giesberts had alluded to subversive "developments in the Reich that were of the greatest importance to the security of the state." Alarmed by the widespread rumors of a projected Right-wing *coup d'état,* Stresemann at 11:30 P.M. telephoned the Assistant Commissioner of Police in Berlin, Ferdinand Friedensburg, who told him that a plot had indeed been discovered and its main outlines pieced together. The *Putschists* had planned to abolish the Constitution, dismiss Hindenburg and replace him by a *Reichsverweser* who in turn would appoint sub-regents for the individual *Länder* and would thus rule as a dictator. As for the means by which they sought to seize power, Friedensburg specified that they hoped to capture Berlin, "in collaboration with elements of the *Reichswehr,*" and for the rest planned to use emergency decrees. The conspirators belonged to the

21. For the complete parliamentary debate, see *ibid.,* pp. 7153–85.

so-called patriotic societies and looked for leadership to the former Pan-German chief, Dr. Class, as well as to the mayor of Lübeck, Neumann, and to Hugenberg, who two years later was to become the leader of the German Nationalists.[22] Afraid that "we [were] in immediate danger of a great internal catastrophe, which fortunately had been averted," Stresemann urged Friedensburg: "Well, crack down on them [*Na, greifen Sie nur ordentlich durch*], and if you run into difficulties about parliamentary immunity, I will intercede with my *Fraktion* for a suspension of immunity."[23] Later that night, the Prussian police, that bulwark of the republicans, did crack down and searched innumerable homes, including those of some leading Ruhr industrialists. The evidence they confiscated suggested that the *coup d'état* had not been imminent. The *Putschists*, it appeared, planned to strike at the time of a real or staged Communist uprising in order to establish a Right-wing dictatorship. For weeks after these nocturnal raids, the Prussian government, and Braun and Severing in particular, were vilified by the Right

22. This cast must have sounded familiar to Stresemann, and he immediately expatiated to Friedensburg on Hugenberg's villainy. On January 22, 1926, two leaders from the *Jungdeutsche Orden,* Artur Mahraun and Otto Bornemann, talked with Stresemann, and Mahraun said that "he had refused all collaboration with these circles—he mentioned Hugenberg, Klass [*sic*], and Major Nicolai, because he wanted a reasonable national policy, not political adventures." In the context Mahraun even suggested that Hugenberg and Class might be the undercover central organization of National Bolshevism—an unlikely charge, but indicative of Hugenberg's repute. German Foreign Ministry files, Office of State Secretary Schubert, microfilm in the National Archives, Vol. 5, Reel 2282, Frames E 137254–7.

23. See Friedensburg's memorandum of June 5, Stresemann Papers, Vol. 38, Reel 3145, Frames H 161760–1; also Stresemann's own notes in *Vermächtnis,* Vol. II, pp. 401–6. Ferdinand Friedensburg, *Lebenserinnerungen* (Frankfurt and Bonn, 1969), pp. 160–73, gives a rather detailed picture of this episode. He stressed the fact that the Right was extraordinarily cohesive in its anti-republican efforts and had close access to Hindenburg, while his own efforts to strengthen the unity of the Left proved futile. Dorpalen, *op. cit.,* p. 103, believes that Hindenburg knew but vaguely what the conspirators had in mind: "From what he did learn, he seems to have dissociated himself—in his indecisive way that left all doors at least half-open."

for these precautionary steps. After it became known that Stresemann had sanctioned the police action, he, too, came under heavy attack, especially from those Ruhr industrialists of his own party whose houses had been searched. On June 3, Stresemann publicly acknowledged his part in the affair, but added that the information subsequently released made it appear doubtful that the Prussian police had had sufficient cause for its action. The incriminating material was turned over to the newly appointed chief public prosecutor, well known for his Right-wing sympathies, who after some dilatory efforts dropped the case altogether.[24]

On May 12, the Reichstag resumed its debate on the flag decree. The leader of the Democrats, Erich Koch-Weser, announced that his party had reluctantly decided to oppose the government.[25] The Nazi representative, Dr. Graefe, sneered at the Jewish press and complained of the "shameless arbitrary rule" that the Socialists were inflicting on Prussia. The Communists celebrated the flag decree as "the well-deserved kick in the pants which the bourgeoisie and the Junkers gave their sometime relief-agents, the Socialists, as thanks for Socialist help in restoring their rule."[26] Vituperation was a common bond between Nazis and Communists, and both, of course, exulted in the embarrassment of their common enemies—the moderate republicans. Count Westarp of the German Nationalists announced that his party approved of the flag decree, but not of the weak-kneed government, and that consequently his *Fraktion* would abstain from voting. After the Nazi and Social-

24. Braun, *op. cit.*, pp. 197–8.
25. Koch's enemies in the Reichstag charged that he was simply taking his revenge for having been cheated out of the promised Ministry of the Interior. In January, 1926, Luther withdrew Koch's nomination at the behest of the Bavarian People's Party, which considered Koch too "unitarian." By an ironic coincidence, not noted by the contemporaries during the crisis, Koch had been the only Democrat in 1919 who voted for the retention of the imperial flag.
26. *Verhandlungen des Reichstags*, 200th session, p. 7203.

ist motions of no confidence had been defeated, the Democratic motion was adopted by a vote of 177 to 146, with 103 Nationalists abstaining. The Socialists, Communists, and Democrats had combined to defeat the government and thus precipitated the thirteenth cabinet crisis in seven years.

This particular crisis had not been anticipated and no one had a quick solution at hand. Every new crisis brought with it the chance of a majority government—by including either the Socialists or the German Nationalists. Republicanism was riding high—it usually did after a particularly flagrant outburst of anti-republicanism; witness the Kapp *Putsch* or the Rathenau assassination—and it seemed an auspicious moment to reconstitute the great republican coalition from Socialists to People's Party.[27] The Center, ever sensitive to shifts in popular moods, favored this solution. The People's Party, that quarrelsome remnant of the National Liberals of imperial days, whose hopes and memories and prejudices remained so close to the Nationalists even though their policies were less intractable or unprofitable, would have preferred a break-out to the Right. But the stubborn fact remained that the Nationalists not only were non-republican, but were frozen in an utterly unrealistic stance on foreign policy. They dreamed of an intransigent, belligerent Germany that would wrest maximum concessions from the Allies—anything obtained peacefully, by compromise, was a reminder that Germany was no longer strutting about like a masterful giant. Consequently Stresemann was still being vilified by them. The Socialists, on the other hand, most happily accepted Stresemann and his promise of a Europe infused with

27. Not that the People's Party was unreservedly republican. As Stresemann noted shortly after the flag decree: "That the People's Party is not republican on principle, everyone has known since the first day of its program." Stresemann Papers, Vol. 280, Reel 3100, Frame H 149591.

a Locarno spirit, but they frightened their opponents with demands for a more radical social program.

Hindenburg's first move was to ask the Luther government to remain in office until a new Chancellor had been found. Luther refused and resigned immediately, but the cabinet remained. Gessler, the perennial Minister of Defense and the cabinet member with the longest tenure of service, was appointed Acting Chancellor, and later Hindenburg turned to him with the bid to form a new cabinet.[28] After a couple of days, he formally declined.

As soon as the crisis had broken, on May 12, the bargaining among various parliamentary groups began. The first on the scene was Dr. Scholz, the parliamentary leader of the People's Party, who on May 12 turned to the Nationalists with a bid for a Right-wing coalition.[29] This, it was reported, was vetoed by the Center, which was already negotiating with the Socialists.[30] Hindenburg meanwhile was toying with the candidacies of Külz, the Democratic Minister of the Interior in the Luther Cabinet, or of Dr. Scholz, whose face, properly scarred by duel marks, and whose distinguished military record, made him *persona grata* to the President. In short, there was neither a generally accepted nor a pre-eminently eligible candidate.

On the evening of May 13, even before Gessler had given up

28. Stresemann, who was no friend of Gessler, had been forewarned about an early Gessler candidacy; on February 6, 1926, Consul Bernhard wrote him that in the next government crisis, the President would appoint Gessler and would thus play into the hands of various conspiracies within the *Reichswehr*. An eastern swing in foreign policy would ensue. "For the *spiritus rector* of all these plans one must look to Lieutenant-Colonel von Schleicher, who dominated completely and in every respect not only the former Chief of the General Staff, Seeckt, but also the [present] Minister of Defense. Schleicher is described to me as a man of vast ambition, with an insatiable lust for power, who with all possible means of intrigue will certainly attempt to realize his plans." Stresemann Papers, Vol. 279, Reel 3100, Frames H 149466–9.

29. *Berliner Tageblatt*, May 12, 1926.

30. Stresemann Papers, Vol. 37, Reel 3145, Frames H 161463–4.

the formation of a government, the leaders of the Center Party, Guérard and Stegerwald, telegraphed Konrad Adenauer, the fifty-year-old Lord Mayor of Cologne, to come at once to Berlin.[31] Adenauer had on several occasions been mentioned as a possible chancellor, and the Centrist leaders now thought that this highly respected and successful mayor would be their most promising candidate.[32] The choice of Adenauer was itself a token of the Center's swing to a strong republican coalition. He was known as a "reliable republican. . . . At the Munich *Katholikentag,* which he chaired, a warm confession of loyalty to the Republic brought him into sharp conflict with the [anti-republican] Bavarian Monarchists."[33] He enjoyed the confidence of the Socialists, with whose votes he had been repeatedly elected president of the Prussian *Staatsrat.* The People's Party, on the other hand, was said to oppose him, largely because "after the Revolution he was said to have supported the detachment of the Rhineland from Prussia."[34] Adenauer's present-day critics have charged him with all sorts of separatist

31. Shortly after his trip to Berlin, Adenauer composed, for his own purposes, a detailed *aide-mémoire* of his negotiations, which appeared for the first time in Paul Weymar's authorized biography, *Konrad Adenauer* (Munich, 1955), pp. 129–43; also an American edition, capriciously condensed and inaccurately translated, *Adenauer* (New York, 1957), translated by Peter De Mendelssohn. The following account draws heavily on this *aide-mémoire.* For a sharp criticism of Weymar's book and the veracity of Adenauer's notes, see the review of the American edition by a leading historian, Gordon Craig, *Herald Tribune Book Review,* March 10, 1957, and the partisan echo of Craig's review in *Der Spiegel,* April 10, 1957. All subsequent references are to the German edition.

32. On November 24, 1923, the day after his resignation as Chancellor, Stresemann jotted down the names of five likely successors, including Adenauer. *Vermächtnis,* Vol. I, p. 255. Adenauer had also been mentioned in 1920.

33. *Berliner Tageblatt,* May 15, 1926; the article continued: "Adenauer has proved himself a brilliant organizer and an intelligent administrator of Cologne, which owes its great rise not least to him." The *Vorwärts* of May 15 wrote: "Adenauer has several times before this been mentioned as a candidate for the chancellorship, but has always refused. He is regarded as one of the most outstanding men among the Prussian administrators."

34. *Berliner Tageblatt,* May 15, 1926.

ambitions but most evidence seems to point to the fact that, although Adenauer favored Rhenish independence from Prussia, he did not want a break from Germany.[35] At the height of the Ruhr crisis in 1923 he may—reluctantly—have contemplated a further step, the creation of a new West German state tied to Germany, but only if this would be accompanied by a simultaneous and complete understanding with France.[36] The charge of separatism, however, remains the sensitive point in Adenauer's past, and neither his political friends nor his enemies have been able to establish the truth so that it will stick. Adenauer himself seems loath to speak on the subject.[37]

"Feeling no inclination to take over the post of Chancellor," Adenauer procrastinated and did not arrive in Berlin until the evening of May 14.[38] Even as he was traveling to Berlin the Pan-European retreat from democratic government was gather-

35. Weymar, *op. cit.*, pp. 72-81, contends that Adenauer's activities in 1919 in support of a West German Republic were a political ruse, designed to kill off all genuine separatist agitation. Admittedly, this seems far-fetched, but Dr. J. A. Dorten, the notorious separatist leader, repeatedly refers to Adenauer as "the traitor," as the man who scuttled the Rhenish cause which at first he seemed to champion. See Dorten Papers, The Hoover Library, Stanford, California, and Dorten, *La Tragédie rhénane* (Paris, 1945), pp. 49–57. As the merest example of the mystery that surrounds this subject, contrast Weymar's report that Adenauer had always refused to receive Dorten and Dorten's account which describes in detail several meetings he had had with Adenauer. On this whole controversy, see now Karl Dietrich Erdmann, *Adenauer in der Rheinlandpolitik nach dem Ersten Weltkrieg* (Stuttgart, 1966), *passim*.

36. See, for example, Adenauer's remarks at the controversial meeting of Rhenish representatives with the German government on January 9, 1924, Stresemann Papers, Vol. 265, Reel 3111, Frames H 146610–25. I am indebted to Edgar Alexander for calling my attention to the full record of the meeting as well as to the published account in Stresemann's *Vermächtnis*, Vol. I, p. 282, which is abridged—in a manner prejudicial to Adenauer.

37. It is remarkable that despite Adenauer's prominence neither a satisfactory biography nor an account of his public life in Weimar exists. Edgar Alexander's *Adenauer and the New Germany* (New York, 1957) is a thoughtful introduction, but he unfortunately did not live to complete his projected two-volume biography.

38. Weymar, *op. cit.*, p. 129.

ing speed. In banner headlines the morning papers announced that Marshal Pilsudski had established a military dictatorship in Poland—another democracy, established in the Wilsonian aftermath of the war, had been snuffed out. How many Germans, one wonders, recognized this warning of the precariousness of parliamentary democracy? How many sensed that all new European democracies were in jeopardy?

On his arrival, Adenauer was met by Stegerwald and Guérard, who assured him that they had "until now always deliberately refrained from proposing me for the post of Chancellor, because they felt I was not to be wasted on a purely temporary or interim term of office." This time a cabinet of the great coalition was to be formed, "a stable and durable majority government."[39] Guérard and Stegerwald reported that the parliamentary leader of the People's Party, Dr. Scholz, had approved the formation of a great coalition, contingent on the resolution of three issues: the revaluation of the mark, the flag decree, and the expropriation of the former dynasties. The Socialists had agreed as well, and everybody expected that these three questions could be settled without difficulty. If need be, Adenauer should form a neutral transition cabinet; after the plebiscite on expropriation, which was to be held on June 20 or before, he could form a permanent, majority government.

Adenauer was impressed by what he had been told and asked himself whether in such circumstances it was not "[his] duty to make a great personal sacrifice and take over the post of Chancellor."[40] The next morning he told the two Centrist leaders that he would pursue the possibility of forming a cabi-

39. *Ibid.*, pp. 130–1.
40. *Ibid.* There was little reason for Adenauer to trade a safe and successful administrative post for a political appointment of uncertain promise and duration. The *Berliner Tageblatt* wrote of his candidacy on May 15: "In truth it takes today a great deal of self-abnegation and true patriotism to put oneself in the firing range of the extreme Right-wing mudslingers."

net further, despite his "doubts and scruples" regarding (1) the Dawes Plan: "It seemed clear to all concerned . . . that already by 1927 the terms of the Dawes Plan would become impossible to fulfill. Therefore, in my opinion, we should not have signed the Agreement." (2) Locarno:

> Although I fully and unreservedly accepted the situation created by the Locarno Treaties, in order to get as much out of them for Germany as possible, I was nevertheless profoundly unhappy about the unsteady, seesaw character of German foreign policy, and could not approve of the manner in which this policy was conducted. . . . Furthermore, as far as I knew, our negotiations at Locarno had been conducted rather unskillfully. . . . All in all, as far as I could judge from the outside, our foreign policy up to the present time had not been exactly happy. On the other hand Herr Stresemann must remain in the cabinet, quite apart from the fact that he was the leader of one of the future coalition parties.

Adenauer refused any delay in the formation of a great coalition: "Under no circumstances would I accept the Chancellorship on the uncertain *expectation* that the great coalition may *some day* be established."[41] He agreed to see Gessler and to consult with Scholz of the People's Party and Hilferding of the Socialists.

Gessler concurred in Adenauer's desire for a stable majority government—a minority government "would be able, at best, to administer, but could not govern." He also told Adenauer to see Stresemann "who was a little worried by my appearance in the capital."[42]

Adenauer saw Scholz first, and told him that he would insist both on a great coalition and on complete freedom to select his own ministers without being bound to accept the nominees of the coalition partners. Scholz's reply was brutally decisive, nor

41. Weymar, *op. cit.*, pp. 132–3.
42. *Ibid.*, p. 134.

did he haggle over petty details. His party, he said, considered a great coalition impossible: "The swing to the Right has to come." If this coalition could not be effected immediately, the party would prefer another minority government, and, despite some grumbling by a few members, would be happy to have Adenauer as the head of such a government. "What was totally out of the question for them was to join the Socialists in a government. Not even a government based on Socialist support in parliament was acceptable to them. As for the President, his views on this were exactly the same."[43] The party might not even remain in coalition with the Democrats, unless Dr. Koch explicitly withdrew "the notice he had given to the present coalition, and unless they accept the flag decree without mental reservations."[44]

Adenauer had failed before he had really begun. Scholz had torpedoed his candidacy, and was told so by Adenauer:

> in these circumstances it was, of course, quite impossible for me to accept the office of Chancellor, and this corresponded to a large extent with my own personal wishes. On the other hand, what he had said could really make one weep, because it revealed the frightful picture of our partisan strife and divisiveness. I could well understand, I said, that there were many elements among the German Nationalists, especially among their supporters in the country, who were of value to the state, but surely it should be the foremost duty of everyone with the well-being of the father-land at heart to win over the many millions of Social Democratic supporters everywhere in the country to the principles of the state and to train them as responsible citizens. This was manifestly

43. *Ibid.,* pp. 136–7. There is every evidence that Hindenburg did not share these views.

44. Scholz and Stresemann had met on May 13 (before Adenauer's candidacy was known), discussed the conditions for the formation of a new government, and agreed that there should be "no negotiations with the Democrats until Koch withdraws his notice." The cryptic account of their talk suggests that they had agreed on a policy for the People's Party. Stresemann Papers, Vol. 37, Reel 3145, Frames H 161463–4.

impossible, I said, if the Social Democrats were simply excluded from all share in the government.[45]

Adenauer then saw Hilferding, who was very much more accommodating. He too wanted a stable government and suggested that, if necessary, Adenauer should first form a minority government, which the Socialists would nevertheless support. If the People's Party should persist in its obstructive tactics even after the plebiscite, the President, Hilferding thought, should threaten it with parliamentary dissolution. Adenauer again rejected any notion of an interim government and expressed doubt moreover that Hindenburg would grant him a dissolution that would favor the Left and Center, i.e., those "parties which, considering the whole character of Hindenburg, must be alien to him."[46] But, whatever Hilferding's concessions and demands, Adenauer had made up his mind to return to the healthier conditions of Cologne, and he so informed Gessler. The latter was much surprised at Scholz's intransigence, and "suspected all this might be due to Stresemann, who feared that I was too strong a man for him to deal with"—a suspicion that Adenauer shared and undoubtedly encouraged. Later in the day, Stresemann and Scholz assured the Center *Fraktion* that Adenauer's impressions of Scholz's attitude must have rested on a "misunderstanding," though Adenauer rather persuasively discounts the possibility of a misunderstanding during an hour-long interview, at which he took full notes. According to Adenauer, "the general view was that Stresemann had used Scholz to make it impossible for me to take over the Chancellorship."[47]

45. Weymar, *op. cit.*, pp. 137–8. Adenauer's formulation of the problem is odd, however correct his conclusion. Despite their occasional revolutionary rhetoric and despite some radical groups within the party, the Socialists were the single largest group stolidly loyal to the state, i.e., the Republic.

46. *Ibid.*, p. 140.

47. *Ibid.*, pp. 142–3. In his notes Adenauer sought to document this charge against Stresemann by a piece of utterly inconsequential gossip.

After Adenauer's withdrawal, the cabinet crisis was solved with great rapidity, largely because of Hindenburg's well-advertised impatience. The cabinet met on the same afternoon, May 15, and Wilhelm Marx, a former Centrist Chancellor and the Minister of Justice in the Luther Cabinet, was for the first time proposed as a possible successor to Luther.[48] On Sunday, May 16, Gessler, Scholz, Stresemann, Marx, and some others met, and Scholz agreed to the Marx candidacy and the eventual formation of a great coalition. "Scholz staged an obvious retreat . . . and granted Marx what he had denied Adenauer."[49] On the evening of May 16, Marx went to see Hindenburg, and on the next day he was appointed Chancellor and all the other ministers of the Luther Cabinet were confirmed in their posts. "The Luther Cabinet without Luther," a characteristic failure to exploit an opportunity, came into office a week after the old government had resigned and remained in office for seven months. The flag decree, incidentally, was carried out, but the flag conflict persisted until the end of the Republic, seven years later.

It is of some interest, if perhaps only as a kind of historical whimsy, to discover whether it was indeed Stresemann who obstructed the Adenauer candidacy. That it was his party which thwarted Adenauer was the general belief of observers at the time and seems incontrovertible.[50] But there were hints

48. Apparently, on the initiative of Stresemann. Letter to writer, June 26, 1957, from John Zeender, who has been working on the Marx Papers. For further confirmation of Scholz's brusque rejection of a great coalition and of Stresemann's genial role in nominating Marx, see *Der Nachlass des Reichskanzlers Wilhelm Marx,* ed. by Hugo Stehkämper (Cologne, 1968), Vol. I, pp. 415–16.

49. *Berliner Tageblatt,* May 17, 1926.

50. *Berliner Tageblatt,* May 17, 1926, notes that Adenauer failed "because he had the right idea, i.e., that in the face of the great difficulties which the Reich faced in the near future, at home and abroad, it required a firm majority government, and that the majority government could be constituted

even then that it was Stresemann's direct intervention which led Scholz to be obdurate one day to one Centrist and conciliatory the next day to another Centrist.[51]

There is certainly ample evidence of Stresemann's long-nurtured dislike and suspicion of Adenauer.[52] On May 17, he saw two important foreign diplomats with whom he discussed Adenauer, and his notes report their unsympathetic views sympathetically. One was M. Hesnard, Briand's confidant and press attaché at the Berlin embassy, who "was surprised that the

---

only through a cabinet of the great coalition. If Adenauer's program did not appeal to the People's Party, apparently his strong personality displeased Stresemann and some other members of the Cabinet, who preferred to remain among themselves." In the Reichstag debate on the Marx Cabinet, on May 19, both Hermann Müller of the Socialists and Count Westarp of the Nationalists asserted that Adenauer's efforts had been thwarted by the People's Party. *Verhandlungen des Reichstags,* 206th session, pp. 7323 *et seq.*

51. Even the editor of the *Vermächtnis,* Stresemann's friend Bernhard, wrote: "This [Adenauer's] attempt failed because of the opposition of the German People's Party, which acted in closest agreement with Stresemann." *Vermächtnis,* Vol. II, p. 392.

52. The sources of Stresemann's dislike ran deep and were by no means exclusively political in character. Precisely a year before Adenauer's appearance in Berlin, on May 16, 1925, Stresemann noted in his diary:

"The Cologne Millennial Festival suggests a comparison with Munich. The Munich celebrations displayed the robust populist genius; here we have Rhenish culture, gaiety, and ancient prosperity. Personally, Adenauer is a brilliant success at Cologne; whether he always acts in the interest of the *Reich* is indeed doubtful. The luncheon at the townhall was wonderful, the magnificently appointed table in particular. The lord mayors of today's Germany are in reality, after the great industrialists, the monarchs of the present. Elected for long periods, many of them irremovable, they are more powerful than ministers, and, broadly speaking, from among their numbers are recruited the parliamentarians and political leaders of today." *Ibid.,* pp. 299–300.

This mixture of envy and suspicion, wrapped in patriotic insinuation, is characteristic of Stresemann's utterances about Adenauer. See, for example, his allusion to Adenauer in a speech before the Central Committee of his party, February 26, 1929: "There is a whisper going through the land of illegal efforts to replace the Constitution by a dictatorship and so forth. Notwithstanding the cordial relations maintained by the Lord Mayor of Cologne with the great powers of Europe which enjoy that form of government, I believe that we are still very far from fascism." *Ibid.,* Vol. III, p. 432.

Center should single out Adenauer, of all people, and noted that Adenauer during the Ruhr struggle had maintained the best relations with the French, and had taken an entirely different position from the then Reich government. Adenauer was also one of the first to wander in and out of Ambassador Laurent's office." The other was Lord D'Abernon "with whom I also discussed Adenauer and his position on foreign policy, and who told me that during the Ruhr struggle Adenauer, after all, had taken an entirely different position from now."[53] For the following day, May 18, Stresemann's Papers contain a "confidential news report," which said:

> During his brief stay in Berlin the Cologne Lord Mayor, Adenauer, in whom certain circles put so much stock, showed in the most diverse ways that he is still the old Adenauer. It would certainly be foolish to wish to fall back on that candidacy once again. One must not forget that Adenauer has in some respects deserved well of the Rhineland, but that he has fierce enemies even there. . . . Under Adenauer's Chancellorship the cabinet would have soon suffered from the gravest conflicts. . . . Adenauer is a personality that is difficult to handle and he is a definite opponent of the Locarno policy. . . . Adenauer is a man of one-sided orientation. Although his candidacy is finished for the time being, it seems important to point out these facts, because at least up till this moment, the idea still haunts many people that Adenauer is the right man for a "definitive" cabinet.[54]

These *ad personam* trivialities matter little, and insinuate rather than inform. Stresemann's worries about Adenauer's views on foreign policy are puzzling, but as long as Adenauer maintains his silence on this point, it will be impossible to render an informed judgment. A few surmises, however, may

53. Stresemann Papers, Vol. 38, Reel 3145, Frame H 161483.
54. Stresemann Papers, Vol. 38, Reel 3145, Frames H 161481–2. According to Henry Bernhard, editor of the *Vermächtnis,* these confidential news reports were written by a journalist close to Stresemann, Wilhelm Vogel. Because of this intimacy and their frequent meetings, Bernhard believes these reports possess a "certain authenticity." Letter to writer, July 1, 1957.

be in place. Adenauer's criticism of Locarno certainly did not spring from Francophobia or from any more generalized hostility toward the Versailles Powers. As a Rhinelander and a devout Catholic, Adenauer seems always to have viewed Germany as a part of a West European community.[55] His actions as mayor of Cologne confirmed this, even under the strain of seven years of British occupation; his moving words of moderation at the end of that occupation, on January 31, 1926, attest the now-familiar mixture of statesmanship and sentiment.[56]

Adenauer may have been anti-Locarno for more parochial reasons, perhaps because Stresemann did not obtain sufficient immediate concessions for the occupied Rhineland. The allusion to the unskillful negotiating at Locarno makes this interpretation more plausible. Adenauer's remark about "the unsteady seesaw character of German foreign policy" also admits of several interpretations. The thought that comes most readily to contemporaries today, that Adenauer must have

55. Adenauer in fact hoped for a permanent and far-reaching understanding between Germany and France. At the height of the Ruhr crisis in 1923, he told Tirard, the chairman of the Allied Rhineland Commission, that French hopes of separation were doomed; "a lasting peace between France and Germany can be attained only through the establishment of a community of economic interests between the two countries." (Stresemann Papers, Vol. 265, Reel 3111, Frames H 146621–2.) Stresemann's friends were right that Adenauer had maintained close contacts with the French—but with Stresemann's knowledge, if not necessarily to his pleasure. Adenauer's forays into foreign affairs, in part imposed on him by the occupation of Cologne and the Rhineland, may have troubled Stresemann, who quite properly regarded foreign affairs as his own province. For a detailed study of this, see Karl Dietrich Erdmann, *op. cit.*, pp. 71–186.

56. "Much we have had to suffer at the harsh hands of the victor during these seven long years. Today, in this sacred hour, let us not talk of that; indeed, we want to be just; despite much that we have gone through, we want to recognize that in the political field the departing enemy has allowed fair play to prevail. Let us hope that our suffering has not been in vain, that now a truly new spirit will prevail among the peoples of Europe. The principles of law and morality, which are valid for the relations of individuals to one another, which pronounce every man free and equal and possessed of equal rights, these must in truth, and not only in words, become valid for the society of nations." *Deutscher Geschichtskalender*, pp. 209–10.

sought to condemn Stresemann's cherished tie to the East, his vigorous continuation of the so-called Rapallo line, is least persuasive. Adenauer, it would appear, did not trouble himself much about the East; to him, as indeed to most of the Europeans at the time, the important powers were France, England, and Germany, the nations tied together by the Versailles Treaty. It is far more likely that Adenauer meant the vacillating policy of toughness and compliance, of pinpricks and promises, which had characterized Germany's policy to the West. More likely still, he was referring to Germany's game of playing England against France, France against England, of seeking D'Abernon's help or enticing Briand's friendship. Adenauer probably would have preferred a consistently pro-French policy. Certain it is that Adenauer had conceived no great admiration for Stresemann's foreign policy, despite the fact that (or partly because) enlightened opinion everywhere considered Stresemann a republican Bismarck. One may surmise that Adenauer's own foreign policy under Weimar would have been, as Stresemann feared, one-sided: he would have tried to attach a strong and equal Germany to a strong Western Europe —at the cost perhaps of renouncing uncertain gains in the East.

Presumably foreign policy was not the only difference between these two men. Stresemann undoubtedly mistrusted Adenauer's domestic politics as well, his fiscal extravagance, his Rhenish-Catholic loyalties, his steady collaboration with the Socialists in the Prussian *Staatsrat*.[57] That Adenauer was unreservedly republican, and never as closely involved with the Hohenzollern dynasty as Stresemann, was at best a matter of

57. His pique over Adenauer's collaboration with the Socialists was expressed in his letter to Jarres (cf. *infra*, footnote 59). Complaining that the collaboration of German Nationalists and People's Party in the Prussian *Staatsrat* had not brought the Center closer to the Right, he remarked that "the election of the president showed that there, too, Center and Socialists collaborated, for the election of Adenauer was pushed through, and the position of the presidency was denied to the larger party, the *Arbeitsgemeinschaft* [German Nationalists and People's Party]." *Vermächtnis*, Vol. II, pp. 415–16.

indifference to the latter. For all of Stresemann's unquestioned achievements for the Republic, for all his wearisome battles on behalf of political reason and responsibility within his own party, he never worked at the task of strengthening the Republic at home with the passion that he lavished on the resurgence of the Reich abroad. May it not have been important in this particular crisis that Stresemann's feelings toward the Republic, at least in the mid-twenties, were still those of an adopted son? He had been grudgingly accepted by the Republic, as was shown by his exclusion from responsible posts until 1923, and he himself continued to cherish the memory of his natural home, the Empire.[58] His most embittered foes were on the Right, as were his deepest sentiments. Time and again his party worked toward a reconciliation with the German Nationalists, and a few weeks after Adenauer's candidacy he corresponded with the German Nationalists about the advantages and disadvantages of an amalgamation of the two parties.[59] To be sure, he hotly refused to surrender to the Nationalists the National Liberal tradition, the legacy of Bassermann and Bennigsen, but this tradition, after all, was not only his personal commitment but his sole political stock in trade, indeed his *raison d'être* as a party leader. Stresemann, true to the German belief in the *Primat der Aussenpolitik,* strengthened the Republic's diplo-

58. In his address to the Party Congress on October 2, 1926, he referred to the "fine phrase about the old Germany, which we love, and the new Germany, for which we live." *Ibid.,* Vol. III, p. 81.

59. On July 5, 1926, Jarres and Gayl, the co-chairmen of the *Arbeitsgemeinschaft* in the Prussian *Staatsrat,* suggested in an open appeal to both parties that this formal collaboration of the two parties should be extended to other legislative bodies. Stresemann refused, but in his letter to Jarres of July 30, 1926, he wrote that such a move would be a tactical mistake as well: it would only lead to closer collaboration of the Left and to a permanent Left-Center government. If, on the other hand, one did nothing, then the Socialists would become more radical, hence totally isolated, and an effective Right-wing bourgeois government would become inevitable. *Ibid.,* Vol. II, pp. 412–16. This, of course, was clearly the opposite of Adenauer's hope (cf. *supra,* pp. 182–3) to lead the Socialists out of isolation.

matic defenses, hoping that greater external power would solidify the inner strength of the Reich.[60] Adenauer, on the other hand, seems to have believed then, as he most assuredly did twenty years later, that the power and well-being of Germany depended at least as much on an active, stable political society at home.[61]

Our account of the May crisis of 1926 has shown, in microcosm, the many weaknesses of Weimar: the instability of governments, the depth and dogged fury of the party struggles which intensified the existing antagonisms among classes, confessions, and regions, the resultant erosion of parliamentary power and the corresponding growth of extra-parliamentary and presidential authority, the mediocrity of political leader-

60. There is something pathetic in Stresemann's weary realization, shortly before his death, that he had failed to mold his party according to his original expectation. See the remarkable letter to his party friend, Professor Kahl, March 13, 1929, in which he discussed the possibility of withdrawing from the party he himself had organized. "We are moreover no longer a party of ideological principle, rather we are becoming more and more a purely industrial party. . . . The *Stammtische,* which in our party speak the loudest, shout their approval most heartily for those who talk like Seldte and Duesterberg [the leaders of the *Stahlhelm*]. I wanted to be a bridge between the old and the new Germany." *Ibid.,* Vol. III, pp. 436–40. He had wanted to be a bridge and failed, and this perhaps describes the ultimate tragedy of Stresemann's position: he remained adrift, belonging to neither side, scorned by his old peers on one side and scornful of his new friends on the other. In Henry Turner's fine study, *Stresemann and the Politics of the Weimar Republic* (Princeton, 1963), the May 1926 crisis is set against the background of Stresemann's role in Weimar politics. Turner's conclusions seem to bear out my impressions. He considers Stresemann to have been "a pragmatic conservative," who despite his flexibility failed in his self-assigned role as party politician. Pp. 221–3, 263–8.

61. It could be argued that Adenauer's particular talents and predilections would have been more appropriate, if obviously less welcome, to the Germany of 1926 than to the Germany of 1949. In the former instance his conservatism could have *preserved* and *strengthened* the existing democratic institutions, whereas in the latter instance, after Germany's total defeat, he abetted the conservative desire to *restore* some of the old traditions, with results that may not always have been beneficial to German democracy.

ship, the endless, sterile fighting over the past, the habit of renewing the sources of dissension at every crisis. Remembering all this one may well ask whether Adenauer, as Chancellor in the late 1920's, could have changed the fate of Weimar. Could any man have triumphed over such obstacles, which were not accidental or temporary, but the consequences of a long and tortured political evolution? Could he have braved the "system," could he have pitted himself against all the forces, political and spiritual, that were subverting the Republic? Even if one concedes the potential impact of a statesman, not in order to glorify the role of the individual but to take cognizance of an oft-repeated phenomenon in history—can one suppose that Adenauer was the right man? Can one read back into these earlier years the maturity, the active, even belligerent political intelligence of the present-day Adenauer, chastened by his people's tragedy which two decades before no man could foresee?[62]

Again: if Adenauer had successfully formed a cabinet in May 1926, could he have kept the great coalition in being, could he have cajoled the recalcitrant members of the People's Party, could he have prevented the fatal emergence of those Right-wing leaders in his own party, *Prelat* Kaas and Dr. Brüning, who proved so utterly indifferent to the survival of the parliamentary Republic? Could he have broken or moderated the narrow selfishness of the industrialists which added so immeasurably to the economic and political burden of the depression? Could he, in short, have strengthened the republican forces everywhere and marshaled them so effectively as to ride out the storm of depression and social collapse? Much of this he undoubtedly would have tried, if only because this supremely able and self-assured politician would have sought to consolidate his own power. And much could have been

---

62. Was the Churchill of the general strike in May 1926 the same leader as the Churchill of that memorable summer of 1940?

achieved: the limits of intelligent statesmanship were never approached under Weimar, and the reservoir of democratic power was never adequately tapped. Chance and the unrelieved mediocrity of its leaders had a far greater impact on the final collapse of Weimar than is usually acknowledged.

Whether Adenauer would have succeeded, no man can tell. In the process of trying he would have afforded Weimar a period of creative consolidation; and a prolonged Chancellorship of Adenauer under the Presidency of Hindenburg, in itself a vigorous combination of austere Protestantism and Catholicism, might have endowed Weimar with that authoritative dignity, that proud harnessing of opposing forces, which alone could have lessened the impact of the seemingly idealistic terror movement which assailed and overwhelmed Germany a few years later. In contemplating Weimar's fate and Adenauer's candidacy one must remember that nothing is inevitable until it has happened.

The Collapse of
Weimar

To explain the phenomenon of Nazism to their fellow citizens was one of the major tasks of German historians and social scientists after 1945. In the immediate postwar era, Allied enthusiasts talked easily about the problems of "re-education." The actual task of teaching Germans to come to grips with their own past proved hard. It required—among other things—the willingness of German scholars occasionally to engage in what the French call the art of *haute vulgarisation.* One of the finest products of this re-examination was a collection of radio speeches on various aspects of Nazism by ten leading German scholars. This essay is a revised version of my introduction to the English translation of that collection, called *The Path to Dictatorship,* and first published in New York in 1966.

Adolf Hitler was appointed Chancellor of Germany on January 30, 1933. His rise to power had been speciously legal; his exercise of power was to be covertly revolutionary. With incredible rapidity National Socialism established a regimented society, characterized by the threat and use of terror, pervasive propaganda, economic progress, and the growing support or acquiescence of the populace. Traditional beliefs and institutions were subverted and the old ruling classes gradually replaced by a new Nazi elite. In 1939, a rearmed Germany plunged Europe into the Second World War, conquered most of Europe, perpetrated the most hideous crimes, and suffered the most stunning defeat of modern times. In twelve years, Hitler's Thousand-Year Reich had run its course—twelve years that transfigured the world.

How could it have happened? How could National Socialism have triumphed in a civilized country? Why did millions of Germans vote for Hitler and why did the German elite fail to denounce this false savior? How could that same elite—with few exceptions—have been coerced or cajoled into supporting a regime of book-burners, how could the Nazis have found thousands of doctors, engineers, and civil servants to help them carry out their mass murders? The magnitude and novelty of the disaster raised these insistent questions—and obscured the answers. Nazism had been difficult to understand from the very beginning: if it had been easier to perceive, it would never have succeeded.

The first explanations were those of contemporaries who remained prisoners of their preconceptions. Fascism was the last-ditch defense of monopoly capitalism in crisis, said the Marxists. The Treaty of Versailles and the Great Depression were to blame, said the liberals who had been too feeble to combat the effects of either. Others pointed an accusing finger at some fault of the Constitution or some conspirators around Hindenburg. These were explanations by alibi: some faction, some event, perhaps some accident, was held culpable. Eventually there was a swing to the other extreme, and on both sides of the German frontier people began to argue that National Socialism was the logical culmination of German history. From Luther to Hitler, so the Western argument ran, a long line of authoritarian, illiberal thinkers had poisoned "the German mind." These exaggerations of outraged foreigners were more than matched by the supine statements of German intellectuals under Hitler who also celebrated National Socialism as the crowning embodiment of German traditions and aspirations. Nazi and anti-Nazi historians were at one in hailing the historic ancestry of the Third Reich; they both helped to endow the Austrian corporal with a formidable pedigree. And to a large extent they were right, however stupid and simplistic they were in particulars.

In 1945, the question of the origins of National Socialism lost its political immediacy for non-German historians. Twenty years later, it is still an intellectual conundrum that despite massive and excellent work has remained unanswered or incompletely answered.

For the German scholar, the question became—in the popular word of the day—existential. Shortly after the German collapse, Ludwig Dehio, a leading and untainted historian, noted that Ranke's dictum that history should record "how it actually happened" now read: "how was it possible?" Postwar Germans needed to discover the true nature of Nazi rule and the relation between Nazism and the more distant German past. What aberration of mind, what deformation of society, what unsuspected institutions and values had contributed to the downfall of Weimar democracy and the rise of Hitler? What national traditions, the Germans asked, were left intact? What portion of the past must be repudiated and what reformed?

These questions engaged—and, as I can attest from countless conversations and many conferences, they continue deeply to engage—those Germans who trouble themselves at all with questions of their past. Most Germans, to be sure, are content to acknowledge the dreadfulness of the Third Reich, about which, contrary to foreign impressions, the majority of Germans today cherish few illusions. Schoolbooks and public media have done a remarkable job of presenting the grisly truth. But they have failed to clarify the connections between the German past and Nazi rule, and all too often the Nazi period appears as an island of barbarism somehow separated from the mainstream of German history. These connections are hard to make intellectually and perhaps harder still to bear humanly: better to concentrate on twelve years of blackness than on a hundred years of historical grayness—better especially for Germans who still prefer to think in terms of neat intellectual antitheses.

Some German scholars, on the other hand, have made immense efforts to uncover the path to the Nazi dictatorship, and thereby have stirred up fierce historical disputes. The great controversy about the origin and conduct of the First World War, which Fritz Fischer's work initiated, is a case in point. Even a seemingly slight volume such as *The Path to Dictatorship* bears eloquent testimony to the distinction and success of this search.

Its authors belong to different generations—and thus experienced Nazism in significantly different ways. Six of the contributors were adults with established careers when Hitler came to power; three of them emigrated to the United States as a consequence and returned to Germany after the war. Four of the contributors—those incidentally who have done the most work on the debility of German democracy—were children in 1933. The missing chronological group, those who were on the threshold of careers when Nazism triumphed, suffered perhaps the most and have on the whole contributed less to the intellectual revival of postwar Germany. The older generation that survived Hitler physically and morally intact had the advantages and disadvantages of having known the world before 1933 in all its oppressive complexity. The younger group is representative of an impressive generation of German scholars and publicists who are today in their late thirties or early forties. They lived through Nazism, too young to have been broken or compromised by it, old enough to remember it as the formative experience of their youth. Without fanfare, without apparent self-consciousness, but with energy, courage, and great talent, they have set out to answer the questions about Hitler's rise and Germany's fall. This group, which in its front rank includes Ralf Dahrendorf, Karl Dietrich Bracher, and Ernst Nolte, took its inspiration from Germany's need for new beginnings in 1945. In their response to that challenge, which was at once political and scholarly, they have renewed Germany's intellectual ties to the West. They have been consistently open to ideas and methods from abroad, and their work in turn has benefited ours. They have broken with some of the metaphysical *hauteur* of their forebears while maintaining a closer relationship to philosophy than is common among ourselves. One of the unintended consequences of Hitler's destruction of scholarship has been this greater openness of German scholars, enforced at first and a habit by now. This collection of essays, originally designed for German readers, admirably suited to American readers, exemplifies this international community of scholarship.

Any serious examination of the fall of Weimar ought to start with the reminder that the 1920's were generally inhospitable to democracy and that a series of *coups d'état* established dictatorial or authoritarian regimes throughout Europe. None of the new democracies created in the aftermath of the Great War, save Finland, survived to the beginning of the second war. The Weimar Republic lasted longer than most; it was too "democratic" to be overthrown by reactionary, military, or Left-wing cliques. It succumbed to a mass movement that had become the strongest party by far, and that cleverly exploited all the weaknesses of Weimar's defenses.

These weaknesses were legion. The Weimar Constitution had made Germany a parliamentary Republic, but most Germans harbored strong prejudices against the talkers and compromisers of parliament. Even in countries with strong parliamentary traditions, the system was widely criticized in the 1920's. In Germany, the parliamentary system was suspect from the beginning. Hostility and contempt were deeply engrained. Bismarck had introduced both a national parliament and an anti-parliamentary stance. Bismarck's Constitution provided for a Reichstag that controlled some of the purse strings but not the government itself. The spectacle of a strong and clever Chancellor like Bismarck playing with a feeble Reichstag taught the Germans—at the very beginning of their unified political existence—the wrong political lessons; no wonder that the historian Theodor Mommsen once accused Bismarck of having "broken the political backbone of the nation." But more than popular antipathies to parliament were involved: in Germany, in contrast to England, a strong civil-service bureacracy and a tough military caste antedated the existence of parliament, and the German bureaucracy certainly intended to preserve its powers, unmolested by any transient parliamentarians.

Parliament belonged to that whole complex of institutions and attitudes which Germans often labeled "Western" and scorned as alien and undesirable. Parliament and political parties were divisive, they argued, and German destiny demanded a Führer who would rally and represent the entire people and resolve all conflicts. Such dreams were amazingly popular—and widely mistaken for political truths, as I tried to show in *The Politics of Cultural Despair*. Resentment against modernity—and against the West as the source of it—was an essential part of German nationalism before 1914.

The upper classes in Imperial Germany were anti-democratic

—as their interests and inclinations prescribed. It is perhaps worth pointing out that people generally idealize their interests and in the long run tend to lose sight of the connection between stated ideals and unstated interests. The rhetoric of anti-democracy in Germany was full of what in another place I have called *Vulgäridealismus,* an effort to justify authoritarianism and social privilege by invoking Germany's philosophical traditions and literary ideals. *Kultur* and democracy were antithetical, they said and believed, though usually these same men complained that *Kultur* had already declined, without democracy. The Great War sharpened the ideological resentment against the West, and leading German writers boasted of their country's differences from and superiority to France and England. This avowal of cultural estrangement, abetted as well by Allied propaganda, was one of the incidental legacies of that terrible ordeal. Germany's defeat by the West—a defeat which to most Germans was more apparent in its political consequences than its military causes—deepened these antipathies still more. It was a grievous time to adopt essentially Western democratic institutions—quite aside from the oft-remarked discrepancy between the newly founded democratic state and the continuing non-democratic society.

Any German state would have been virtually bankrupt and deeply divided in 1919. A democratic state could be and was incessantly taunted and vilified just because it was democratic. The anti-democratic sentiment, powerful and pervasive throughout the history of Weimar, was not identical with Nazism. The upper classes in Germany, already hostile to democracy before 1918, continued to be so *a fortiori* after 1918. This made them vulnerable to National Socialist propaganda, but it did not make them National Socialists. It diminished the chances that German democracy would survive a crisis. The Germans under Weimar continued to live on the emotional presuppositions and intellectual baggage of Imperial

Germany. Gustav Stresemann became one of Weimar's outstanding leaders by the simple and yet difficult feat of overcoming some of his prejudices in favor of political realism—and by possessing an instinct for power.

The leading parties in Weimar produced few such men. The largest party in Weimar—as in prewar Germany—was the Social Democratic Party, and for nearly ten years it allowed itself to remain out of the government—as it had always been in Imperial Germany. The sense of power and the readiness to assume leadership were underdeveloped among the Socialists, who had learned to cherish their party organizations, their state within a state, as the best means toward that uncertain end—a socialist society. The leadership of the SPD was drawn from the prewar generation as well, and they too carried with them the expectations and the burdens of an earlier society. Their patriotism had been proven many times, most dramatically and most questionably when in November 1918 they took over the receivership of a defeated Empire—and in their few months of power concentrated on preserving national unity rather than on effecting social reform. The form of the state, not the structure of society, was changed in 1918–19, and yet no classes had suffered more from the inequalities of this structure than those represented politically by the Socialists. There was timidity among Socialist leaders, even as there was mounting militancy and courage at the bottom and among the younger leaders who came to the fore in the early 1930's. The character of Socialist leadership recalls the plaintive remark made by a Labour Member of Parliament in 1931, after the Tories had taken Britain off the gold standard: "But nobody had told us that one could do that." A lot of things needed to be done to make Germany into a democratic society—and nobody told the Socialists that they could do some of these things. They remained imprisoned by the two formative experiences of their infancy: Marx and Bismarck, by the myth of the inevitability of the socialist revolution and by the actuality or specter of repression. Both enjoined passivity.

The Socialists were essentially guilty of sins of omission. Other parties of the Left and Middle contributed more actively to the collapse of Weimar, for as Erich Matthias has remarked, "Adolf Hitler and the Republic's notorious enemies do not bear the whole responsibility for Weimar's failure and the destruction of the parties that supported it."[1] Matthias's judgment is a scholarly echo of what in 1935 Kurt Tucholsky, embittered and in exile, put much more scathingly. Indicting the German Left and German Jewry, he wrote: "One has suffered a defeat. One was beaten up—as no party with all the trumps in his hands has been beaten up for a long time . . . Now we need a self-criticism so strong that compared to it brimstone is like soap."[2] An intellectual's typical hyperbole, but the Left was equally typical in the meekness of its self-criticism.

The tragedy of Weimar was that every party contributed to the demise of the Republic—and to its own demise. By the late 1920's, the democratic elements of the Catholic Center Party came to be pushed aside by an ascendant Right wing, with strong authoritarian tendencies. Rather than seeking a democratic coalition to oppose Hitler, some Centrists indulged in the hope that they could use Hitler for their own purposes. The same delusion characterized the Communist Party, blindly subservient to Moscow, and, after 1928, resolutely embarked on a course to destroy not the fascists but the "social fascists," as they obligingly called the Social Democrats. The Communists tacitly collaborated with the Nazis in several important

1. Erich Matthias, "The Social Democratic Party and Government," *The Path to Dictatorship*, trans. by John Conway with an introduction by Fritz Stern (Garden City, N.Y., 1966), p. 52.

2. Kurt Tucholsky, *Ausgewählte Briefe, 1913–1935*, in *Gesammelte Werke*, ed. by Mary Gerold-Tucholsky and Fritz J. Raddatz (Reinbek, 1962) p. 336.

parliamentary votes and in the Berlin transport strike of November 1932. Centrists and Communists paid for their mistakes, though the catastrophe that overwhelmed the latter was far greater than anything the Centrists had to endure.

Others did Hitler's work too—and more directly and knowingly. Thirteen million Germans voted for him in 1932. The voters came from the middle-class parties that virtually disappeared between 1930 and 1933, as well as from the young who cast their first vote for the party that promised a national regeneration. But the masses of voters would not have been enough; the active collaboration of the governing elite—of bankers, industrialists, old-time civil servants, and political soldiers—was necessary in the end to undermine Weimar so that Hitler could appear as the last available savior. Not all of these men of little power, frozen in their old fear of socialism and their new horror of Bolshevism, were as cynical or as candid as Kurt von Schleicher, who in 1932 wrote: "If the Nazis did not exist, it would be necessary to invent them."[3] In June 1934, the Nazis suspected Schleicher of wishing to uninvent them—and they killed him.

Hitler established his rule in 1933–4 with amazing swiftness. Lenin is said to have remarked that "nowhere but in Russia would it have been so easy to seize power and so difficult to keep it." For Hitler, the reverse was true. Some positions of power were immediately seized, some guarantees of civil liberties immediately suspended, some opponents tortured and killed, but for the rest, the appearance of continuity, of order and normality were preserved and only intermittently disturbed. German society was not openly transformed, as the Bolsheviks had done in Russia; the old forms of life were allowed to linger on, subject only to the sudden and irresistible intervention of the new rulers who could neutralize or suspend all laws.

3. Francis L. Carsten, *Reichswehr und Politik, 1918–1933* (Cologne and Berlin, 1964), p. 377.

Hitler's insatiable will to power was once more abetted by the multitude's will to passivity. The *Gleichschaltung,* the co-ordination, of German life, which many consider the essential form of the Nazi revolution, could not have been carried out without the technical help of tens of thousands of civil servants and the acquiescence of millions.

Complicity and silence, not refusal and dissent, marked the early reaction to the Nazi regime—at the very time when the opposition of even a small minority would have had incalculable effects. Bracher once referred to "the dirty motives of careerism, personal enmities, and profitable informing on others" as bringing about the conspiratorial relationship between citizens and regime that became the basis of Nazi rule.[4] Fear and potential or already realized profit explain much, but not all.

That so many Germans felt no particular attachment to liberalism and democracy also facilitated their acceptance of Nazi rule. The insidious propaganda of the Nazis and the continuous display of national strength and purpose impressed most Germans—and many foreigners; the more so as the regime registered actual achievements as well. The Treaty of Versailles was being dismantled, unemployment ceased, production rose, the nation worked again—even if the likely end was war and the risk of self-destruction.

In the prewar era, then, Nazism was popular and virtually unopposed. Some historians have overestimated the early resistance to Hitler; to do so unwittingly belittles the heroism of the few people who did in fact resist. Even in a democratic society dissent is difficult in a period of crisis; in a totalitarian society it requires a degree of moral certainty and heroism that few men possess and none can demand.

So many men and events, ideas and institutions, social customs

4. Karl Dietrich Bracher, "The Technique of the National Socialist Seizure of Power," *The Path to Dictatorship,* p. 124.

and prejudices shaped Germany's path to dictatorship that no single book can hope to encompass them all. The historian, moreover, wonders where it all began and what alternative paths might have been open.

The essays in *The Path to Dictatorship* say least about what is already best known. They tell us little about the Great War with its shattering impact on every facet of German life and its legacy of resentment. They barely touch on the contribution of the German army to the rise of Nazism, though that contribution was important, as Gordon Craig, J. W. Wheeler-Bennett, and F. L. Carsten have shown. They omit the role of Protestant clergymen and German academics who were overwhelmingly hostile to Weimar democracy, and who either accepted or failed to disavow the idealistic pretensions of Nazism. Nor do they deal with Germany's economic plight—beginning with the calculated inflation during the war and the equally calculated inflation during the Ruhr invasion, to the reparations tangle and the terror of the Great Depression—which favored but did not cause Hitler's success. Finally the book omits a detailed study of Hitler—which Alan Bullock has done in so exemplary a fashion—and of National Socialist ideology or organization. This omission emphasizes the implicit thesis of the book: the disintegration of the Weimar Republic and the rise of Nazism were two distinct if obviously overlapping historical processes. By 1932, the collapse of Weimar had become inevitable; Hitler's triumph had not.

These two processes have deep roots, which reach back to the unification of Germany in 1871 and beyond. They merge most clearly in the final years of the Weimar Republic, from 1928 to 1933, and the book, though its title suggests a longer and more conventional span, rightly concentrates on those last years. We possess, moreover, an astounding array of facts about that dramatic period, though the understanding of these facts depends on a knowledge of the earlier period.

Weimar suffered because some of the most important institutional and intellectual barriers to German democracy were set in 1866 and 1871. It was then that Bismarck forged a new mold for German politics and by so doing foreclosed or lessened the likelihood of other solutions. Historians can, of course, go back further: to the reasons, say, for the success of Bismarck and the failure of 1848, to the reasons for the failure of the Prussian reform movement in 1819. But the lure of infinite regress should not prevent the historian from finding a sensible point of departure for his inquiry. The creation of Imperial Germany is such a date.

Bismarck unified Germany and inserted into an older political and social system enough modern features to preserve it. A parliament based on universal male suffrage was created, but executive authority and bureaucratic predominance were carefully preserved. Industrial capitalism was encouraged by the state, but after 1878 economic liberalism was spurned and the *embourgeoisement* of the country was not properly achieved. The proletariat was allowed to organize but barred from political power and virtually denied the possibility of social advancement.

It was a curious system, and Bismarck's successors found it increasingly difficult to run. The ruling classes were afraid that the forces of modernity would yet break through the barriers that remained; the proletariat was torn between expectation and frustration. For all the power, prosperity, and seeming smugness of Imperial Germany, there was *Angst* in Germany, too— *Angst* before one's enemies at home and abroad.

The vaulting nationalism and imperialism of the late nineteenth century absorbed some of this double fear, even as it had absorbed some of those earlier, xenophobic ideas about the Germanic *Volk* that had been born in the struggle against Napoleon. Modern nationalism in Germany, even more than elsewhere, became the property of the conservative, propertied, and educated classes who sought to legitimize their power by invoking nationalistic slogans about the incompatibility of the German spirit and Western liberalism or materialism. From the 1870's on, anti-Semitism was often annexed to nationalism as well: The Jew as the prototype—and profiteer—of modernity was depicted as yet another sinister danger to Germany. It is important to note that anti-Semitism appeared simultaneously among the rabble-rousers soliciting votes and the elite—witness Treitschke's attack against the Jews in 1879—pleading for the preservation of German values. Lagarde and Treitschke embedded anti-Semitism in an "idealistic" set of values and thus elevated it to cultural respectability. The fewest people understood Nietzsche's denunciation of "these latest speculators in idealism, the anti-Semites, who like to appear in a Christian-Aryan-bourgeois-respectable guise and who endeavor to stir up all the bovine elements of the nation by a misuse of that cheapest of propaganda tricks, a moral attitude—a misuse that exhausts all conceivable patience."[5] In illiberal Germany, to be anti-Semitic bespoke essential virtues—virtues that even Jews cherished. The path to dictatorship in Germany was long, tortuous, and amazingly crowded.

By its political institutions and its social system, Imperial Germany inhibited the development of democracy. It also spawned ideas of nationalism and racism that inspired Nazi ideology and facilitated the acceptance of that ideology by millions of Germans. The failure of Weimar and the success of Hitler had common sources in Imperial Germany.

The antagonisms and resentments of prewar Germany were briefly overshadowed by the common exultation at the outbreak of the war. But this long-cherished utopia of national unity and the end of internal conflict receded rapidly as the conduct of

5. Friedrich Nietzsche, *Zur Genealogie der Moral,* in Vol. II of Friedrich Nietzsche, *Werke in drei Bänden,* ed. by Karl Schlechta (Munich, n.d.), p. 896.

the war in fact exacerbated earlier antagonisms in Germany. The Weimar Constitution inserted still other elements of modernity into public life, indeed parliamentary democracy itself, but the forms of society and the personnel of the governing elites changed little. The defeat and the peace treaty had embittered the nation, and democracy frightened or disappointed all classes. The Republic barely survived, though from 1924 to 1928 it experienced some degree of stability while a succession of bourgeois governments secured diplomatic gains abroad and the economy prospered at home. Even democracy made strides —in municipalities and in some of the states, for the history of Weimar was not without its promise and achievement.

In 1928, the two processes—the disintegration of Weimar and the rise of Hitler—began to coalesce. In that year, the Socialists gained an impressive victory at the polls—and frightened their enemies without satisfying their followers. To constitute a proper coalition government took a year, and Germans jeered at the inefficiency of democracy. In that year of still growing prosperity, the Nazis made significant inroads among university students, and the desecration of Jewish cemeteries reached an all-time high. In the last years of Weimar, both professors and students proved peculiarly vulnerable to the idealism of the avowedly anti-intellectual Nazis. In 1929, Stresemann died, the depression struck, and the final agony of Weimar began.

A curious crisis ensued. The impact of the depression sharpened class antagonisms, and the uneasy collaboration between Socialists and conservatives collapsed. At the instigation of Schleicher, Brüning became Chancellor and embarked almost at once on a Right-wing authoritarian course. He resorted to government by presidential decree, dissolved a Reichstag with a comfortable democratic majority, and found that the next parliament mirrored the terrible radicalization of German politics: Nazis and Communists had scored great gains. A new generation of voters turned its back on the Weimar "system" and sought revolutionary answers to unprecedented needs. Brüning hoped to stem the tide of radicalism by engineering further foreign successes and an economic revival, while rebuffing parliament and relying more and more on Hindenburg's presidential powers. In May 1932 he fell victim to the very power he had so unwisely aggrandized. For three years, while Hitler was on the doorstep of power, the ruling groups of Germany sought to find an authoritarian answer that would supplant or radically alter parliamentary government. At a time of increasing misery, the gulf between government and governed was allowed to grow wider, and a handful of men frivolously thought they could use the Nazis to weaken the Socialists, all the while maintaining themselves in power. Papen and Hindenburg's camarilla dreamed of a "new state," which in effect would have been the old imperial regime in a new guise. As Marx once said—in regard to Louis Napoleon—certain types recur in history; the first time, they appear as tragedy, the second time as farce. Papen and his cohorts in irresponsibility were such a farce, even if the imperial regime was no tragedy.

In those months of ever worsening crisis, the ghosts of an earlier era appeared as if for a final *Totentanz*. People misread the signs, misunderstood Hitler, and reverted to anachronistic struggles and maneuvers: the Socialists feared the reactionaries more than they feared Hitler, the conservatives thought they could use or imprison Hitler so that he would deliver his mass support into their fine aristocratic hands. Both the conservatives' dream of authoritarianism and the Socialists' meek acceptance of a return to authoritarianism at their own expense and despite the militancy of many of their younger leaders and of the rank and file, suggest a kind of psychological regression, a shrinking back to a past beyond recall. In the face of dangers and uncertainties, many of the older Germans unconsciously reached back to the habits and presuppositions of their earlier political experiences; at the end of Weimar, they acted as they had during the critical years of the Empire. Hitler with his single aim of grasping power faced divided and deluded opponents.

Hitler clearly appealed to the great national past, and after its guardians finally called him to power, he identified himself as the heir of Prussian traditions, most dramatically on that day of pageantry in Potsdam in March 1933. But in the twelve years of his rule he liquidated the remnants of Imperial Germany as ruthlessly as he did the vestiges of Weimar democracy. Not Hitler's rise to power but his end marked the true break in German history. The path to dictatorship, so deeply embedded in the German past, ended in 1945 because so much of that past was dead, buried in the rubble of the Third Reich. A smaller, different Germany may at last have found the path to democracy.

Germany Revisited

Berlín 1954

In the summer of 1954, I was a visiting professor at the Free University in Berlin. At the end of that time, I wrote the following piece, which was first published in *Commentary* in February 1955. It is reprinted here without a change, except in the title. The piece may serve as a measure of how radically things have changed in the intervening years; my perspective has changed too.

In the last eleven years, I have visited Germany dozens of times and have attended and spoken at many conferences. New ties of friendship have been formed. I believe I can now see Germany through German eyes as well as through my own. I even spent instructive weeks in the "other Germany," both before and after the building of the wall.

A peaceful, truncated Germany is today the leading country of Western Europe. The Brandt government—measured by its collective intelligence and political good will—may be the best government Germany has ever had. The very fact that an *émigré* could have become Chancellor is an indication that the past has become largely irrelevant.

By the same token, Hitler, too, has become irrelevant. The anguished concern of the generation of the 1950's with its immediate past has been replaced by an angry confrontation with the present. The United States, likewise, has become marginal to the consciousness of young

Germans—except perhaps as the current embodiment of evil. Gone are the days of Marshall Plan gratitude and gentle American tutelage. The older Germans are proud of their regained power and the young have known America only as the despoiler of Vietnam. Uncritical admiration of America has turned into mindless rejection, and there is a trace of *Schadenfreude* as the teachers of yesterday are seen as the culprits of today. Most thoughtful Germans ask —as do many Americans—what will become of America, will its cities die, its society disintegrate, its liberal tradition wither away?

But the German scene, though calm on the surface, is far from reassuring. To take but one instance: a democratic Germany had to reform its universities, but the gap between tradition and democratic aspiration was so great that compromise proved difficult—and change may have come too late. Revolution may have overwhelmed reform, but it is too early to tell whether German universities as centers of free learning and research will be able to survive. Among the students, a new utopianism has gained ground. Like youth elsewhere, they seek freedom from all restrictions and coercion. Yet another generation is seeking to break away from the repressive forms of bourgeois society. The original force behind student unrest was largely romantic and anarchic, but in the land of Marx and Hitler, the anarchist impulse was quickly transformed into tight, desperately intolerant doctrine and practice. A new Leftism with a simplistic ideology and a frightening willingness to use authoritarian means is steadily advancing.

In one sense, the German past remains present. The outsider—and the critical German—never sees German developments with that residue of historic confidence with which he views even a patently ailing England. The legacy of the German past is apprehension: what next?

As I watch the current, often covert conflict within universities and generations, as I see new adversary relations handled in old ways, I am confirmed in my view that the German past and present have a specific relevance to the study of liberalism. Liberalism—at its best, the institutionalization of decency—in practice is all too often dull, inadequate, and tolerant of what should be intolerable. Illiberalism, in turn, is often exciting and, in the short run, efficient. It is also the institutionalization of suspicion and the perpetuation of nonage. Even in today's democracy, the

Germans occasionally manifest the fact that they never went through a liberal phase. Their history can be read as an object lesson in the failure of illiberalism.

It is difficult to think of Germany dispassionately, and on my way there last spring I found that I still felt intensely what I had tried so hard to overcome. In the 1930's, when we felt the hatred of Nazism as a moral imperative, the distinction between Nazi and German often became blurred; and the strongest passions seemed feeble when, at the end of the war, we uncovered the totality of crime, and even our generals broke down and cried. But after that, the very enormity of Nazism speeded exoneration. For such crimes no people could be held responsible, and to affirm collective guilt somehow suggested Nazism in reverse. I had wrestled with these perplexities, but I could rally neither reason to sustain my rejection of Germany nor sentiment to support my conclusion that the German nation cannot be held accountable.

Ten weeks in Berlin helped me to understand afresh. At some point I became conscious that the last layer of ideology and hatred had peeled off. It was not a matter of *tout comprendre, c'est tout pardonner,* but of recognizing intellectually and experiencing emotionally that there are no "Germans," no "they" on whom blame can be pinned, but rather an aggregate of individuals and groups, cherishing few hopes and many hatreds and living without common traditions. And I came to understand how this divisiveness, this absence of consent and tradition, has had an immensely weakening effect on German politics. My own hatred did not survive my proximity with the Germans; I left Germany in August purged of hatred—though not disloyal to the feelings of the past, and full of forebodings about the future.

I was unaware how far this process of education had gone until one moment when I felt an intense humility and sorrow which cut through all earlier passions. The occasion was the memorial service for the victims of the 20th of July revolt against Hitler. Only a few cabinet members and the relatives of the dead attended the ceremony in the new, American-built Auditorium Maximum of the Free University. The audience sat in silence, as at a funeral, no one applauding as Heuss and Adenauer walked down the aisle to their seats or as the last notes of the second movement of the *Eroica* died. Heuss, in his gentle Swabian accent, spoke quietly and quickly, without pathos, recalling the anguish of the men who had chosen themselves murderers of murderers and had paid for their courage in torture and death. These few men, terrified of their responsibility, gaining moral certainty only in the retribution which followed their failure, had sought to arrest and alter fate, had plotted conspiracy on a world-historical plane. As Heuss relived those memories, I struggled with my own feelings, saying to myself that their purposes had not been ours, that their sacrifice had been born of German nationalism, not atonement; but before such moral heroism my quarrels ceased. Heuss concluded, "Our debt to them has yet to be fulfilled." The orchestra played *"Ich hatt' einen Kameraden,"* but softly, transforming a battle song into a funeral elegy. And as I stood there, among sorrowing men, I sensed that more than a hymn was being transformed.

The audience slowly filed out, still silent except for some sobbing, and as I walked around in the adjoining hall and looked at these people—old, distinguished, and sadly proud, dressed in mourning, faces hardened and humbled by suffering, I felt a sense of shame for my indiscriminate hatred. For in that audience I saw a country's elite, perhaps rescued from its callous provincialism only by a catastrophe, but an elite nevertheless, and one which had been condemned, or self-condemned, to political passivity. These were the men who should have led their people twenty or forty years before, and neither sought to nor were sought, and even now, with few exceptions, were without public responsibility. As I walked home that day, I grasped that the once popular view of German history, as an irreversible process of failure and falseness since Luther or Bismarck, missed the true tragedy; uniform wickedness does not describe the German experience, but a succession of "might-have-beens," of great promises never realized. A Manichean struggle, with Satan always the winner.

What rendered the sacrifice of the 20th of July senseless was not the accidental survival of Hitler. The conspirators had played for the soul of their people, and lost. Ten years had to pass before German officialdom formally acknowledged the heritage of that resistance, and now when acknowledgment was finally made, indifference ran too strong, and the slanderers of the movement, rejoicing over Otto John's defection on the anniversary itself, were ready to peddle their poisonous slogan, "Once a traitor, always a traitor." What was thus vilified was the only movement of resistance in Germany which had at the end united diverse men from all regions and traditions: Junker officers and bourgeois bureaucrats, clergymen and labor leaders. How different the German spirit might be today if their memory had been cherished! Honoring three thousand martyred patriots could have inspired a proud unity when every other loyalty and tradition had snapped. But the German people rejected their sacrifice. In the future a few will remember, some others will keep an embarrassed silence; most will learn to disavow these men, and so exonerate themselves for their support of Hitler or their passivity.[1] But as the Germans abandon this legacy, per-

---

1. One of the best-known German historians, now retired, spoke to me of a Socialist participant in the 20th of July attempt, whom I know, as an "opportunist." I objected that to have risked one's life and endured torture for nearly a year did not strike me as typical opportunism. His answer: "We couldn't all get entrance tickets for the concentration camps."

haps we should claim it, as a reminder that the Nazi era had its millions of spineless servants and its handful of heroes.

Nor did the Germans find any other identification with a past tradition which could have moderated the divisiveness of their society. Nothing struck me so much this summer as this thinly disguised *Zerissenheit* in German life. I am not thinking of the imposed division between East and West, or of the traditional divisions of class and interest, or of the new and inescapable division between Nazi and anti-Nazi. It is more than all that— it is the division between each and all, a kind of Hobbesian war without weapons.

On our very first day in Berlin, our landlady, Frau Geheimrat M., warned me against trusting any German. "We aren't what we used to be," she said. And I was to hear this theme in endless variations. Most of the Germans I met were not troubled by extermination camps or war crimes—these were either ignored or charged to the villains at the top. What troubled them was the suspicion that the Third Reich and its catastrophic end had corrupted the Germans themselves. Each seems to have his own particular recollection of those weeks at the end of the war when millions were on the move, and each remembers how Germans robbed, looted, and betrayed fellow Germans. But I know that those same weeks also evoked noble deeds of generosity and self-sacrifice, and these seem forgotten. The contrast struck me the more since I think historically the Germans are peculiarly given to these laments of moral depravity and are correspondingly susceptible to the specious idealist who promises regeneration. Their sense of moral or aesthetic failure has often been injected into German politics, in the stab-in-the-back legend after the First World War, or Hitler's promise to "cleanse Germany" of the "decadence" of modernity (and here the Jew became the image of modernity, as he had been to many German ideologists since 1870). That non-political, speciously moral tone of German politics is still in evidence, and in part must be attributed to the absence of a commonly accepted political tradition—such as the Western countries evolved in the process of building up their democratic states—and to the misgivings which Germans have about themselves. In short, the uncertain political idiom or allegiance is unable to restrain the powerful non-political forces of collective resentment which break into the political society. Hence the significance of this moral uncertainty which lingers from the Second World War.

The Germans' memory of their own meanness feeds also on the trials of the first years of occupation. One story can serve as representative of many. A prominent professor of medicine was barred from his university post by our military government because, though a non-Nazi, he had in the 1930's accepted the rectorship of the university and in his inaugural address had spoken some words of perfunctory praise of the new regime. He had had one hundred copies of the speech mimeographed, distributed ninety-eight to his good friends, and kept two. After the war, he offered one of his copies to the American officer investigating him. The officer said: "Thank you, but I have already received forty-seven unsolicited copies."

Prosperity brought back the amenities, but the suspicion of German against German has continued, shifting now from the individual to the group. It is group against group, with each protesting, and believing, that the other is out to kill. It is as if the Germans were locked in a continuous and particularly vicious American presidential campaign, only here everyone believes all the campaign charges and counter-charges. I talked to a bank director from Cologne, himself in exile during the Third Reich, who insisted that the labor unions were bent on destroying private property and that co-determination—foisted upon Germany, he darkly hinted, by American labor unions— was the opening wedge to disaster. Again, the director of an Evangelical *Gymnasium* in Berlin, a generous man doing an admirable job, warned me of the Catholic Church's plot to establish a totalitarian regime in West Germany and of the corrosive impact of liberalism which threatens all "values." And on my last day in Berlin a professor of a Protestant seminary, a leading participant in his church's fight against Hitler, confessed to me that he despaired of the church's vitality and integrity in West Germany: "If I were younger," he said, "I'd go and fight it out in the East; as it is, I thank the Lord I don't have to live among West Germans."

His feelings were typical of Berlin, where everyone seems to cherish a lusty hatred of the West Germans, considering them smug and heartless. And indeed my two weeks in West Germany taught me that the Bavarians, Swabians, and Rhinelanders do resent the troublesome claims of the Berliners, even as they resent the East Germans who stand as a muted reproach to their enjoyment of prosperity. Weak indeed is the national sense of a people that could so rapidly move so far apart. Even at the height of the uprising of June 17, 1953, the East Germans who risked their lives condemning their Quisling government and its continued injustices made only feeble gestures in the direction of reunification. As a Prussian conservative wrote in the 1840's, Germany's national characteristic is its divisiveness.

To read such judgments, even to understand that historically the Germans are for all their occasional outbursts of chauvinism a peculiarly non-nationalistic people, is much different from discovering this for oneself in immediate, spontaneous words and gestures. This I did while serving as an examiner on a Fulbright screening committee in Berlin; here I could drop pleasantry and the polite silence about fundamental questions which I had to show toward my own students. We interviewed some forty students from the various faculties of the Free University—bright, well-educated people who were articulate and informed about everything but their own past. Hardly any of them had tried to analyze the terrible problems of Germany's last decades. With the significant exception of some young theologians, they neither accepted their past as a part of themselves, nor had come to grips with it in any other way. What they carried was a faint, blurred picture of the last one hundred years, or of the fatality of the last twenty, with no more sense of personal involvement than an American might feel in talking about a rigged convention. The divorce between German intellect and politics, the continuing absence of a live, pervasive political society which I had so often postulated in the abstract, was here on exhibit, as it were.

Quite a few of the students protested their anti-Nazism by assuring me, "But . . . we lost everything at the end of the war." Asked how it happened, they cited Versailles, the inflation, or the depression as responsible for Hitler, and Yalta for everything after Hitler. These were the automatic answers that reflected their unwillingness to penetrate the past and sort out the good from the bad. Certainly the past, whether remote or recent, is no source of pride to them; it is not even a part of their experience. I remember asking a particularly engaging young fellow, a Junker scion as it happened, to mention one German political figure of the last two hundred years whose picture he might put on his desk. "None," was his reply, and I thought to myself: who, after all, who? But I also remembered Burke's injunction to the French: ". . . respecting your forefathers, you would have been taught to respect yourselves." What of a people that neither celebrates nor distorts its history, but ignores it?

This escape from the past reinforces the German propensity to blame others for their misfortunes. Collective guilt is, as I have said, a harsh and perhaps even a meaningless concept; and yet I had expected to find that the conscience of the Germans would have been tried. Except to a few, the mote in the Allied eye seems already much bigger than the beam in their own. At every level, even among the most detached and conscious anti-Nazis, I found this emphasis upon Allied "mistakes," expressing the general resentment over Allied unity against the Germans. Why unconditional surrender? Why after D-Day did not the Western powers join us in a crusade against the Soviets? And, again and again: why the "sell-out" at Yalta? And when I suggested—more often than I wished to—that it had been Germany's aggression which had in the end brought the Soviets to the Elbe, that we had been compelled to fight with the Soviets against the immediate evil, there would be silence or grudging assent, with a glance at the bookshelf where W. H. Chamberlin's *America's Second Crusade* or books of that sort—all diligently translated—bore witness that this new stab-in-the-back legend can be substantiated by the utterances of many Americans.[2] And so, with what Germans like to think is America's blessing, the belief grows stronger that the European collapse began in 1945—with the victory of the Allies.

Anyone looking for German contrition will have to be content with their boundless self-pity. Each German has his own horror-story and each city its peculiar tragedy. And why deny them? When I first saw the center of Berlin—for blocks nothing but rubble and silence, or the bombed-out shell of the Anhalter Bahnhof with signs warning of rat-poison—I too was overawed. I tried not to think of this terrifying wasteland as retribution, but later it occurred to me that this may be how many Germans —quite unconsciously—regard it. Why would the West Berliners now collect funds not to restore or demolish the Gedächtnisskirche but to preserve it as a ruin? Could it be to remind

2. Germans often see us either as dupes of our idealism or as victims of traitors. Alger Hiss is well known in Germany and in the Bundestag debate over Dr. John, Adenauer's Minister of the Interior referred knowingly to Hiss, as if to suggest that such things, after all, happen in the best of families. In this connection it is interesting that during my stay in Berlin I did not hear a critical remark about Senator McCarthy, while many students praised him as America's "leading anti-Communist."

themselves that punishment has been received, that the debt is paid? Why be contrite about war crimes and genocide, which a few Germans may have been guilty of, when Germans indiscriminately were bombed, starved, and harried?

In a sermon for the 20th of July, delivered before President Heuss and broadcast to the nation, the Bishop of Berlin praised God's mercifulness, declaring that even in the most horrible days of German suffering His mercy had remained. During this painful recital of German suffering there was not even an allusion to the sufferings of others. In despair at what I thought a culpable omission I wrote him, humbly suggesting that his authority and the uniqueness of the occasion might have made it appropriate at least to acknowledge the tragic fate of the victims of German deeds. I mailed the letter quickly, before second thoughts could restrain me, but his answer, swift and untroubled, reassured me: "When I was talking of German suffering I was also thinking of those who died at German hands." How nice, I thought at first, and then it dawned on me that the link between German suffering and German cruelty may indeed have been there in his silent thought, and that self-pity is a form—and the only important form in Germany today—of unappeased conscience.

It is not as if I spent the summer as a human Geiger counter, attuned to radiations of repentance. The pace was too quick for that. But so many of the chance remarks and political events acquired deeper meaning in the light of how Germans regarded the past. For overtly their life during the past nine years seems to have been routine and unreflective, and the "poets and thinkers" more divorced from the life of the people than ever. And I plunged into their workaday life as fully as possible.

I still remember that first night on the military train between Frankfurt and Berlin, when we pulled into the Soviet Zone at the break of dawn and I saw the first Soviet soldier. He appeared at the end of a tunnel, out of nowhere, in the middle of nowhere, a solitary soldier in high boots, with a tommy gun slung across his back, like a dull picture in a magazine, but here he was in reality and in the heart of Europe. In time, it is true, the sight of Russian soldiers became usual, but it was left to an acquaintance of mine to tell me that the presence of the GI from Texas or Nebraska was truly more startling than the Russian, who had, after all, traversed Europe before. True enough, perhaps, but the American soldier was a friend, and I had never known how much such unknown friends could mean.

I had been told in New York that Berlin was the most "exciting" place in Europe, what with the Russians at the other end of the subway line and a kind of competition in culture between the worlds. I was looking forward to at least a miniature version of David Riesman's delightfully profound fantasy of the Nylon War, but while Berlin is the most significant place of co-existence, and while America successfully exploits this fact, the city does not really sustain the importance attributed to it.

There is, in fact, a deceptive normality to Berlin, especially if one is thrown at once into the academic life at the Free University. Ruins and Russians become an accepted part of life, and the well-appointed stores (to say nothing of the countless *Konditoreien,* dripping with whipped cream) add a bizarre note to this city which at times celebrates itself as the outpost of freedom. West Berlin is almost a dull place, at least in the summer, and even the tough humor of the Berliners cannot dissipate the fear that the city will degenerate into utter provincialism. Imagine Washington with the federal government moved to Cambridge, Massachusetts, the museums rifled, the Library of Congress emptied, and the roads blocked. What sustains Berlin is the struggle between Americans and Russians, and the magnificent determination of the Americans to win that struggle. The airlift constituted the most dramatic instance of that resolve, but America's assistance in the establishment of the Free University may well prove to be the most enduring monument to the deeper meaning of our role.

In a country where success stories are less common than with us, and where universities are judged as much by age and tradition as by performance, the success of the Free University is truly remarkable, and justifies the pride which its faculty and students exude. The Free University is six years old (Heidelberg is nearly six hundred years old), has ten thousand students, from East Berlin and the Soviet Zone as well as from West Berlin and West Germany, and a faculty which can hold its own among faculties throughout Germany. Even the older German universities, so aloof and incredulous six years ago, are beginning to accept the Berlin upstart as a permanent achievement of those students and few teachers who in 1947-8 rebelled against the ideological pressure of the Communists at the old university in East Berlin.

The unique origins of the Free University molded its character. Unlike most West German universities, the Free University draws its students from every walk of life. It has a system of student participation in university administration, unique in Germany, which surpasses, I believe, similar experiments in America. Student delegates sit in each faculty as well as in the university senate and, in theory at least, "co-determine" policy.[3] But even in Berlin the old vices of German academic life are partially reappearing. As in West Germany, only on a less alarming scale, the old *Korporationen,* with their compulsory dueling and voluntary anti-Semitism, seek to regain their place. Dueling and drunkenness, however, have little appeal to students who are dependent on odd jobs and financial help for their existence.

3. Illustrative perhaps of many current efforts to conciliate antagonisms by "co-determination" was the unintentionally humorous remark by a high university official praising student participation since "they are so responsible that they hardly ever speak up or give us any trouble."

Nor did I find any evidence of resurgent nationalism or any other extremism. The students treated my—to them—unusual interpretations of German history with sympathetic seriousness, and I came to share the belief of many democrats that this may be the first generation of German students not poisoned by chauvinism or militarism. The Free University, by force of circumstance, has bridged that gap between the political and academic life which was, and in West Germany still is, so characteristic of German universities. The Communists "forced these students to be free," and American generosity (continuing in the form of substantial Ford Foundation grants) provided the material basis for their freedom.

The spirit of the Free University, however, is all its own. It is a mixture of pride, humility, and seriousness, and sufficient good humor to overcome the persistent difficulties of inadequate facilities. While the hoarier forms of extracurricular life may be creeping back and the relative informality of its early years may be receding before revived pomposity, I think the university will for a long time to come justify the affection of its own students, as well as of the Fulbright students from America whose loyalty is almost alarming.

As for Berlin's more general pretensions to cultural vitality, I am afraid I remain unconvinced. True, I came toward the end of the season, but saw enough not to be inconsolable that I could see no more. In the magnificent new Schiller-Theater I saw the old *Hauptmann von Köpenick,* a crude play crudely produced and received. The audience, passive, even inattentive through most of the evening, responded only to the vulgarity in word and posture of a man waiting his turn to go to the toilet. In the East, the programs were superior, but the productions seemed threadbare and unimaginative. I remember wandering into one of Gorky's last plays, *Ssomow und andere,* which in the first act probes the mind and mood of counter-revolutionaries in a hostile but not stereotyped manner, and the brave activists in the audience were somewhat at a loss how to respond to this criticism of the regime. I also saw *Don Carlos,* with its dramatic plea *"Sire, geben Sie Gedankenfreiheit,"* for which the play had been banned under the Nazis. The passage received hesitant applause, but the Communists made up for it by giving the villainous Grand Inquisitor in the tragic finale a deathlike face that made him resemble Adenauer. Contrary to Western opinion, however, the Eastern theater seemed all in all no better than the Western, though in fairness I should add that I missed Brecht's *Mutter Courage,* which is generally acclaimed as the greatest contemporary play and production.

The drama in the East, however, was not in the "social realism" of the stage, but in the sordid realism outside. From this side of the Atlantic, I had looked forward to East Berlin as a kind of forbidden experience. The first time I went there alone, I almost wished it *were* forbidden. I stayed only ten minutes, long enough to feel the terrible anguish of helplessness and the fear of arbitrariness. I remember arriving at the Eastern subway station, finding my way to the street amidst slogans and posters, and recoiling from the sight of the first *Volkspolizist,* that dreadful combination of Nazi face and Soviet uniform. I left again, thinking that those who scoff at "bourgeois values" or sham liberties ought to come here; one does not ordinarily notice the air one breathes, but tamper with it, and you choke.

It was a different sensation on a U.S. military bus, where the trip to the East was cheerfully depressing. The Eastern sector seemed like a different world, deserted, downtrodden, and destroyed, as against the buzzing, elegant, and dynamic West— just the contrast one always reads about. On that tour, a regular army service authorized in the remote days of active co-existence, I went to the gigantic Soviet War Memorial in their half of Berlin, part of which was built from the tiles of Hitler's Chancellery. It is a formal garden, with bas-reliefs depicting scenes from the war, and on a hill at the end, a towering statue—World's Fair style—of a Soviet soldier clutching a Russian child in one hand and a sword slaying the swastika in the other. Inside the memorial chapel is the coffin of the unknown soldier, and above it a German and Russian inscription recalling the struggle against the "Fascist hordes." The ideological cliché, even in the presence of death, jolted me back to the present. For it is an impressive sight, a monument not only to the Russian dead, but to the death of so many hopes and illusions.

It took me weeks to get up enough nerve to return to East Berlin alone. When I did, each excursion seemed like an adventure into past and future: so much reminded me of the Nazi past and so much had the flavor of a terrifying future. On almost every remaining wall a picture of "Big Brother"—in various guises—and on the street the police *do* watch you. The future is previewed in the celebrated showpiece known as Stalinallee: a magnificently wide boulevard, on either side of which are apartment houses built of cream-colored stone and tile, decorated in the Oriental manner with mosaic pattern and paintings. In a city so wrecked as East Berlin, Stalinallee cannot help but impress, and depress too. Is this pretentious ugliness, this fancy slum, really the ultimate fulfillment of the Communist society? And can the Communists be unaware that this showpiece of the entire "proletarian" world embodies the cruel inegalitarianism of their society which provides only for the few even as it promises to the many?

I confess Stalinallee did have a lure for me that I could not resist: the Karl Marx Buchhandlung. If there has to be a lure, books may be preferable to food, and I did not make it a practice, as many West Berliners and Americans do, of devouring the delicacies of the "people's restaurants," with caviar less than fifty cents a portion. But the bookstore, larger than Scribner's and Brentano's put together, was different, and I must have gone there six or seven times. There were thousands of books in all languages, though the "peoples' democracies" were most heavily represented; and there was a second-hand division where "bourgeois" editions of old classics could be had for next to nothing. In my search I discovered and bought a set of Herder's works, and noticed later that it carried the official stamp: "From the Jewish ghetto in Theresienstadt." The salesmen treated me with excessive politeness though I had from the first insisted upon my nationality, and I acquired a sense of security there which I felt nowhere else in East Berlin. This was dispelled quickly enough when one day from the upstairs window of the store I saw a car full of policemen parked outside, waiting for someone or something. The next half hour, until the car departed as mysteriously as it had come, was uncomfortable, and I was reminded of the protagonists of *1984* who had felt so safe in the antique store—and who were finally caught precisely in this mausoleum of the past. Much shaken, I took a taxi to the subway station closest to West Berlin and resolved that this was to be my last visit. That night I remarked to an American colleague who was grumbling about West Berlin that its justification was East Berlin, and that that was enough for me.

Our conversation that night turned to the political future, and to the question of whether the West could maintain its prosperous stability and attendant superiority over the East. That question needs to be asked, for this past summer marked a turning point in the development of postwar Germany. Between 1948 and the spring of 1954, Adenauer's Germany achieved a spectacular economic recovery and a degree of political stability which probably has no parallel in modern German history. That period, however, seems to have come to an end: formally with the promise of sovereignty, but more significantly in a fluidity in German life which may ultimately crystallize in a pattern less satisfactory to us than that of the recent past. Put differently, between 1945 and 1954 Germany had no live political option. She is freer now, at home and abroad, and the stability that was partly imposed from without will be severely shaken.

Let me say at once that I do not belong to those spiteful pessimists who see Nazis in every nook and cranny. Our newspapers regularly report the rise of neo-Nazism, the triumphant return from prison of some notorious SS leader, or the desecration of Jewish cemeteries. Such desecrations may well have happened, though not as daily occurrences, as one recent observer claims; but for all their human meanness, these acts would assume political significance only if a neo-Nazi movement did in fact exist. As far as I could see, it does not. Our reporters too often confuse neo-Nazis with ex-Nazis, who, undoubtedly, are making a disheartening comeback. But there is a difference, if not necessarily an edifying one, between the former Nazi who has not recanted but does not seek to restore, and the new Nazi who, like a nineteenth-century Bonapartist, yearns to do it all over again. Of the many Nazis who have made their way back I know of none who openly advocates the restoration of totalitarianism or any of its characteristic features. My guess is that there are very few "Bonapartists" in Germany today, if only because Hitler was no Napoleon.

The danger to West Germany does not come from the extreme Right, or from the extreme Left, which is virtually nonexistent. It comes from the removal of external restraints and the other successes which Adenauer has achieved. And it manifests itself in a weakening of Adenauer's hold and an incipient splintering of the middle. West Germany has suffered from "too much and too soon," and the adage that nothing succeeds like success is not here applicable.

In his sincere efforts to attach West Germany to Europe, Adenauer has had the support of the United States, the fanatic following of a few German youths who had become obsessed by the "European idea," and the acquiescence of the large majority of West Germans who could not think of a better policy. While the European idea as a mystique is dead, the achievements of his rule remain and are to be crowned shortly by the ratification of the Paris treaties. But these successes make him all the more vulnerable. He has accomplished all that he could, things that only he could have achieved, and now he can be criticized and attacked with impunity.

This falling way from Adenauer's policy began even before the death of EDC. The appearance of adventurers this spring— Dr. Brüning and Herr Pfleiderer—was a mere straw in an easterly wind. Dr. John's defection and the subsequent pilgrimage of Adenauer's party colleague Schmidt-Wittmack to East Germany suggest more dangerous squalls and, incidentally, for the first time since the division in 1948, gave the East a temporary propagandistic edge. Then came the rejection of EDC, for which Bonn was apparently no better prepared than we were. In a series of anxious improvisations the United States sought to strengthen Adenauer, seemingly unaware that our unqualified help may easily weaken his position. For when our Secretary of State demonstrates to the German public that he finds the road to Bonn faster and more pleasant than, say, the road to Paris, the Germans conclude that Adenauer is no longer indispensable, that with the certainty of American support a bolder policy can now be embarked upon. By giving Adenauer too much we have encouraged his people to give him too little, and the immediate result may be seen in the intense agitation over the Saar, which some months back would have been unthinkable.

But even granting the eagerness of some Germans to break away from Adenauer's sober policies, they will sooner or later come up against the ultimate limitations on their freedom of action. The East-West conflict has enabled Germany to regain its sovereignty and strength, but from this time on will impose ineluctable restraints. Germany—whether unified or not—has at last been dwarfed by the very powers she herself brought to Europe by her aggression and whose continued presence in Central Europe is now guaranteed by their mutual fear. Thus West Germany's potential for good on our side outweighs her conceivable capacity for mischief. And since I do not believe that the West Germans will join the Soviets—if only because the continued presence of Allied troops would make this most difficult—or that the Soviets will voluntarily abandon East Germany, it is unlikely that reunification will become a live possibility, though it will probably emerge as the center of constant political manipulation which will give it the *appearance* of a serious question.

There is, at present, no strong irredentist feeling in West Germany, least of all among those social groups that are sharing in her prosperity. Unification, they know, would pose dangerous problems and impose heavy economic burdens on the West. The Soviets have expropriated the large land-owning class in Prussia and nationalized most sectors of the economy, and the West would either have to accept this settlement or try to put Humpty Dumpty together again. Potentially this is a most explosive issue, since the Socialists could not accept restitution or the Centrists the *fait accompli*. It is probable, therefore, that the present tendency to pay lip service to reunification and to concentrate on one's own business will continue. Most East Germans, one might add, hate their Communist regime, but after twelve years of Nazi propaganda and nine of Soviet, it is unlikely that Bonn's parliamentary democracy attracts them enthusiastically. And so one arrives at the pedestrian conclusion that Germany will continue to live as a divided nation—which would, of course, constitute no great reversal of its historic traditions.

In domestic politics, it is the same story of the self-defeating quality of Adenauer's success. He has been the most successful statesman, and among the successful the most admirable, of modern Germany. He is also a great man, not unaware of his exceptional stature, and he has become impatient with smaller men, lesser minds, and ultimately with opposition itself. His leadership and the imposed restraints from abroad held his party and coalition together, but the signs of political discontent are multiplying. He may patch up the cracks as they appear, but the coalition will not survive him, and given the sorry state of the opposition, one realizes that his mantle will not automatically fall on another: neither an Attlee nor an Eden is waiting in the wings, but at best a well-meaning Caprivi. And at such a time, the political power of certain groups, notably big business and the bureaucracy, which Adenauer has kept in check, may emerge in alarming strength.

When I first came to Germany I doubted that the Germans could really develop a democracy. The summer months taught me that I was wrong, but I left Germany with the fear that a promising beginning is being severely threatened. Franz Neumann, whose tragic death this summer deprived us of one of the most penetrating observers of modern Germany, wrote four years ago: "The West has so far won the battle for Germany." This was still true six months ago, but new dangers will arise when the present coalition disintegrates, probably at the same time that American influence will at least be weakened by the establishment of the new Germany army, a force that historically has never tended to sustain democratic or even civilian government.

In the ensuing struggle it will be difficult to find another broad union, and as so often in German politics, the opposition to the existing regime is divided and unprepared. The Socialist Party remains the most sincerely democratic group but lacks personalities, program, and power. It still seems to be torn between its imaginary revolutionary tradition and its real, conservative attachment to democracy; at the SPD *Parteitag,* which

I attended, the leader of the party demanded "the erection of a new society, not the restoration of the old," and, a few paragraphs later, denounced Adenauer for scuttling a local coalition between his party and the Socialists. Does he really suppose that the German conservatives will legislate a socialist program, as English Tories upon occasion do? Or does he think that because the SPD now wants to be like the British Labour Party, its political opponents will obligingly turn into a Conservative Party, ready to share power and responsibility equally? Lastly, the trade unions, by accepting political neutrality as the price of unity, have agreed, at least formally, to their own political impotence and thus deprived the Bonn Republic of one of the pillars of Weimar. If Bonn nevertheless remains stronger today than Weimar ever was, it is primarily because its enemies are weaker and not because its defenders are stronger. And still I fear that the day will come when we will discover that political instability, a monopoly on which we have angrily attributed to the French, could take a far more dangerous form in Germany.

All this, however, is still in the future. Set against the vicious tone and violent action of the Weimar period, the tone of present-day German politics is polite, perhaps even dull—as H. Stuart Hughes has noted in *Commentary* (November, 1954). That fewer cries of "traitor" and "swine" have been bandied about in the Bundestag than in the old Reichstag may attest an improvement in manners, and it certainly bespeaks the powerful though indirect restraint which our occupation represents. In the recent debate over Dr. John, Adenauer's Minister of the Interior, Schroeder promised that once "the shackles [of occupation] are removed" one would be able to talk more freely. These shackles have in fact protected the Republic, and their removal may unleash the more violent political passions which so far have been suppressed. Then it is likely that the deeper divisions in German society, which I have already mentioned, will show up in political life as well, and that the ugly tone of negation and resentment, which I sensed running strong underneath the surface, may erupt and poison the new society.

If and when that happens, the lack of young leaders will intensify the crisis of the new German democracy. The best Germans have always disdained politics, and during the Weimar Republic men of the stature of Heuss and Adenauer were hardly known—or quickly assassinated. In the Bonn Republic, politics seem no more attractive, and today's youth, so far as I could tell, is not likely to seek active political responsibility. Among the older generation, the most promising men were exiled, or killed in the 20th of July movement, and the silent sympathizers of that movement find it repugnant to work alongside ex-Nazis. And here we do share some responsibility with the Germans: not that we failed in "de-Nazification"—the task, it will be remembered, was quickly and properly turned over to the Germans, who botched it—but that we too readily retreated from our moral condemnation of those who publicly benefited and only "inwardly" suffered from the Nazi regime. We thus may have helped, unwittingly to be sure, to alienate those Germans who refused all advancement under the Nazis and who in the postwar years could have been encouraged to enter positions of power. (Only a few weeks ago, a resolutely anti-Nazi professor, visiting this country, complained to me that a prominent ex-Nazi had been invited to attend an important festivity at an American university: "I felt as if I had been slapped in the face.") As it is, when the present septuagenarians retire, their places will be taken by default, and the decline of political life in Germany will have commenced.

The last person I talked to in Germany was a Scandinavian priest, imprisoned and tortured by the Gestapo, liberated at the end of the war by the British, and since then the head of an international students' house in a small German university town. For nine years he had tried to reform his former enemies, and he was proud of his past successes. His words of parting I repeat sadly—and in that sadness perhaps lies my own best gain from the summer: "I am leaving Germany. The atmosphere is becoming unbearable."

Index

S

R

A Note About The Author

A recognized authority on modern Europe, Fritz Stern is Seth Low Professor of History at Columbia University. Born in Germany in 1926, he came to the United States in 1938. He received his B.A. from Columbia College in 1946 and an M.A. and Ph.D. from Columbia University. He has also taught at Cornell, Yale, and the Free University of Berlin, and is permanent visiting professor at the University of Konstanz in West Germany. He was a member of the Institute for Advanced Study at Princeton in 1969–70, and has been awarded fellowships by the Guggenheim Foundation, the American Council on Learned Societies, and the Center for Advanced Study in the Behavioral Sciences at Stanford. Mr. Stern is the author of *The Politics of Cultural Despair* (1961), and he edited *The Varieties of History* (1956) and (with Leonard Krieger) *The Responsibility of Power* (1968). He has contributed to many general publications and scholarly journals, and is a regular book reviewer for *Foreign Affairs*.

A Note on the Type

The text of this book was set in a face called Times Roman, designed by Stanley Morison for *The Times* (London) and first introduced by that newspaper in 1932.

Among typographers and designers of the twentieth century, Stanley Morison has been a strong forming influence, as typographical adviser to the English Monotype Corporation, as a director of two distinguished English publishing houses, and as a writer of sensibility, erudition, and keen practical sense.

Composed by Cherry Hill Composition
Pennsauken, New Jersey
Printed and bound by The Hadden Craftsmen, Inc.
Scranton, Pennsylvania

Typography and binding design by Virginia Tan